THE GINGER KID
The Buck Weaver Story

Buck Weaver, the Ginger Kid
(Courtesy of George Brace)

THE GINGER KID
The Buck Weaver Story

by
Irving M. Stein

WCB Brown & Benchmark

Library of Congress Cataloging in Publication Data:
STEIN, IRVING 1923

THE GINGER KID

Library of Congress Catalog Card Number: 91-73931
ISBN: 0-697-16276-1

Printed in the United States of America by The Elysian Fields Press, 2460 Kerper Boulevard, Dubuque, IA 52001.

10 9 8 7 6 5 4 3 2 1

Mission Statement of The Elysian Fields Press Imprint

The purpose and philosophy of The Elysian Fields Press is grounded in an appreciation of baseball as a central mythology of American culture. We wish to explore in print, via periodicals and books of essay, history, fiction, biography, poetry and anthology, the unifying romance of baseball as it connects us with our larger heritage and the natural cycles of generation.

In loving memory of my parents

Morris and Ida Stein

". . . the 'ginger kid' played a splendid game . . ."
Irving E. Sanborn
Chicago Tribune **sportswriter**

"Buck Weaver liked to play ball better than anyone I have ever seen."
Eddie Collins
Original member of the Hall of Fame
and White Sox second baseman

"Buck Weaver . . . the No. 1 third sacker in the game's history."
Clarence Rowland, vice-president
Chicago Cubs and former White Sox
manager, as quoted in the
Chicago Sun-Times, **1959**

"Buck Weaver at third was probably as expert as any who ever played there, and some consider him the ablest of all."
Harold Seymour
Baseball: The Golden Age,
Oxford University Press

Contents

Foreword

One of the absolute "musts" in sports broadcasting is doing your homework. When the light goes on and the broadcaster starts to talk, that's the fun part. Sure there's pressure, but you wouldn't be there if you couldn't handle that. You already know you have the gift (I guess you can call it that) of being able to speak rapidly and be understood. But before that cue light blinks or the director says, "Take it away!" you'd better be prepared to go with it.

There's an old saying that if you steal from one writer it's plagiarism, but if you steal from enough it's research. Most of us in sports broadcasting are great researchers. "So what are you up to right now?" "Oh, just having a second cup of coffee and stealing ad libs from the paper" or "Just reading a terrific sports book—man, have I got some lines for when the Dodgers come to town!" Or else you take that player (or manager or coach) to dinner, have a late drink with him, sit with him on the plane or train. Homework.

This is why I appreciate Irving Stein's biography of Buck Weaver. As you get into this story you quickly realize the monumental research job it represents. Mr. Stein has waded through several carloads of mold to bring us several quarts of penicillin.

I knew Buck Weaver. I knew many of the writers and baseball figures quoted. I knew personally men such as Jim

Crusinberry, Irving Vaughn, Harry Grabiner, Charlie and Stormy Bidwell, Judge Kenesaw Mountain Landis, Fred Lieb, Babe Ruth, Ty Cobb, Red Faber, and Ray Schalk. Just to name a few. No other effort I've read shows the tremendous shoe-leather rolled-up-sleeves forget-a-decent-night's-sleep-tonight effort Irv Stein has painfully—but apparently joyfully—put out to bring us this book and set the record straight. See if you don't agree with me that if Buck Weaver doesn't belong back in the game then neither do some of the most revered heroes sports has ever known. For they were men for their times—or, more to the point, *of* their times—and those unruly times carried conditions sometimes too loose, too tempting, and too strange for mere flesh and blood mortals to handle.

Jack Brickhouse
WGN-TV, Chicago

Introduction

I first heard the name of Buck Weaver in my childhood as a rabid White Sox fan. I was that kind of kid who gets so distraught when the home team loses, he won't eat his dinner. Some Chicago baseball announcer—I don't remember which one since back then about six stations broadcast the games at the same time—compared Luke Appling's early days at shortstop with Weaver's. They were both wild-throwing, rifle-armed infielders, but both settled down: Appling developed into a Hall of Famer and Weaver shifted to third base to become the premier performer at the hot corner in the American League. He might have become a Hall of Famer.

As a follower of the White Sox you couldn't help but hear occasional references to the Black Sox scandal of 1919, when a bunch of Sox players threw the World Series to the Cincinnati Reds and were kicked out of baseball. Occasionally you heard a vague reference to one innocent ballplayer who was booted out with the rest. As the years passed, Buck Weaver's name came into focus as the unfortunate ballplayer.

As I grew to adulthood, I came to wonder why no one had written a book about Weaver and the drama of the 1919 World Series. For a while, I considered the subject for my master's thesis in history. But I knew such research would consume more time than I cared to invest to earn my degree.

Years went by before any author investigated the Black Sox story. Finally, Eliot Asinof wrote his fine, detailed study of the fix, *Eight Men Out*, published in 1963. I read it soon after it appeared, but it didn't impel me to action. Then, for some inexplicable reason, I re-read *Eight Men Out* in the mid-seventies. This time I became intrigued by Weaver's plight; I think an ingrained American sympathy for the underdog compelled me. There was just something wrong with the story: What had happened to Buck violated a sense of justice and fair play. The more I delved into the facts of his life, the greater appetite I had to learn more about the man. By coincidence, soon after I completed my early drafts, Hollywood, too, became interested in the tale and *Eight Men Out* was produced as a feature film in 1988. It starred John Cusack in the sympathetic role of Buck Weaver. One prominent movie critic wrote that the film would have had greater dramatic impact if it had focused on Weaver rather than spreading its attention thinly on all eight players.

To research Weaver was an inviting project for me. I had a background in history and journalism and had taught these subjects in high school for many years. And I love baseball, even though I wasn't very adept at playing it. In my last American Legion game I struck out four times in a row on a diamond in Lincoln Park in Chicago.

I started keeping notes on Weaver in 1979. My research at that time was sporadic and haphazard. I found I couldn't give the project the time and attention it deserved while I was teaching, so I quit my high school teaching job, taking early retirement, and went to work discovering Weaver's life. Not certain if there was even enough material for a book, I naively leapt into the project without a commitment from a publisher or the assistance of an agent.

While my affection for Weaver is quite obvious—I have pictures of Buck and his wife hanging in our hallway at home, right next to our family portraits—I've tried to present a balanced view for and against Weaver in the baseball crisis of 1919. By the time you finish reading the book, I hope you'll be able to reach your own conclusions regarding the Ginger Kid's ouster from organized baseball and his life-long struggle for reinstatement.

Irving M. Stein
Skokie, 1991

Acknowledgments

My indebtedness extends to many people who have contributed their knowledge, culled their memories and guided me forward to bring this biography to fruition. Foremost in my gratitude is Bette Scanlan, Buck Weaver's niece, who generously gave of her time to provide us with information that gave us an insight into his personality and character. She recalled the years from the early thirties until his death in 1956. The late Ed McEvoy, who was eighty-five years old when I interviewed him in 1984 in Pottstown, Pennsylvania, shed light on Buck's childhood and his early playing days. Both McEvoy and Doug Ludwig, president of the Stowe Old-Timers Baseball Association in 1984, explained how local residents feel about Buck to this day. McEvoy, a former semipro ballplayer himself, founded the Stowe Old-Timers Baseball Association in 1928.

My deepest thanks to Chicago sportswriter, Bill Gleason, who led me to Miss Scanlan. He also added to the Weaver story. Other individuals who helped fill the portrait of Buck Weaver or add to the background of the times include the late Nick Etten, former New York Yankees, Philadelphia A's and Philadelphia Phillies first baseman; Charles A. Comiskey II, grandson of the founder of the White Sox; the late John P. Carmichael, a great sportswriter with the Chicago *Daily News*; and Charles Bidwell Jr., owner of

Sportsman's Park race track in Cicero, Illinois. I received help from author Harry Stein and Jeff Kernan, Research Associate at the National Baseball Library of the National Baseball Hall of Fame, and from F.L. Stabley, Librarian for the *York Dispatch*, York, Pennsylvania. Archie Motley, Curator of Archives and Manuscripts of the Chicago Historical Society, led me to a rich source of information.

I wish to thank Arthur Edelson, Joe Lurie, Edward Contorer, Edward Sager and Marty Silver who shared their childhood memories of Buck.

I have used the facilities of the following libraries and wish to thank their staff members for their advice and assistance: Northwestern University, Evanston, Illinois, Skokie Public Library, Skokie, Illinois, Chicago Public Library, Chicago, Illinois, Evanston Public Library, Evanston, Illinois, National Baseball Library of the National Baseball Hall of Fame, Cooperstown, New York, Library of Congress, Washington, D.C., University of Illinois Library, Urbana, Illinois, Chicago Historical Society Library and Newberry Library, Chicago.

Through inter-library loan, the Skokie Public Library also provided me with microfilm and books from the University of Illinois Library, Urbana, Illinois, the Illinois State Library in Springfield, Illinois, the University of Missouri Library in Columbia, Missouri, the Beloit, Wisconsin, Public Library and the Arlington Heights, Illinois, Public Library. Through correspondence, I also received information from the Carnegie Library of Pittsburgh, Pennsylvania, and the City of Milwaukee Public Library.

Newspapers particularly helpful to me were the editions of the *Chicago Tribune*, Chicago *Daily News*, *San Francisco Chronicle*, *York Dispatch*, *New York Times*, The *Sporting News*, Beloit *News* and the *Chicago Sun-Times*. *Sporting Life* and *Baseball Magazine* were informative periodicals. The Kenesaw M. Landis Scrapbook of the Chicago Historical Society offered a rich lode of newspaper stories on the baseball commissioner.

Many thanks to my editor, Steve Lehman, who polished

up my writing and clarified my thoughts and whose suggestions made for a better story.

Thanks to Executive Managing Editor Ed Bartell for his courage in taking on a first time author and to Professor Harold Seymour for leading me to The Elysian Fields Press.

I also wish to express my gratitude to Jack Brickhouse, one of Chicago's three Hall of Fame baseball announcers, who took time from a busy schedule to read the story and write the foreword for *The Ginger Kid*.

To my friends and relatives who gave me encouragement and advice, a special thanks.

Finally, I'm especially indebted to two people. One is my youngest daughter, Leslie Ann Handler, who encouraged me "to go for it." She read the manuscript several times and kept encouraging me in moments of doubt. The other is, of course, my chief advisor and partner, who functioned as critic and editor during the years we researched and put the biography on paper, my dear wife, Lois.

1

"Greatest Kind of Find"

Buck entered the courtroom feeling confident. He purposely ignored his former teammates already present and clustered together. When he sat down, he was careful to put some distance between himself and the other seven ballplayers. All eight were facing conspiracy charges involving the throwing of the 1919 World Series to the Cincinnati Reds. By now the former eight Chicago White Sox were lumped together as the notorious "Black Sox."

But unlike the others, Buck hadn't touched a cent of the crooked gamblers' tainted money. And he had performed throughout the Series with his usual elan on the field. Yet he had been named as one of the conspirators. Vainly he had sought a separate trial. Now he was primed to tell his side of the story as soon as he could take the witness stand. He hoped sitting apart from the other ballplayers would reinforce the idea that he was not in league with them.

"I am dead anxious for the trial," Buck told a reporter a few months earlier. "Don't say Buck is cringing, that he's hanging his head, that he's trying to run away. Just ask the public to withhold judgment until they hear all. I will tell everything about myself, but there is one thing I won't do and that is say anything against anyone else. I hate a squealer. I know in my heart I never helped throw a game. If my conscience wasn't clear in this respect I would never think of taking a ball in my hands again."

Buck probably first took a ball in his hands as a youngster still in grade school in Pottstown, Pennsylvania. Pottstown is located about 40 miles northwest of Philadelphia and its pleasant hilly environs is cut by the Schuylkill River. Pottstown owes its existence to an iron master, James Potts, who built Pott Grove Manor in 1752. The Manor was General George Washington's headquarters for five days in September, 1777, during the Revolutionary War.

George's father worked as a laborer at the Glasgow Iron Company mill which dominated the industrial town of 13,000 people and built a row of duplexes for its workers on Glasgow Street. In one of these duplexes, at number 504, a Pennsylvania Dutch couple, Daniel and Susan Weaver, celebrated the birth of their first son, George Daniel Weaver, on August 18, 1890. At the time of George's birth, Pottstown had almost tripled its population in the previous decade, with workers attracted to two iron foundries, three rolling mills, two blast furnaces, a nail factory and carworks. Its chief manufactured products included iron bridges and agricultural machines.

Cultural and social life centered around the twelve churches in town. For finishing schools, there were the Cottage Seminary for young ladies and the Hill School for boys. The town supported one daily newspaper and three weeklies and a national bank.

Danny, as George was called, blossomed into a free spirited youngster. He was a tough kid and relished wrestling with his peers in front of the confectionary store down the street from his house. Known as a prankster, Danny caused concern among adult onlookers as he rode a wheelbarrow recklessly down the center of Glasgow Street.

Glasgow Street separated Pottstown on the west from its neighboring smaller town of Stowe, which happened to be a hotbed of baseball activity. As many as 2,000 fans, not much less than the total population of Stowe, came out to watch amateur and semipro games. Living in the midst of so much enthusiasm for the national pastime convinced Danny to take up the game at an early age. In his mid-teens, he already was skilled enough to play for the St. Mary's College team of Phoenixville, a town located only a dozen miles from Pottstown. If there were eligibility rules, St. Mary's College apparently winked at them.

At the age of 18, Weaver was one of the most talked about semipro players in his community. Most of the time Danny cavorted at shortstop, but he also roamed the outfield. "Danny was a spunky, aggressive player who wanted to put on a good show. He wanted to draw attention and draw people to the game. He was a little rambunctious. It was worth the price of admission just to watch him work out. He was a hustler,"recalled Ed McEvoy, who was Weaver's neighbor and saw him play. A veteran minor league ballplayer named Curt McGann was so impressed by Weaver's intense and highly spirited play that he nicknamed him "Buck," and the name stuck, according to McEvoy. Buck never advanced beyond elementary school but had no hankering to end up in the iron mill like his father. He saw baseball as a possible escape from the drudgery and boredom of mill work.

That chance to escape arrived after the major league season ended in the fall of 1909. A team of major leaguers barnstormed into Stowe to challenge the local favorites. Charley Dooin, manager of the Philadelphia Phillies, was impressed by Buck's natural talent, and took him aside to give him some pointers on how to improve his game. Buoyed by such attention, Buck had intended to ask Dooin right there and then for a job in professional baseball but "I never got up my nerve," he recalled years later. There were others who also recognized Buck's potential. Jack Lapp, a catcher for the Philadelphia A's, escorted Buck to Mike Kennedy, an A's scout, who quickly noted Buck's raw talent. Years later Weaver reminisced in an interview with author James T. Farrell, "I didn't know nothin'. Kennedy, the scout from Philadelphia, saw me and he asked me to sign a contract for $125 a month. One hundred-twenty five a month! Why I never saw that much money."

Apparently Buck hadn't signed at first because Kennedy had switched during the winter to Cleveland. He then convinced Buck to sign a contract with the Indians. But as the season got underway, it seemed Cleveland had forgotten him. Buck complained to the ruling baseball commission which then ordered Cleveland to pay Weaver his back wages. Two weeks into the season the Indians sent Buck a check for $62.50. "Boy, was that money!" Buck exclaimed many years later.

Cleveland originally assigned Buck to Saginaw in the Southern Michigan League, but there is no record that he saw any action there. He was soon transferred to Northhampton, Massachusetts, of the Connecticut State League.

Buck had a nightmarish start. Suddenly the nineteen-year-old rookie literally couldn't see the ball. At shortstop he lost track of balls hit squarely two feet in front of him. His debilitated vision led to numerous errors, and he was just as useless at the plate. Buck told his manager about his sight problem but his skipper ignored him. But when Buck struck out twice in his fourteenth game, the manager screamed at him, "Here's your release; you're terrible!" Perhaps in his intense drive to succeed, Buck fell victim to a form of hysteria. Was it possible that he became so emotionally unstable on the field that the problem manifested itself as temporarily failing eyesight?

Buck should have been relieved to get dismissed from the sluggish seventh place Northhampton team. His temperament certainly didn't mesh with that lackadaisical ball club. The respected baseball weekly, The *Sporting News*, indicted the Northhampton team for being the slowest on and off the field and accused their manager, Bill Luby, of being "about the most deliberate man in the entire circuit in getting to his position."

With the strange Northhampton episode behind him,

Buck did get up enough nerve to ask for a job. He traveled to Philadelphia and watched the Phillies play on a Saturday afternoon at Baker Bowl. Weaver later confided, "When I seen them fellows hit and run, I said, 'Hell, I can play!' " He asked manager "Red" Dooin for a chance. Dooin did take Buck on, offering him a contract with York, Pennsylvania, in the Tri-State League for $175 a month. Buck jumped at the chance.

Weaver joined the York White Roses in the middle of June, 1910. *Sporting Life*, a baseball weekly of the time, commented, "It is believed that York has a good man in Weaver . . ." York was desperate for help since it was mired in last place and was destined to remain there all season. Three days after Buck joined the ball club, the White Roses already had wilted with a paltry record of 6 wins and 25 losses. The team was so bad the manager quit and went home because he said he "could not pick his own players."

Buck moved right in and saw action in left field and at third base besides manning his regular post at shortstop. The eye trouble that plagued him at Northhampton departed as suddenly as it had arrived. Despite their season-long residence in the cellar, the White Roses now had a player who could give their fans some exciting moments. The York *Dispatch* reported on Weaver's whirling performances: "Weaver covered a lot of territory in left field and gathered in several balls that looked like sure hits." "The work by Weaver . . . stopped balls intended for base hits." "Weaver was a sensational shortstop . . ." "Weaver Starred But Team Loses." "The York team continued high standard of hitting established last few games led by Weaver . . ." "Weaver sent the crowd into hysterics when he helped the team recover three runs in the same inning when he homered into left field."

However, there were unsettling moments. When Buck committed three errors at shortstop one day late in the season "that proved costly," the *Dispatch* reporter concluded Weaver was a "popular little shortstop but too wild." Buck at 5 feet 10 inches was hardly little by 1910 standards. But was there substance to the reporter's charge that Buck was "too wild"?

When the player draft was held at the end of the season, Buck had hoped "Red" Dooin would pick him. But the Philly manager passed over him in favor of a pitcher. However, superscout Ted Sullivan of the Chicago White Sox liked what he saw in Weaver and purchased him for $750. The White Sox then assigned Buck to the San Francisco Seals of the Pacific Coast League for the 1911 Season.

Buck, pleased with his two hundred dollar a month contract, arrived at spring training at Modesto, California, in February. Buck later reminisced about those early days with San Francisco: "I didn't get nowhere in spring practice. They had Oscar Vitt playing third base. I'm a goof—I didn't know nothin' from nothin'. Oscar was sick. He would field a few balls and call it a day. So I practiced. I didn't know they considered Vitt the best third baseman in the league. I said to myself, 'Brother, I can take your job.'

"I sat on the bench for about three weeks. One day the center fielder got hurt. The manager says to me, 'Georgie, can you play the outfield?' I told him, 'I can play any place.'

"A ball was hit just over the infield. I run. I keep running and make the catch right here off the ground. And then I come to bat and swing. The ball sails and hits the fence. I make a two base hit. The next time I bat, I hit the fence again. See, I got the breaks. But after that, I told myself, 'Georgie, my boy, now you're in.' "

And Buck was right. Harry B. Smith, a *San Francisco Chronicle* sportswriter, commented, "Tab this fellow Weaver. He did plenty of work . . . to convince those who have seen him that he can deliver the goods. . . . I don't know just what Weaver will do at bat, but as a fielder he is fast and bound to be a sensation. This afternoon, even though it was only a practice game, and considered a joke at that, he went far over toward the left-field fence to grab a foul, and what is more, he got it with one hand." Look at one of the small, primitive fielding gloves of the day and you'll understand why catching a ball with one hand was so astonishing. Smith went on about Weaver: "It [is with] his general style in handling himself around shortstop that he impressed the fans."

More than the fans were impressed. Another *Chronicle* story gushed, "Weaver is one of those boys who can't 'play' at baseball, he goes full tilt." Manager Danny Long ". . . made it plain that he thinks Weaver is the greatest kind of a find and that he will force a place for himself on the team."

That Buck did. He was tested at all outfield stations, second base and shortstop. When Buck was forced out of the lineup for a week early in May with a "bad case of a Charley horse," the *Chronicle* observed, "Weaver is still out of the game and is missed very much, for he looks like one of the best ball players seen here in years." In a Memorial Day game, the *Chronicle* reported, "That boy Weaver covered the entire outfield . . . and was a regular greyhound."

Baseball was the fuel that fired up Buck's natural exuberance to new highs. In one game while playing center field he threw up his hands and yelled every time his pitcher threw a strike. "He certainly put a lot of life into the contest," said the *Chronicle's* Smith. As the season wore on Buck stayed put at shortstop where his acrobatic fielding earned him raves from the press such as "sensational" and "marvelous." His unbridled energy wasn't always appreciated by his infield teammates, however. They complained that Buck's speedy and powerful throws threatened to cripple their hands. Buck's play at shortstop won the attention of a young sports cartoonist for the *Chronicle* named Robert Ripley. He drew a four column cartoon showing Weaver with his arm cocked ready to fire the ball. So impressed was Ripley by Buck's talents that he drew him ten times the size of his teammates. Later, Ripley himself rose to national fame with his "Believe It Or Not" cartoon series.

It was now obvious that Weaver had become valuable baseball property. Near the end of July, the owners of the Seals claimed Weaver as their own and said they were anxious to sell Weaver to a major league team before the season ended to avoid the draft. Reminded that Buck had come to the Seals under options from the White Sox, San Francisco denied it. Publicly the White Sox said nothing. A month later, however, when Chicago recalled Weaver for the following spring, San Francisco didn't complain.

Buck hurt his leg about the time the White Sox recalled him, forcing him out of the lineup for two weeks. Uncharacteristically, he wasn't in a hurry to get back into action. "Of course, if we were fighting for the pennant, I would take a chance of crippling myself but under the conditions there is no reason why I shouldn't follow my doctor's orders and be careful." The Seals were resting in fourth place and would soon drop another notch before the season ended.

On his return Buck suddenly became so erratic that fans began howling, "Error a Day Weaver!" Commented the *Chronicle*: "The Seals hitherto sensational youngster, who has been heralded far and wide as the 'find' of the season and one of the most natural ball players ever shown on the coast . . . . has certainly been off form . . . In the last seven games played Weaver has made no less than eleven big errors. He has been unable seemingly to hold or throw a ball with any degree of sureness and his fall down has been one of the reasons why the Seals have lost so consistently of late."

Manager Long said, "The boy really needs another year before tackling the tough game in the big league. I think Weaver realizes it, too. . . . I have written to Comiskey and hope that he will let Weaver stick here another season." Charles Albert Comiskey, the Sox owner, would not reconsider, even though only two shortstops in the league fielded worse for average than Buck's .898 mark. But his final batting average of .282 was the third highest on the team.

When the *Chronicle's* Smith named his all-star team at the end of the season, he left Buck off the team. He explained why: "A couple of months before the season closed and George Weaver would have been given a mark. He was hitting like a fiend and fielding well. But of late his work has suffered. Weaver, to be frank, has endeavored to play an individual game and hasn't apparently been much of a listener to older heads than himself. He has the fault of trying to swing hard on every ball that is pitched to him without regard to the conditions of the game itself." Ironically, Smith did not go into details about Buck's fielding.

2

The Big Show

Weaver remained in California during the winter working
on a stock ranch near San Francisco. He grew stronger physically as he tackled the tough tasks of ranch life and earned
a little money. But he was disturbed by letters from his dad
that his mother was seriously ill and getting worse. Much
as he wanted to see his mother, a railroad trip back to Pennsylvania and then another one to the 1912 White Sox spring
training camp in Waco, Texas, would drain him of all his
earnings. On the day he and his new teammate, Ping Bodie,
were to leave San Francisco for training camp, Buck received
a telegram from his dad saying his mother had died. Buck's
dad advised him not to try to come home for the funeral because it would have been impossible to report on time to the
White Sox. He told his son to "join the team and keep a stiff
upper lip."

Traveling with Ping Bodie probably made the trip much
more bearable for Buck. Ping was a jolly, roly-poly outfielder
known as the "Frisco fence buster" who also played for the
Seals before joining the White Sox. Ping's fielding, however,
forced fans to hold their breath as he zigzagged under fly
balls. He was one of the first Italians out of San Francisco
to reach the big leagues. Born Francesco Pezzola, he acquired
the nickname Ping as a child from a family friend. His father had worked the gold field around Bodie, California, so

the children adopted the name Bodie. Ping formally was known as Frank.

Buck would have to wrestle shortstop away from Lee Tannehill, a veteran who had been with the White Sox ten years and who was expected to be on the job when the season opened. Besides Tannehill, there was a batch of other young hopefuls blocking Buck's path for a place on the roster. Said *Baseball Magazine*, "Comiskey's White Sox offered better chances for juveniles than any other club in either league."

Weaver was eager to take advantage of those better chances, especially when Tannehill injured himself in a precamp workout and was out of action. In the first intrasquad game he helped provide Comiskey, who sat in the stands, with "a contented smile when the game was over."

Comiskey already knew he had something special in Buck Weaver. Few people could have been a better judge of baseball talent than the owner of the White Sox. A genuine pioneering giant of the game, Comiskey, like Weaver, was consumed by baseball. He was the only owner of a major league ball club who had been a player. Originally starting out as a pitcher on the sandlots of Chicago, he continued pitching in college and in the semipros. When his arm went lame, Comiskey switched to first base. As a first baseman, he played in the major leagues thirteen years with the St. Louis Browns and Cincinnati Reds and managed both ball clubs. He won four pennants with the Browns in the American Association, then a major league, during the 1880s and one world championship beating the Chicago White Stockings of the National League in 1886.

Comiskey is generally credited with being the original first baseman to play off the bag. Until his time, first basemen remained anchored with one foot on the base. He drifted off the bag, stationing himself sometimes on the edge of the outfield grass. He even cruised into short right field for popups, an unheard of maneuver in his day. When he scurried away from first base to snare ground balls, fans were flabbergasted to see the pitcher racing off the mound to cover first. Besides making the pitcher an extra first baseman, Comiskey taught his infielders an array of new tactics: to shift positions for different batters, to play in on the grass for a possible throw to the plate to cut off a run, to maneuver for possible bunts, to back up throws and to synchronize their moves to speed up double plays. Comiskey's ideas were quickly copied by other teams to revolutionize not only infield play but the game itself.

Together with a former Cincinnati sports editor named Byron Bancroft Johnson, Comiskey founded the Western League in 1894, transformed it into the American League in 1900 and after a bitter struggle won equal footing with the National League in 1903. He took over the Chicago franchise in his home town and called his team the White Stockings, the original name of the Chicago Cubs. On the advice of *Chicago Tribune* sportswriter Irving E. Sanborn, Comiskey shortened the name to White Sox to satisfy newspaper headline writers.

Comiskey, who was affectionately called "Commy" by his friends and newspapermen, also gained the nickname, "Old Roman." There doesn't seem to be any one incident that inspired the name, nor was there a moment when the title was bequeathed. Several stories abound. By the time Comiskey left St. Louis after the 1889 season, a sportswriter lauded him as the "Noblest Roman of the Baseball Empire," probably for his popular innovations and his fierce competitive spirit. Gus Axelson, in his biography, *Commy*, pointed to his aquiline nose, popularly called Roman, that earned Comiskey his stately sobriquet. His grandson, Charles A. Comiskey II, the last of the Comiskey clan to own a piece of the White Sox, said the family handed down stories that his grandfather had won the "Old Roman" moniker in the early years of the century because of his sartorial flamboyance.

Comiskey wasn't the only one impressed in 1912 by Weaver's demeanor. Buck's bubbly manner was the talk of the camp. *Chicago Tribune* sportswriter Sam Weller wrote, "He goes through the work as if it were the greatest fun in the world." During infield practice when Buck "showed more activity around shortstop than anyone who has tried for that Sox job . . . ," coach Kid Gleason purposely began slamming the ball far to Buck's left and right. Buck stretched all the way back of third and then scooted behind second and fired the ball like a bullet to first base. If Buck fumbled or missed the ball, he yelled for another hot smash his way. One afternoon Buck seemed extraordinarily enthusiastic so the captain of the team, veteran third baseman Harry Lord, "cautioned him to ease up a bit or he might wear himself out . . ." Even when practice ended Buck hated to quit and was the last player to leave the field. In exhibition games "he fired a steady stream of Frisco language that did much to inspire his mates and disconcert the opposing players." On the field he never seemed to lose his "pepper" no matter what happened. In those first days, though, Buck would break down in tears in the loneliness of his room, still grieving over the loss of his mother. Perhaps he regretted not going home while she was still alive.

By the end of spring training Buck had won the job at short. However, there were questions about his hitting and base running. Buck showed speed but needed coaching on how to run the bases.

That coaching would come from William "Kid" Gleason who would become like a father to the rookie shortstop. Gleason, also in his first year with the White Sox, had been plucked out of retirement by new White Sox manager Jimmy Callahan.

Gleason made the majors as a twenty-two year old right-handed pitcher with the Philadelphia Phillies in 1888. He immediately was tagged with the nickname "Kid" because of his youth and short height at 5 feet 7 inches. The Kid twirled eight years, having a phenomenal year in 1890 when he won 38 games against 17 losses with a 2.63 earned run average. He concluded his pitching career with the Baltimore Orioles with 129 victories and the same number of defeats.

At Baltimore he was converted into a second baseman and later saw action with the New York Giants, Detroit

Tigers and again with the Phillies. Gleason's playing days ended abruptly in 1907 when he was hit in the groin by a foul line drive in pre-game practice. He laughed about the accident but he could never play again.

Besides pitching and playing second base in his long twenty-two year career, the Kid performed in the outfield, shortstop, first base and even went behind the plate for one game. His years of experience and versatility caught the eye of Jimmy Callahan, the new White Sox manager. Apparently, Callahan knew something about Gleason's teaching abilities and patience with young ballplayers. He asked the veteran to join the ball club as his assistant and coach.

Spring training in those years had a way of testing the endurance and stamina of ballplayers beyond normal expectations. For an exhibition game at Corsicana, for instance, the Sox stayed at a hotel that had only one bathtub. Luckily, dressing rooms were found next to a swimming pool on the other side of town. There were no street cars and hardly any sidewalks so the players slushed in their uniforms about a mile to the ballpark in rich black mud.

It started to rain about a half hour before the game so it looked as if the match would be canceled. But about 1500 excited fans ignored the rain and mud. "They just began trooping out, some in rubber boots, some in hunting boots, and some in low tan shoes. Not only men came. They brought their wives and daughters and umbrellas, and demanded a ball game. . . . Those who didn't have a quarter climbed the trees outside the fence or stood in wagons and looked over the crowds."

The players huddled in the grandstand before wading ankle deep in mud. Great ovals of it stuck to their shoes as they stepped out of it. The crowd cheered and laughed.

"Lord sent the crowd into a spasm by putting a liner over the right field wall right through a crowd of colored gents watching the game from a dray wagon." Somehow the players were driven back to their dressing rooms after the game and "had only a half hour to get into street clothes and catch a train back to Waco."

Closing out five weeks of spring training in Texas with a rain postponement led Weller to conclude: " . . . one is forced to admit that Texas is a great state for raising cotton and coyotes. . . . if President Comiskey takes the club elsewhere next spring it's bound to be agreeable to all the athletes."

It was a rare warm day for the opening of the season. Temperature at game time climbed to 71 degrees. The sun beamed brightly and a gentle breeze loafed leisurely out of the southwest. Hardly a typical April 11th in Chicago, and the fans made the most of it.

The crowd swarmed to Comiskey Park. They walked or rode street cars, autos, cabs and "el" trains. Some hardy fans challenged the technological age by driving up in tally-hos, coaches drawn by four horses, and carryalls, light vehicles pulled by one horse. When the nearby garage filled, drivers parked on side streets where they were greeted by boys who yelled, "Mind your auto, mister?" Often, the harried owners obliged. They didn't want to miss any of the opening ceremonies. The car watchers, who should have been in school, then climbed telephone poles and trees and occupied rooftops to catch a glimpse of the game.

Inside Comiskey Park, one half hour before the game, fans already sat in the aisles and packed the standing room area in the rear. The bleachers bulged beyond capacity as the crowd "hung over the fence in center field." Just about 30,000 spectators jammed the ballpark, smashing previous highs of 25,000. "Never since baseball began in Chicago have so many people been out for an opening game," vouched *Chicago Tribune* sportswriter Walter Eckersall, a former All-American football player at the University of Chicago. It would be the largest opening day crowd in the American League. In the bleachers men sat in shirtsleeves, something fans could not remember ever happening before on opening day. The fans downed more soda pop and ice cream than hot dogs and pop corn.

Scheduled to start at 3 o'clock, the game was delayed a few minutes to allow Mayor Carter Harrison to reach his seat. Then the White Sox took the field. They were attired in their familiar striped white uniforms with the big S emblazoned on the left side of their jerseys and the O and X inserted in the loops of the S. The dome of the caps were white with stripes with dark peaks. The stockings were solid white.

As Buck raced out to his position, the fans saw a twenty-one year old, slim, broad-shouldered rookie with a swarthy complexion, blue eyes and brown hair, about 5 feet 10 inches tall and weighing a trim 168 pounds. His lithe, athletic body moved with effortless grace as he took infield drill. Buck's facial features were unique. He had a narrow cleft chin with high cheekbones and a broad forehead. His face could be best described as shaped like the letter V. On the field he seemed to be wearing a perpetual smile or grin.

Before the game Buck must have gazed in wonderment at the most spaciously designed park in the majors proclaimed the "Baseball Palace of the World." The foul lines extended symmetrically to 362 feet in left and right field and it was 420 feet to dead center. No wonder Comiskey Park quickly gained the reputation as a pitcher's ballpark. And not by accident. The generous outfield dimensions were suggested, perhaps in self-interest, by Big Ed Walsh, the White Sox formidable spitballer, already a legendary figure. His ideas were incorporated by young architect Zachary Taylor Davis, who later designed Wrigley Field as well.

Comiskey Park, originally called White Sox Park, opened July 1, 1910, and could accommodate 32,000 fans. Although the playing field attested to Comiskey's love of the game itself, he showed his tight-fisted control of the purse by installing narrow, straight back and cramped seats in order to squeeze more fans into the park. Yet this same man offered his loyal White Sox followers the lowest priced admissions in the majors.

After the White Sox won the opener against St. Louis, Buck wrote in a short piece under his byline in the *Tribune*, "It's great to play a game in the big leagues. That was the biggest crowd I ever saw. I never thought there would be so many people out for the first game. But I wasn't scared at all and just made myself forget there were 30,000 people looking on and went ahead and played ball just as if I was in Frisco. Of course, I was awfully glad I got a hit in the first game and scored the first run for the boys, but I might not have scored if Ed Walsh hadn't hit that one to the fence. It was easy for me then. Besides scoring the first run I also made the first 'boot' on the team and I'll very likely make a lot more of them before the season is over, but I'm going to give 'em the best I have all the time."

Buck couldn't have been more right about making errors or playing with unrelenting intensity. The next day Weller reported: ". . . 'Buck' made a horrible mess on two of his first three fielding chances, and there have been youngsters who would collapse under such conditions. But 'Buck' came up smiling instead of fretting after the second mistake and fought 'em harder than ever. He had nine more chances at the ball before the game was over and he handled every one of them perfectly. The fact that he pulled himself together makes him look like a better ballplayer than had he handled all twelve of the chances without a mistake."

Early in May Buck earned another nickname. He was forced out of a game when he suffered a spike wound on his left hand tagging a runner out at second base. His replacement was hit by a pitch which fractured his right wrist. The next day Buck returned to action with his left hand in bandages. Sanborn, who was the dean of the Chicago sports press corps, noted: "Weaver plugged the hole at shortstop by going into the game with a left hand done in bandages. In spite of that handicap the 'ginger kid' played a splendid game . . ."

Most of the summer Buck roamed all over the left side of the infield, stretching far behind third and scooting behind second or charging in behind the mound to snap up slow rollers. His explosive throwing arm cut down dozens of would-be base runners. And the youngster ignited the infield with his constant chatter of support. But as in San Francisco his brilliance was dimmed by too many fumbles and wild heaves. Buck's troubles were compounded by a disappointing dip at the plate. Though he grew steadier as the summer rolled by, he could only muster an anemic .224 batting average for the season. Yet manager Jimmy Callahan resisted any notion to pull Buck out of the lineup. Comiskey shared Callahan's unusual patience with the obviously talented youngster.

Callahan also may have developed a fatherly interest in his mercurial fielding shortstop. He, like Weaver, grew up in a working class mill town—Fitchburg, Massachusetts, about fifty miles from Boston. Dropping out of public school when his father died, Callahan went to work as a sewing machine boy in a worsted mill at 75 cents a day for almost a 12 hour shift with "a whole half hour for lunch."

Later, while employed as a plumber's apprentice, he began playing semipro ball. When his boss issued an ultimatum, plumbing or baseball, Callahan chose to hone his skills on the diamond. He reached the majors as a pitcher with the Chicago Nationals in 1897. He also played short and spent some time in the outfield.

In the midst of a successful career with the Cubs, Callahan was lured by Comiskey to the White Sox in 1901 in the beginning of the baseball war between the National and American Leagues. He took a brief turn at managing the Sox in 1903 and part of 1904 before voluntarily leaving the team in 1906. He became owner, manager and player with the Logan Squares, one of the most popular and successful semipro teams in the Chicago area. By the close of the 1910 season he was forced to give up the ball club because rising real estate values drove rentals skyward. Suspended by the National Commission for independently leaving the majors, Callahan obtained an official release from Comiskey so he could regain his eligibility with the White Sox. He rejoined the team in 1911, batted .281 in 120 games, played left field and stole 45 bases. Comiskey named him manager for the 1912 season.

But by August 1 even Callahan had seen enough of Buck's bewildering play. He committed four errors in a var-

iety of ways. He "missed a smash to start the game," "booted" another grounder, "muffed" a pop fly and "pegged poorly
to first." The White Sox called up a rookie infielder named
Ernie Johnson and by August 5 Buck was watching the game
from the dugout. It looked like a long exile for Buck. Johnson was playing well and winning favorable comment from
the local sportswriters. When Buck trudged out to the bullpen to throw one sportswriter observed, Buck had "a better
chance to get back into the game as a slab man than as a
shortstop." Weaver rode the bench for more than a week.
Then suddenly Johnson became ill and had to leave a game
"suffering a slight touch of ptomaine poisoning from eating
crab in Cleveland. . . . The youngster has been wised up
that it is not safe to eat sea food west of Philadelphia, and
won't do it again."

Buck returned to the lineup for the rest of the season.
He resumed his chameleon-like performance, finishing with
a woefully weak fielding average of .915 on a frightening
number of 71 errors, the worst record of any regular shortstop in the majors. But at the morning workouts, Buck was
doggedly seeking to correct his weaknesses. One month before the season ended, he started practicing batting left-
handed. By the time the pennant race was over, Buck was
handling the bat as well from the left side as the right. Callahan predicted Buck would increase his batting average fifty
points as a switch hitter.

As for the White Sox, their 1912 campaign started out
quite promising. They jumped off to a quick lead. By the
middle of May they had won 18 of 20 games. But Hughie
Jennings, manager of the Detroit Tigers, warned, "Chicago is
playing wonderful ball, but it cannot maintain such a pace
as it is setting. Here is Walsh pitching half of his club's
games." Jennings was right. Walsh couldn't do it alone. The
Sox fell to fifth place by July 5. Comiskey searched for
pitching help. On the advice of Ring Lardner, a *Chicago
Tribune* baseball writer who had been the sports editor of
the Boston *American*, Comiskey claimed veteran right-hander
Eddie Cicotte on waivers from the Boston Red Sox. Cicotte

had been with the Red Sox for four years but wasn't getting along with Boston management. "He was suspended without pay so much of the time that it was like having no job."

A month later, Comiskey, pointing to the future, purchased a catcher named Ray Schalk from the Milwaukee Brewers. Weller reported: "He is rated by many critics as the best catcher in the American Association this year, and he's a young fellow just coming to the front, so it's possible that in a year's time he will be worth all of $15,000 to the White Sox. He is not a large fellow, but is a fine fielder and a good batter and base runner." In his first game on August 11, he "played like a major leaguer right from the start."

The end of the regular season did not mean the end of Buck's problems for the year. It had become the custom for the White Sox and Cubs to play each other in a post-season city series if they were not engaged in such trivialities as a World Series. Players, newspapers and fans regarded the exhibition city series with the same emotional intensity and excitement as a World Series. Often the attendance at the Chicago ballparks outdrew the more prestigious inter-league event. The local newspapers covered both series with their top sportswriters and afforded the games equal treatment. As in the World Series, the major league offices worked out the assignment of umpires and division of gate receipts. The city series also offered the ballplayers a chance to pick up some extra cash. That was no small matter since their shares in the city series were a hefty percentage of their contracts for the year. Even though there was always danger players could be seriously hurt in these post-season games, the dollar rewards brushed aside such concerns. Playing his usual gung-ho game, Buck was the only player injured in the series.

In incredible, ferocious competition, the first game ended in a nine inning 0 to 0 tie. Neither team gave ground in the second game as they battled to a twelve inning 3 to 3 tie. With two out in the eigth inning of the second game, Buck chased a Texas Leaguer into short left field with his back to the infield. Charging in was regular third baseman Harry Lord who was playing left field. Each ran "with the throttle wide open . . . tearing madly toward the same spot. The roar of the crowd deadened all warning cries . . . and made it impossible for the players to hear each other . . .

"Just as the ball came down Weaver made a final lunge, reached it, but was struck on the jaw by Lord's knee or shoulder . . . as Harry plunged forward, expecting to catch the ball himself." Both players fell to the earth "completely out" with the ball resting between them. Before the Sox could recover the ball, the base runner was safe at third.

Both players were carried from the field before the stunned, silent crowd. Lord walked under his own power to the clubhouse, dressed and left the park. But Buck was carried, still unconscious, to the clubhouse and placed on a rubbing table. Club physician James H. Blair rushed to his side. Buck came to in about fifteen minutes but still couldn't recognize some of his teammates.

Dr. Blair put Weaver under the shower, helped him dress, then accompanied Buck in a cab to Buck's rooming house. On the way Buck fell unconscious again. Dr. Blair ordered the taxi to the hospital where he worked on Weaver until 9 P.M. "without being able to bring him back to normal condition." Later that evening Blair said Weaver "seemed to be resting easily . . ." He had suffered "a slight cut on the upper lip, a scratch over one eye and a slight bruise on the left side of the head just in front of the ear." That bruise led Blair to fear a possible skull fracture but no X rays were taken.

Buck ignored Blair's advice to stay in bed the next day, Saturday. He dressed, left the hospital and went to the game where he watched from the press box as the Cubs won, 5 to 4. He told reporters there was nothing seriously wrong and promised to be back in the lineup on Monday. Buck still didn't play Monday, though, as the Cubs won their third straight game. It looked as if the Cubs had the series guaranteed, but the White Sox rallied to win four straight in a rousing comeback.

The Sox comeback gave Buck a chance to play again. He took batting and fielding practice before the Sox's second win but he didn't feel up to playing. Buck did celebrate his return to shortstop for the third White Sox win by smashing "a terrific line drive to the lumber pile in left-center and by a splendid sprint made it good for a home run." The Sox slaughtered the dazed Cubs, 16 to 0, in the last game, with Buck pounding a double and triple. Buck showed no ill effects from his injury.

For their incredible comeback each White Sox player earned a winners' share of $809.15 while each losing club player was rewarded with a check for $567.72. Buck Weaver's salary for the entire regular 1912 season was $1,800. Major league stars averaged less than $4,000 a year while average ballplayers collected between $2,000 and $2,500 a season. Factory workers in 1912 earned about $550 a year.

Even though the baseball season finally drew to a close, Buck Weaver could not completely relax. On the last day of the year the *Tribune* headlined: "FIGHT AHEAD FOR SOX SHORTSTOPS." Buck's job was hardly secure.

3

Buck's Roller Coaster Season

During the winter Buck visited Oscar Vitt, his old teammate and buddy from the days with the San Francisco Seals. Vitt, now with the Detroit Tigers, owned a cabin in the California mountains and invited Weaver to be his guest. To help Vitt with the daily chores and incidently help himself round into shape, Buck began chopping wood. He then noticed when he swung left-handed, he always hit the groove in the wood while missing the groove when he swung from the right side. His sureness from the left side convinced Buck more than ever to become a switch hitter.

In reminiscing his decision to bat left-handed with author James T. Farrell, Weaver said, "But I didn't start swinging right away. First I just stood up at the plate like this."

"He illustrated his stance with his feet close together," Farrell recalled in his *My Baseball Diary*.

Buck continued: "I let them pitch to me. Then I practiced taking one step forward like this. I didn't try to hit the ball. I just wanted to get my swing and my confidence. Then I practiced getting away running. I got my confidence that way. And then I knew I could hit anything. I'd have the ball always comin' in on me. If a left-hander was pitching, I'd bat right handed where my power was. The ball would still be comin' in to me. All of them pitches would be comin' in."

Buck didn't have to travel far this time to get to spring

training. Comiskey had become disenchanted just as the players had with the weather conditions in Texas the previous year. He decided to move the spring training site to Paso Robles, California, a health resort town located about 200 miles south of San Francisco.

Not many distractions disturbed the serious business of getting ready for the coming season. The main attraction of the isolated resort was the natural sulphur spring which sprang out of the ground at 100 degrees ". . . and ran into the swimming tank just right for a hot bath." Only about 2,000 people lived in the village in which the largest building was the hotel where the players stayed. The hotel, about a half mile from the playing field, did not provide private baths and showers so the players used the "swimming tank or the showers or tub baths in the natatorium, which is about 100 feet from the hotel."

As for amusement there was a motion picture theatre that changed its bill once a week. Weller observed, "The nearest thirst parlor to Paso Robles is six miles away, which greatly aids those who are sticking on the wagon." At least one Saturday night there was an informal party in the ballroom and Buck, who somehow had become an accomplished dancer, "gave an exhibition of the Frisco Rag." Weaver always seemed ready to entertain a crowd whether it was baseball or some other endeavor.

Unfortunately spring training did not cure Weaver's penchant for messing up plays at short. Callahan chose to ignore Buck's errors. He said, "There's no chance to keep that kid off the team with all his enthusiasm and aggressiveness." The *Tribune* commented: "Competition for the job of shortstop seems to have inspired Weaver to further efforts for he has shown even more pepper in the spring training than he did during the season."

But were enthusiasm and aggressiveness enough to win a spot on the big league club? Baseball observers may have wondered why the Sox held on to Buck Weaver considering his puny .915 fielding average and his astronomical 71 errors in his first year. He didn't come through as a consistent hitter, either. Logic seemed to indicate that Buck might need more seasoning in the minors as manager Danny Long of San Francisco had cautioned in 1911. Then again one could not gainsay Buck's spectacular execution of plays seldom seen on the baseball diamond. His acrobatic gracefulness drew admiring cheers from the crowd, friend or foe. Then too, the spirit of the entire team was lifted by his presence.

Highly respected sportswriter Hugh S. Fullerton of the *Tribune* failed to be impressed by Buck and touted a rookie shortstop named Joe Berger: "Sadly enough, it seems as if Weaver is the shortstop. He is a fair ballplayer, but has not lived up to his promise of last spring. Not disparaging his work at all, he isn't of the caliber that wins pennants. I had high hopes Berger would make the job. He has not looked good to the experts travelling with the team and Callahan does not seem to take him seriously. He certainly will be kept and probably will get a chance later."

Only one day after Fullerton's prediction that Berger would get a chance later, Callahan benched Buck in favor of Berger. Weaver may have had cause to worry but he had withstood challengers before. One of his serious challengers, Ernie Johnson, had just been shipped to Los Angeles.

Berger impressed the onlookers. The *Tribune* headlined: "Berger Replaces Weaver at Short and Delights Coast Fans by His Showing." "The feature of both games for the coast fans," Weller wrote, "was the presence of Joe Berger at shortstop for the Sox. The natives out here think he's going to set the world on fire this season when he displays his prowess to the ball fans in the east.

"Joe made good, getting a double, two bases on balls and being hit once by a pitched ball in the morning game. He bagged a single and a couple of passes in the afternoon. In addition, he handled everything in the field like a coming star, and the crowd had many opportunities to applaud him."

All Buck could do was sit on the bench in the morning game and take over left field for manager Callahan after three innings of the second game. Buck stayed in left field as a large, colorful crowd watched one of the last spring training games at Yuma, Arizona. Though the roof of the grandstand had recently burned down, the fans gathered under a burning sun with the temperature over 90 degrees in the shade. Many men and women rode up on horseback and viewed the action from the saddle along the foul lines. More spectators arrived in automobiles, big wagons and buggies. A musical group called the Alabama Minstrels, scheduled to perform that night in town, provided music between half innings. Also in town that day were "several hundred Indians from the reservation across the Colorado river . . . to take in the sights. They wore long hair, hand paint and feathers in plenty, and all were barefooted."

Buck warded off Joe Berger's challenge and was back at shortstop on opening day. He launched the season in a blaze of superb play. The *Tribune* headlined: "WEAVER STAR ON DEFENSE" and the story chortled: ". . . the stunts of young Weaver turned in about four or five plays that were thrillers . . ." In Detroit, "Weaver evoked prolonged applause from the hostile crowd . . ."

Near the end of May, Buck ". . . got tangled up inside with some bum eats and the trouble was diagnosed as ptomaine poisoning." He stayed in Chicago while his teammates started a road trip. But Buck recovered quickly, grabbed a train for Cleveland where he played both ends of a double-header. Advised Sanborn: "After watching him play eighteen innings we asked Manager Callahan to inject ptomaine poisoning into all his players. Weaver led the Sox in hitting with two clean swats in each game and fielded like a threshing machine . . ."

Shortly thereafter, the White Sox obtained first baseman Hal Chase from the New York Yankees. To get Chase the White Sox surrendered infielder Rollie Zeider, who was plagued by bunions, and a lumbering, clumsy first baseman named Babe Borton. Mark Roth, a sportswriter for the New York *Globe*, commented wryly, "The Yankees traded Chase to Chicago for a bunion and an onion."

Chase, nicknamed Prince Hal because of his fancy glove and sprightliness around first base, also held a lifetime batting mark of .285 since coming to the majors in 1905. Admittedly, he would make some of Buck's misfired throws look a little more secure. But he already had the rancid odor of a "fixer" and thrower of ball games. Yet the baseball powers preferred to hold their noses and do nothing.

Chase would not toil long in a White Sox uniform. In June of 1914, a year later, he jumped to Buffalo of the newly formed Federal League. The Federals, started in 1913 by multi-millionaire businessmen, challenged the established majors by offering big monied contracts to recognized stars. Otherwise the rosters were filled with fringe major leaguers, has-beens, minor leaguers and sandlotters. A number of talented players jumped to the so-called "outlaw" league but the league could not convince the federal courts to rule significantly in its favor on issues dealing with the reserve clause and charges of monopoly. By the end of 1915 the Federal League had passed into history.

About the same time an attempt was made to organize the professional players into a union called the Players Protective Fraternity. In a few years that too fizzled soon after a threatened strike was called off. While many major leaguers belonged at one time or other to the union, Buck never joined. He said he had confidence he could deal fairly with the owner of a ball club on a one-to-one basis.

Much of the 1913 season seemed to be a carbon copy of the previous one for Buck, at least on defense. By the middle of summer, the White Sox infield was being compared with the inimitable defense of the Philadelphia A's. After a particularly outstanding afternoon, Sanborn wrote ". . . if the Sox would continue to handle ground balls as they did yesterday, all infields of the past would be discounted.

"In the center of all the brilliancy was Young Buck Weaver. His fielding prowess was almost super human. At least four times he brought the crowd to its feet by his sensational actions."

In another game Buck displayed his daring by chasing a high foul fly towards the concrete wall beyond the left field foul line. It looked as though he would crash into the wall but he slid just as he made the catch. When his momentum carried him into the wall, he finished "with one leg hanging over into the pavilion but held the ball and was uninjured." The catch "brought a storm of applause."

But soon Buck began to couple his defensive gems with so many blunders that the crowds and writers were again calling him "Error a Day" Weaver. On some days that was being kind. Sanborn, who was generous in his praise of Weaver when he played well, could just as easily sting Buck with sarcasm when he played poorly. Near the end of July when Buck blew four chances in one game, Sanborn commented with biting wit, "Buck Weaver had a terrible day in the field and unfortunately it came when a lot of batters were hitting the ball at him."

In late August Callahan started a rookie pitcher named Linn Scroggins. Scroggins walked the first batter who then stole second. Sanborn followed with his verbal barrage: "He made the next batter hit to Weaver, who with aeons of time to spare took plenty of aim and made a wild throw to first.

"Probably the shortstops in Oklahoma aren't in a habit of throwing down their pitchers in that way, for the blow completely upset Scroggins and he was taken out after he pitched three straight bad balls to the third batter. . . . Next time [White Sox scout Ted] Sullivan stands sponsor for a pitcher he probably will insist on bringing along said pitcher's own shortstop by way of support."

Perhaps Sanborn's merciless criticisms stung Buck so much that it disturbed his concentration on the field. Maybe. Maybe he was down on himself because he was making as many errors as he had the year before. (He would finish the season with only one less.) Whatever the reason, Buck failed to sprint to first on a ball he hit back to the pitcher. It was a shocking display because usually no one was "in the game" more. Before a hometown crowd of 20,000, Buck jogged to first and the pitcher's throw got away from the first baseman, "rolling about six feet from the bag." But "because Buck had stopped running," the first baseman recovered the ball in time for the out.

Worse yet, in late August in Chicago Sanborn targeted Buck for another blast: "The worst bonehead play I ever saw . . ." With two out, Philadelphia had runners on first and third. Eddie Collins took off for second on an attempted steal. Buck took the throw and tagged Collins. Without looking for a call from the umpire, he rolled the ball to the pitcher's mound, thinking he had the third out. But the umpire signaled "safe" and the runner on third scored with the tying run. The Sox lost the game, 2 to 1.

One thing about Sanborn was he didn't spare his criticism. When the fourth place White Sox lost a twin bill to Cleveland on Labor Day, he left no doubt what he thought of the ball club. "Chicago's White Sox looked like the worst team that ever donned uniforms in any league today when they lost both halves of their double bill. . . ."

For Buck it really wasn't that bad a summer. In fact it turned out to be unexpectedly bright. There were joyful personal moments such as when the White Sox played in Philadelphia. About twenty to thirty of his friends from Pottstown and Stowe would take a train in to watch Buck play. Buck would arrange to have seats for them right behind the Sox dugout. Buck would stay in Pottstown overnight with his dad every time the Sox came in. That June "a delegation of Weaver's friends and fellow citizens from Pottstown came across the river and presented him with a gold watch and chain in token of their esteem. For some time, Stowe and Pottstown have disputed the honor of being the birthplace of the coming great shortstop."

Though Buck was born in Pottstown according to his baptismal papers, baseball records show Stowe as his birthplace. Glasgow Street divided Pottstown from Stowe starting at the Pottstown curbstone. The house in which Buck was born was on the Pottstown side of Glasgow Street. It was easy to see how partisans of both towns could claim Buck. Buck must have informed the baseball record keepers he originated in Stowe where he played most of his hometown baseball. In any case he allowed both towns to claim him.

Buck could not have been down on himself long. In the last month of the season he raised his batting average from .247 to .272, high enough to lead the team in hitting. For that surprising accomplishment, he won a silver bat and ball donated by a Chicago businessman. Buck had raised his batting mark almost fifty points from the previous season as a switch hitter just as manager Callahan had predicted. As his hitting became more robust, Buck's fielding grew steadier. He committed only three errors in the last two and a half weeks of the season—nothing spectacular, but considering Buck's problems, a pleasant improvement.

In a game against New York Buck showed how much he had regained his confidence and sense of leadership. In a display of surprising spunkiness, the youngster who had recently turned twenty-three dared to advise a starting pitcher how to pitch in a tough situation. With the bases loaded, Lefty "Tex" Russell had just walked the weakest hitter on the Yankees to force in a run. Buck hustled to the mound and suggested that "Tex" would have better control if he would go with his full windup since the bases were still loaded. Russell rebuffed Buck's counsel. He snapped at Weaver, telling him to go back and play shortstop and let him do the pitching. The two players exchanged some heated words. "Tex" was showering rather than pitching before the inning was over. Russell's exit prompted Sanborn to write, it "may convince Russell it is possible hereafter to accept a suggestion from a teammate in a pinch without lowering his dignity."

The White Sox finished in fifth place and again beat the Cubs in the city series. Each Sox player earned a check for $807.22. Buck's pay for the entire season was $2,500. It was no wonder the city series was taken seriously.

4

The World Tour

Buck was the only regular White Sox player to sign up when Comiskey and the manager of the New York Giants, John J. McGraw, announced they were taking their teams around the world that fall and winter. He already had played 151 games during the 1913 season, more than any of his teammates. Yet Buck couldn't resist a chance to play more baseball. Joining Weaver were two starting pitchers, Jim Scott, Buck's roommate, and "Butcher Boy" Joe Benz. Manager Jimmy Callahan would head the playing delegation. Other Sox players agreed to play stateside but begged off leaving American shores. They said they wanted to spend time with their families, work other jobs or just relax for the winter. McGraw faced the same problem. Both Comiskey and McGraw filled their roster with rookies and players from other ball clubs. Comiskey even persuaded two American League superstars to put on Sox uniforms for the global ride—outfielders Tris Speaker of the Boston Red Sox and Sam Crawford of the Detroit Tigers. A rookie outfielder of the Giants named Jim Thorpe, the American Indian hero of the 1912 Olympics, came aboard for the trip.

Sixty-seven persons would sail from American shores including seventeen wives and manager Callahan's two small children. Two Chicago sportswriters, Gus Axelson of the *Record-Herald* and Joe Farrell of the *Tribune*, would report the journey. Frank McGlynn represented Pathe Moving Picture Company which would make a film documentary of the world tour. Comiskey and McGraw somehow convinced two of the top major league umpires to come along. Magisterial Bill Klem of the National League joined colorful Jack Sheridan, the umpire-in-chief of the American League. One New York sportswriter, Sid Mercer, covering the tour, lambasted most of the regular team players for not making the trip.

By this time Buck had become quietly engaged to beautiful, twenty-three year old Helen Cook. Helen was part of a four sister singing and dancing act called the American Girl Quartet. Buck may have asked her to come along but she probably said she didn't think it proper and stayed behind. Helen and Buck had been introduced to each other by the manager of a San Francisco hotel where they were both staying. Helen and her sisters were touring the country on the Pantages vaudeville circuit. Helen was a breathtaking young lady. At 5 feet 6 inches in height, Helen was tall for a woman of her era and her richly endowed figure attracted the admiring glances of many men. She had pretty features—blue eyes, dark brown hair and a thin nose resting on an oval face. The young lovers discovered a happy coincidence. When Helen and her sisters were not on the road, they lived with their parents on the south side of Chicago, only a few miles from Comiskey Park.

The teams played their first barnstorming game in Cincinnati on October 18 to satisfy August Garry Herrmann, the chairman of the three-man National Commission of baseball and owner of the Cincinnati Reds. He reciprocated with one of his traditional feasts of food and drink, radiating an abundance of gemutlichkeit. Cincinnati wasn't called the Rhineland for nothing.

The official sendoff was launched the next day at Comiskey Park with a brass band playing, banners and flags flying and ballplayers decked out in brand new uniforms. Especially designed for the world tour, the uniforms bore a patriotic motif of red, white and blue colors with patches of the American flag and the national shield. Wrote Weller: "On the whole, the two teams made a swell appearance which should knock the natives of the Orient silly."

Comiskey leased a deluxe special train, made up of three sleepers, an observation sleeper and a combination buffet and baggage car to haul the baseball caravan westward to the Pacific Coast. The train chugged out of the La Salle Street station about 11:00 P.M. on October 19. It would steam across the country for a month until it reached Seattle. The globe trotters would play games almost daily and try to sleep as the train pitched and swayed through the countryside at night.

The long baseball trail was marked by many picturesque, bizarre, comical incidents and situations. As cold weather gripped Peoria, the "fans in the bleachers ripped loose the boards of the wooden structure and burnt small fires, around which they warmed themselves."

At Sioux City, Iowa, a host of Indians from nearby reservations came to cheer for their kin—Thorpe and Giant catcher John "Chief" Meyers. Blue Rapids, Kansas, declared a holiday and closed its schools and businesses so its citizens could attend the game. With about 500 cars flitting about town, "Main Street resembled State Street in Chicago."

A stunt pilot temporarily stopped the game in El Paso, Texas, when he landed in the infield. Business was shut down in Douglas, Arizona, the home of the "largest copper smelters in the world." An army band gave the players ". . . a royal welcome." At the game the crowd included a large number of Mexicans whose "vivas" could be heard amid the cheers of the Americans.

At Oxnard, California, Giant infielder Hans "Lobert, regarded as one of the fastest baserunners in the game, enlivened the afternoon by racing once around the diamond against a pony. The horse won by a nose. Lobert would have won, the spectators believe, if he had not been forced to watch the horse."

While it was cold and rainy in a game at Medford, Oregon, Giant right fielder Lee Magee made a dramatic catch with one hand while holding an umbrella over his head with the other. On "Apple Day" at Portland, Oregon, a crowd of 6,000 fans tossed "boxes of fruit to the players from the grandstand and bleachers." The final game in the States was cancelled because of rain in Seattle but the baseball fans of the city presented the players with a gigantic 125 lb. fruitcake in the lobby of the hotel. The cake was decorated with pictures of the Polo Grounds, the home field of the Giants, and Comiskey Park. At the top of the cake were candy statues of Comiskey, McGraw and Callahan.

Only one serious accident marred the entire trip. It happened just before the game started in Tulsa, Oklahoma. The overcrowded right field bleachers collapsed. One spectator, an army private, was killed as about 700 screaming spectators were hurled to the ground. Ballplayers from both teams rushed out to help with the rescue efforts.

When the tour arrived on the West Coast, baseball fans, thirsting to see big leaguers play, swarmed the ballparks in Los Angeles, San Diego, San Francisco and Oakland. Long lines of fans in front of ticket windows delayed the start of the games in Los Angeles. For the first game a reporter noticed that "more than $1,000,000 of automobiles were parked outside the playing field when the contest started." A harbinger of the future. The two games in Los Angeles drew wildly cheering crowds of 11,000 and 15,000. San Francisco matched the excitement in Los Angeles. The barnstormers drew 6,000 in the first game and a standing room crowd of 10,000 in the second. Undoubtedly, Buck Weaver, in a White Sox uniform, helped lure fans who were curious to see the former Seal shortstop in action. In San Diego, 6,000 enthusiasts overflowed the stands onto the playing field. The diamond became so cramped that a base runner racing to second on a double "upset four bystanders."

Buck gained favor with fans everywhere. A contributor from California to Ring Lardner's "Wake of the News" column in the *Chicago Tribune* wrote, "Buck Weaver's right at home here. I've never seen a place where he wasn't." Lardner was already famous as a short story writer.

Even in those exhibition games, Buck played with an intense, fierce desire to win. In a game at San Francisco Buck wasn't even involved in a play but he yelled at umpire Bill Klem for calling a runner safe at third when Ray Schalk's throw apparently caught the Giant baserunner "clearly off base." Later in the game he smashed into a double play and was called out on a close play at first. He was so angered by Klem's call he stalked off the field. At Portland in the "Apple Day" game, "Buck Weaver's verbal feud with umpire Klem cropped out again . . . and Weaver was sent to the clubhouse in the third inning" when "Klem objected to the player's remarks from the bench."

Besides the big crowds in California, there was another welcome note for staying in the Bay area. The tourists could luxuriate by sleeping in hotel beds and showering and bathing in leisure for one of the few times on the entire trip.

By the time the ball clubs reached Seattle the first leg of the journey was over. Thousands of Americans residing in small towns and hamlets as well as blossoming cities saw some of their baseball heroes for the first and probably last times. In 1913 few people owned automobiles and the first major highways had yet to be built. Besides, there was no major league baseball south or west of St. Louis.

Everyone bound for overseas boarded the Empress of Japan on November 19 at Victoria, British Columbia. Even though most of the players were members of other ball clubs, newspapers regarded these opponents as Giants and Sox. The *Chicago Tribune* trumpeted: "Globe Trotters Sail For Japan, Sox and Giants Complete First Leg of Tour . . ." The *Sporting News* headlined: "Giants and White Sox Depart For Foreign Shores."

Almost from the start, a rough and angry sea battered the twenty-four year old Empress of Japan. According to the ship's captain, an officer of the English navy reserves, it was the worst streak of bad weather the ship ever encountered. The ship's log on November 29 noted: "Overcast weather and blowing a storm of hurricane force. Mountainous sea running. Steamer straining heavily and shipping much water."

Most of the tourists were laid low by seasickness except the Callahan children who "romped gleefully" about the ship. When a calm sea returned, Weaver, who had a fine tenor voice, joined three other ballplayers to form a quartet. The ship's band, made up of "jolly tars from every nation," accompanied them.

On Dec. 6, the Empress of Japan, four days overdue, was reported nearing Yokahama; the American consul-general, Thomas Samons, headed out in a tugboat to meet the visiting Americans and lead them into dock. Despite their exhausting journey, the tourists submitted to a whirlwind schedule. Samons escorted them to their quarters at the Grand Hotel in Yokahama and immediately ordered rickshaws to haul them to the railroad station for their trip to Tokyo. In Tokyo the ballplayers were rushed out to the playing field of Keio University.

Cheering students greeted both teams. They knew the game and were familiar with the reputations of some of the players, particularly Speaker and Crawford. The president of the university threw out the first ball as members of the diplomatic corps, Tokyo officials and high ranking members of the university looked on.

The next day so many fans jammed the ball ground that the gates had to be closed at 9:00 A.M., an hour before game time. The Japanese college boys were about to play a mixed squad of Giants and White Sox. In the first inning the Japanese students turned the stands into a bedlam as a Keio batter "whacked a corking three bagger off Jim Scott . . .

"Never since the beginning of the world," Farrell wrote, "have so many kimonos been destroyed in one sitting. Then the run came over, something the picked world girdling team never looked for and something beyond the wildest dreams of the boys themselves. The baseball ground became a sight never to be forgotten by an energetic rag picker." That was the finest moment for the Japanese youngsters for in the end the Americans won, 16 to 1. The White Sox outslugged the Giants in the afternoon game, 12 to 9.

Farrell interviewed a gentleman named Jiro Murao of the University of Keio who was regarded as the "Father of Baseball" in Japan. He told Farrell he hoped Japan would take its place side by side with the United States as the first and only other nation to accept baseball as its national game. McGraw also expressed confidence that the Japanese would take to baseball with enthusiasm and skill. He said, "Someday the streets of Japan will have signs reading: 'Baseball today, Japan vs. United States.' The Japanese are great imitators. You'd be surprised to see how quickly they pick up the tricks of the game. The manner of throwing curve balls puzzles them, but they can run the bases and field the ball very well."

Though baseball held the spotlight on the tour, other diversions crowded the daily schedule. Regardless what city they visited, the Americans were treated as reigning celebrities. Often they were regarded as almost official representatives of the United States. Welcomed by high ranking government officials, they were guests at breakfasts, luncheons, dinners and banquets. Toasts and speeches from guests and hosts filled the air. Guided sightseeing tours, parades about town, souvenir shopping in exclusive shops or from poor vendors buzzing about their ships, and visits to theatre and sports events crowed the daily calendar. At times the women exclusively attended teas while the men enjoyed smokers. Before leaving Yokohama, there was a farewell banquet, a ride around town in "rickeys" and a tour of tea houses with their quaintly attentive geisha girls.

With the Americans back on board, the Empress of Japan steamed south towards Shanghai, China, with a coal stop at Nagasaki. Nagasaki had the reputation of being the fastest loading coaling station in the world. And it was all done by hand—from the coal barges to ocean liners. Fascinated, the Americans leaned on the rails as they watched and listened to the monotonous chant of 750 coal passers. The workers kept time in a sing-song way to the march of little coal-filled baskets. The baskets advanced from the barge hand-in-hand through rows of men, women and children to the hold of the ship. The Empress sailed from port with 17,000 tons aboard, packed in five hours.

From Nagasaki, the Empress sailed across the Yellow Sea and dropped anchor at the junction of the Whangpoo and Yangtse Rivers on the Chinese coast. The Americans then transferred to a fast tender for travel up the Whangpoo. An overwhelming welcome of shrieking whistles, flag dippings and great ovations along a route of 12 miles greeted them as they were escorted by two American gunboats to Shanghai.

Waiting at the dock were a thousand cheering American sailors. A brass band played Sousa's "Liberty Bell March." Officials of the Shanghai amateur baseball league mustered all the autos they could find and whisked the visitors off to the Astor Hotel, considered the swankiest lodging in town.

The Shanghai game was to be played within the foreign compound where 15,000 Americans and Europeans resided. But the day of the game turned out to be "damp, drizzling, miserable . . ." Hundreds of people patiently waited in the rain. Many brought light lunches to fortify themselves in case of a long delay. When the game was cancelled, "it was a very blue crowd that filed away from the beautiful race course . . ."

Disappointed that a game could not be played in Shanghai, Comiskey and McGraw quickly arranged to have a game played in the English crown colony of Hong Kong. Before landing everyone was vaccinated again and then paraded about in sedan chairs "resting on the stalwart shoulders of the natives . . ." One game was played on an uneven football field before a crowd of 7,000 curious onlookers who were admitted free. They persisted in pushing out on the field and disturbing play. The players were happy to leave for Manila after the game.

When the Americans pulled out of Hong Kong harbor, they had become passengers of another ship, the St. Albans.

The Empress of Japan, anchored nearby, fired a parting salute from a small cannon. Though the largest ship plying the
waters between Japan and Australia, the St. Albans was
tiny compared to the vessels tracing the more popular ocean
lanes. On this voyage the ship carried the largest passenger
list in her history. Steerage and second class quarters were
packed. The baseball tourists were the only first class occupants, except for three other people.

Upon landing in Manila on December 17, the Americans
were greeted by top government officials and a ninety piece
band. On hand were the governor-general, the commanding
general of the army, and the admiral of the U.S. Pacific fleet.
Almost all the resident Americans flocked to the dock. Before the first of two games, General Franklin J. Bell told the
players as they stood around home plate: "It is unnecessary
for me to assure you of the hearty nature of the welcome extended by Manillans, the large number of fans which greeted
you at the wharf and the record crowd that has turned out
to witness your skill in field and at bat are sufficient evidence of how local baseball enthusiasts feel about your visit,
which has been awaited for months."

The next day the second game was cut short in the
eighth inning because the players had to catch the St. Albans sailing for Brisbane. Almost one minute before midnight, New Year's Eve, the St. Albans slipped into dock at
Brisbane, ready to welcome the year of 1914. "Fireworks,
cannons, whistles, skyrockets, every known racket maker,
greeted the ocean weary travelers" as they hugged the ship's
railings, watching the spectacle that erupted over the city.
For more than six weeks since the baseball troupe left Seattle, there had been scant contact with the United States so
when an official climbed aboard ship with a bag of mail, the
Americans welcomed him with a rousing cheer.

The traveling troupe could not have had much sleep,
for that same morning at 10:30 they took the field and entertained the largest crowd ever seen in the Brisbane cricket
stadium. The Giants won a snappy 2 to 1 game with rookie

Urban "Red" Faber of the White Sox on loan to New York hurling the victory. After the game the Americans made another quick getaway, this time to Sydney.

As the world travelers docked in Sydney, a band of forty-six boys from ten American cities struck up "Yankee Doodle." The young musicians were on a world tour, heading in the opposite direction. Now they would delay their departure to act as the official musicians for the ball clubs before and after the games.

The mayor's key of welcome to the Americans seemed to be a signal ". . . for all of the welcoming committee's automobile drivers to violate speed laws in an endeavor to be the first to reach the Sydney cricket grounds . . ." Australian prime minister Joseph Cook welcomed the tourists during luncheon on the grounds. The luncheon was a prelude to more dances, banquets, horse racing, theatre parties, a prize fight and more sightseeing. Sandwiched in between were two ball games between the Sox and Giants and two games between the Americans and Australian teams.

A crowd of 11,000 watched the Sox rally in the ninth to nip the Giants 5 to 4 to win the first of two matches. Buck played a dramatic role in the victory. The Sydney *Daily Telegraph* reported in its quaint way the "sensational" ninth inning: "The White Sox' prospects had greatly improved in the last few sessions and their chances of overhauling their opponents looked rosy. The crowd by this time had a good grip on the game, and in true sporting fashion their sympathies were extended to the under dogs. One to tie, two to win—that was the state of the game when the White Sox entered their last effort.

"Daly opened up and put plenty of ginger into a clout which sailed out toward midfield. Donlin springed in and just got his hands around what proved a marvelous catch. Chicago's defeat after this achievement appeared certain.

"A safe hit by Evans between the first and second sacks saw him to the former. Bliss with a one bagger saw Evans to second. With two down Weaver mounted the box. The crowd had its eyes on Evans on third. If he could steal home an extra inning would be ordered and possibly the White Sox would win.

"Such was the desire of the spectators who listened to the stentorian voice of the umpire calling out 'Strike one' 'Strike two.' Before it could be realized Weaver smashed Hearn's third strike magnificently to left field. It was a fine hit resulting in a two bagger and it sent Evans and Bliss speeding across the plate. The pent up enthusiasm of the 'fans' broke forth in rounds of cheers."

Aboard the train steaming from Sydney to Melbourne on January 6, the Americans wondered how many more festive occasions they would be compelled to endure when they read a Melbourne newspaper: "The reception accorded the world's baseball tourists by the people of Melbourne is to be greater than that given them by the populace of Sydney."

True to their word, the governor-general and his wife welcomed them immediately at the railway station. The travelers were escorted to municipal hall for a formal reception attended by a gaggle of dignitaries including the premier of New Zealand. The governor-general and his wife then invited everyone to a garden party at their beautiful mansion home.

For the baseball festivities, the Melbourne and Australian governments announced half day holidays and the cream of the social set was among the 10,000 people who attended at the cricket grounds. Prior to the games, the cricket club trustees served luncheon with the governor-general officially handing the ballplayers the key of welcome for all Australia. In the first game a specially selected Melbourne team was easily defeated by a mixed American squad, 14 to 0. The Giants whipped the Sox, 12 to 8, in the regular exhibition game.

A Melbourne newspaper reporter showed nationalistic disdain for baseball. His attitude was quite opposite the glowing description by the Sydney journalist who seemed to be genuinely caught up with baseball fever. He wrote: "There are nine men on a side, and the New Yorkers, as they stepped on to the ground, looked like a formidable and rather a fearsome contingent. In size they are above the average; one or two of them would easily turn the scale at 14 stone (a stone is fourteen pounds) and they add to their bulky appearance, by wearing loose and baggy garments, surmounted by white hats pulled down well over the eyes.

"It is hard to say which they most resemble—a band of Arctic explorers, braced for a march due South, or a contingent of prize fighters getting ready for the ring. The man who acts as catcher—a position corresponding to that of wicket keeper at cricket is fearfully and wonderfully arrayed against all possible mischance of the game. He carries a heavy glove in one hand, he has his legs encased in pads of considerable size and thickness and he wears around his body a sort of leather buckler that would be a fair protection against a Macedonian phalanx.

"One would not be surprised to see him mount a charger and gallop three times around the ground, defying all and sundry to mortal combat. It is rather a disappointment to find that he intends to do nothing more than stand in the base immediately behind the striker and catch the occasional balls that come his way.

"Several Americans have said it is not their wish or expectation to displace cricket in Australia. It is perhaps just as well they do not expect to do so. They would probably be disappointed. To say that baseball is very much like rounders—that juvenile game which the young Australian plays with his sister until he reaches a certain age—is to state an obvious truth."

The Americans were entertained in the evening at Luna Park, the Melbourne Coney Island, which was jammed with people who loudly cheered the visitors after a band played the "Star Spangled Banner." The world travelers then proceeded to the Melbourne race track for a final farewell banquet. The next day New York trimmed Chicago 4 to 3 in 11 innings.

No more baseball would be played on the continent. The Americans had looked forward to a big day of fun on a one day stopover in Adelaide, northwest of Melbourne on the southern coast. But the visit had to be cut to a mere hour and a half when the tour's new sailing vessel, the Royal Mail steamer Orontes, announced a change in its departure time.

When the Orontes pointed its prow out of Adelaide the Americans had climaxed ten days of toasting the king of England and president of the United States at parties morning, noon and night in Brisbane, Sydney and Melbourne. Their last stop on the continent would be at the western port of Freemantle. They arrived on January 13 for a half day stopover after a trip many of the tourists said was as rough as the one crossing the Pacific. There was just time enough for an auto trip to the nearby beautiful town of Perth. It was in the midst of Australian summer so it may not have been such a welcome ride. Crawford complained: ". . . if it would only snow once in awhile." Farrell moaned: "A breeze in Perth is like a breath from a furnace."

Back aboard ship the world tourists set sail for Columbo, Ceylon, in the Indian Ocean. Buck this time joined a dancing quartet, calling itself the Tango Four. Besides Buck there were Fred Merkle, the Giant first baseman, Tris Speaker and Herman "Germany" Schaeffer, an infielder with the Washington Senators. They got hold of a record player and some records and entertained their fellow passengers with their version of the tango. If there was a chance to dance or sing, Buck was there.

It was in the midst of the most exotic natives and tropical plants that Sir Thomas Lipton, the renowned tea merchant and sportsman, greeted the globe trotters in Colombo. Lipton was looking after his business interests on the island. A warm, engaging man, he proved to be a charming host. He had prepared a luncheon and a ball at the local hotel. Lipton remained glued to the tourists during their entire one day stay in Ceylon. He autographed menu cards, accepted a baseball signed by all the players, danced with the ladies, and gave the Americans 1,000 pounds of tea.

In contrast to the many beautiful gardens that adorned the landscape in Columbo, the baseball tourists, as they rode about town in rickshaws, saw throngs of ill-clad natives jammed in the streets selling trinkets, bargaining for fruit or foodstuffs, or begging. Many of the natives' mouths looked as if they had just been beaten up in a street brawl due to the popular diversion of chewing betal leaves, a pungent narcotic plant that reddens the gums.

As for the game played, a "tremendous crowd of 5,000 gathered at the race track" to see the Sox win a 5 inning match. Farrell quipped, "Had it not been advertised as baseball, not five in the audience would have known what they were looking at."

The Americans picked up stateside newspapers in Columbo for the first time and learned that a welcoming home committee was being formed to greet them in New York and Chicago. Chicago fans started the idea and New Yorkers took it up. The secretary of the National League, John H. Heydler, named a committee of Ban Johnson, president of the American League, and five club presidents from both major leagues, to give the world travelers an official welcome home. The committee planned an elaborate banquet on March 7 in New York.

The Ceylon interlude quickly over, the world tourists faced nine more days aboard the Orontes as it steered through the Indian Ocean, the Arabian Sea, Gulf of Aden, the Red Sea and into the Suez Canal. As the ship eased up the canal, little boats swarmed about with their native skippers offering olivewood carvings, shells and coral for sale. Each item had eleven different prices. To deal with such wild price fluctuations, the Americans nominated Buck to negotiate with the boatmen. Despite his youth, Buck had earned the respect of everyone because of his special knack of bargaining with itinerant vendors in all the ports they visited. Therefore, he was given the responsibility of making all the purchases of trinkets along the canal.

The tourists left immediately for Cairo after landing at the town of Suez. Before the game on Sunday, February 1, the Americans ventured out of Cairo for an excursion into the desert for an inspection of the Pyramids and Sphinx.

Automobiles transported the tourists to Gizeh where they switched to donkeys and camels. Not everyone could adapt to the camel ride. Pitcher Joe Benz felt like pitching something other than a baseball and had to be assisted to the base of the Sphinx. The respect for antiquity was broken when New York catcher Ivy Wingo threw a baseball over the Sphinx which was caught by Cardinal infielder Steve Evans.

The Sunday game proved to be a gala occasion for Cairo bigwigs and a social triumph for the United States consul general and diplomatic agent, Olney Arnold. Seated in the front row of the newly built stands were his royal highness, Abbas Hilmi II, Khedive of all Egypt, and his retinue. The crowd included the governor of Cairo, the commander of the British-Egyptian army and fifty members of the diplomatic corps. In a well-played 3 to 3 10-inning tie, the crowd vigorously applauded the catching of ordinary fly balls in the outfield.

Sunday evening the Americans were treated to a dinner party and afterwards were left on their own to tour the crowded streets of Cairo. On Monday morning, decked out in tarbushes or Turkish fezes, the tourists, seated on camels and donkeys, proceeded to inspect the system of ancient fortifications outside Cairo. Later in the day, as the Giants beat the White Sox, the crowd sat quietly while the Sox pulled off a triple play.

At the Monday night dance at the Heliopolis Hotel, twenty-eight Arabs rolled up the rug in the main dining room. Before the fashionable crowd took to the dance floor Buck joined Steve Evans in showing them how to dance the tango.

The Prinz Heinrich sailed out of Alexandria on February 5 with everyone on board but one. Umpire Jack Sheridan, an undertaker during the off season, became engrossed with the mummy collection at the Cairo museum and missed the boat. Sheridan would catch up with the tour in Rome, missing only one game played at Nice, France. Games scheduled for Naples, Rome and Paris were all to be canceled.

The confusion and misunderstanding tied to the baseball schedule took on the appearance of Italian light comic opera. First, the hosts in Naples booked the game the same day the Americans were due in Rome. In Rome the board of public safety called it a "brutal game" when its members saw Callahan hit McGraw with a pitch just when the two Americans were trying to prove the game was safe. When the safety board did finally agree to allow a game to be played—provided a safety net was strung around the stadium—it started to rain. The downpour continued until the teams left for Nice.

With baseball games canceled, there was extra time for sightseeing in Naples and Rome. Because the American consul-general, Dr. John Edward Jones, was a friend of both Comiskey and McGraw, the tourists were treated to a tour of the ruins of Pompeii and saw excavations not yet open to the public. Some of the Americans motored 150 miles over the Naples highway, "the most famous and picturesque route in the world." They caught glimpses of the towns of Salerno, Amalfi and Sorrento. Magnificent villas showed off their stateliness along the ocean beach road. Several ballplayers sailed to the island of Capri.

Four days in Rome allowed the Americans to touch most of the historic bases. There was the visit to the Vatican and an audience with the Pope; the Colosseum, the Forum, the catacombs and the ride along the Appian Way. One night they attended a local music hall where the Italians, if they didn't like an act, booed and hooted until the performer left the stage. Comiskey was restricted to his hotel room all during his stay in Rome suffering from some kind of gastric disturbance. He had originally taken ill on the train ride from Naples. He first was attended to by Dr. Jones. Jones consulted an Italian specialist who suspected stomach trouble or a cardiac condition. The doctors allowed Comiskey to rejoin the traveling troupe in Paris.

A holiday atmosphere blanketed the Riviera as the Giants and Sox took the field at Nice on February 16. American tourists, European nobility and the continent's wealthy motored to the long awaited game. The crowd was abundently speckled with "handsomely gowned women among the spectators" which "added to the gayety of the scene." An aviator executed some trick flying over the field and Jim Thorpe put on an exhibition throwing the discus and "putting the shot," showing the athletic skills that won him gold medals in the 1912 Olympic Games. The American consul threw out the first ball. During the action the French, perplexed by the rules of the game, nevertheless cheered for balls hit into the outfield. The ball clubs left for Paris the next day.

Unfortunately rain arrived in Paris simultaneously with the Americans, washing out all the scheduled games. But one evening newspaper claimed rain was an alibi to get out of playing. It said "on one occasion the excuse of bad weather was a good one but on two other occasions the game should have been played, although the conditions were by no means perfect." The newspaper also said it was whispered about town that the players were too tired to play because they had spent too much time looking over the gay lights of Paris. An unidentified American reporter cabled the *Tribune*: "The correspondent knows to his personal knowledge that this charge is not true." McGraw said they weren't going to play under poor field conditions. The object of the tour, he said, ". . . was not to make money, but a desire to give an exhibition of the game properly played."

Of the social gatherings in Paris, the height was a reception in honor of the Americans hosted by the American ambassador, Myron T. Herrick and his wife at the U.S. Embassy. An American millionaire wine merchant, George Kessler, served a luncheon at his home, but the players did not touch the "choicest champagnes and 1824 brandy." Maybe the ladies did.

Bad weather allowed Buck more time to shop the elegant boutiques and stores of fashionable Paris. He made an extravagant purchase of forty pairs of kid gloves. He must have made a fabulous deal. In any case the other players were sorry they hadn't purchased more, since duties were waived for them when they returned to the United States.

For a while it looked as if the one game scheduled in

London faced a boycott. There appeared to be a mysterious lack of interest. Tickets weren't selling and the London press practically ignored the event. Then it was discovered that a New York newspaper reported earlier that McGraw supposedly had said the Americans were superior in comparing American and British soldiers athletically. When McGraw heard the story he hurriedly assured the British he knew nothing of the British army and therefore would not criticize its soldiers. King George V then quickly announced he would see the game and demand for tickets immediately boomed. Every reserved seat was sold the same afternoon of the king's announcement.

As a fitting tribute to the Americans, 30,000 people, the largest crowd of the world tour, packed the Chelsea cricket grounds on February 24 to see the final match between the Comiskeys and the McGraws. Before the contest American ambassador Walter Hines Page presented Comiskey, McGraw and Callahan, all attired in high hats and frock coats, to King George. The players too, as a group, were presented before the royal box.

The White Sox nipped the Giants 5 to 4 in 11 innings when rookie Tom Daly, a catcher playing first base on the tour, slammed the ball over the center fielder's head and circled the bases for a home run. Buck was the only player on either team to rap out three hits. One of his smashes helped the Sox tie the score earlier in the game. Ambassador Page called it the "biggest thing Americans ever had staged in London." Only a few days before the London game, Jimmy Callahan, according to reporter Joe Farrell, "declared that the trip has made a wonderful player of Buck Weaver and that he will be of great value to the White Sox the coming year."

The major social event of the London stay was a great luncheon at the Savoy Hotel attended by more than 300 people and hosted by Harry Gordon Selfridge, the owner of a giant department store.

Finally, what must have been a travel weary group of Americans boarded the ill-fated Cunard luxury liner Lusitania on February 28. On May 7, 1915, just a little more than a year later, the Lusitania would be torpedoed by a German submarine off the Irish coast.

The Lusitania cut through fog and snow past Sandy Hook and the Statue of Liberty into New York harbor on the morning of March 6, 1914, exactly as originally scheduled. While the ship majestically eased towards shore, welcoming groups of Chicagoans, New Yorkers and baseball's top officials sailed out to greet the ocean liner, even before it reached the Statue of Liberty. In a rented ferry boat a delegation of 100 Sox fans hired a band and serenaded the world travelers with the music of Berlin and Van Alstyne. The fans cheered and yelled themselves hoarse. A large yacht loaded with New Yorkers steamed up to salute McGraw and his Giants. Some of the most influential personages in baseball boarded the Lusitania. They included Ban Johnson, president of the American League; Frank Farrell, president of the New York Yankees; Ben Shibe, president of the Philadelphia Athletics and Charles Ebbets, president of the Brooklyn Dodgers. The major league executives presented keys of welcome to Comiskey and McGraw on behalf of the entire country.

The suntanned players stepped off the gangplank attired in their newly purchased Bond Street clothes amid the cheering of 5,000 fans who had jammed the dock to welcome the homecoming Americans. Newsreel cameramen struggled to get pictures of the returning heroes.

From the harbor, the globe trotters were escorted to the newly built, fireproofed, luxurious Biltmore Hotel on Forty-Third Street. The next evening on March 7, more than 700 fans, players and leading baseball figures attended a sumptuous banquet in the Biltmore's main ballroom on the nineteenth floor. It was one of the largest, highest and most beautiful ballrooms in New York. Decorated in a Louis XIV style, the room was done in blue and gold with arched windows and an ornamental balcony. It was a fitting scene to honor the travelers on the completion of their world tour.

The Chicago contingent of the world tourists arrived

back in Chicago on Monday, March 9; 2,000 fans cheered them when they steamed into La Salle Street Station at 8:55 A.M. The Comiskeys spent seventeen weeks and traveled 38,000 miles through eleven different countries since embarking from Chicago. Admiring Chicagoans capped the 119 day world expedition with yet another mammoth banquet at the Congress Hotel the evening of Tuesday, March 10. The hotel offered a breathtaking view of Lake Michigan, Michigan Avenue and Grant Park which coursed the shore of the lake directly below. The dinner was served in the resplendent Gold Room on the second floor. It was "declared by many competent critics to be the finest banquet hall in America."

The Chicago banquet marked the end of the tour. The ballplayers had engaged in fifty games, thirty-one in the United States and nineteen overseas against each other and against native teams in Japan, Philippines and Australia. In head-to-head competition the players wearing White Sox uniforms beat the Giants 24 games to 20. Ring Lardner, as a *Chicago Tribune* columnist, could not resist a wry comment: ". . . the two traveling clubs were known as the White Sox and Giants. That one of them was not really the White Sox is shown by the fact that it boasted two (2) .350 hitters." There were two tie games. Comiskey, hoping to break even financially, realized a profit of $75,000. The games in the United States alone brought in $100,000.

Comiskey and McGraw looked forward to another tour at the end of the 1914 season. But their plans never got off the ground. On June 28, 1914, the Archduke Francis Ferdinand Hapsburg, heir to the throne of the Austrian-Hungarian empire, and his wife were assassinated. Exactly one month later, on July 28, Austria declared war on Serbia and several days later practically all of Europe went up in flames. World War I had begun.

5

The Nervous Bridegroom

Weaver arrived at spring training camp at Paso Robles, California, on the morning of March 19, 1914, and "jumped in at shortstop as if he never had been seasick in his life . . . Weaver celebrated his first reappearance on American soil by whaling a two bagger against the right field fence . . ."

But Buck was not brimming with joy. He and teammate Jim Scott had expected to get a piece of the profit from the world tour. Since Comiskey offered none, they talked about the possibility of jumping to the Federal League if contracts were attractive enough. Comiskey did raise Buck's salary to $4,000 a year, an increase of $1,500 over the previous season.

By the time the season opened Buck dropped any talk about the Federal League. Sanborn was impressed: "At short nobody seems to have a chance with 'Buck' Weaver who improved wonderfully in his batting last season after being placed in the leadoff position. He has retained his ability to bat from either side of the platter . . . and hits the ball harder from the left side than any other batsman of recent years who had switched from right to left handed batting."

Sanborn still expressed concern about Buck's fielding. "Weaver's sole fault has been failure to take his time on slow runners when fielding ground balls. His tendency to make every play as fast as possible has kept him 'fighting the ball' thereby making for himself a lot of hard chances which he could handle easier. This is not a bad fault in a young player because it requires only time to break it."

Sanborn also suggested if Buck couldn't correct his way at short, he be moved to second where there would be more time to make the plays. Sanborn's comments were one of the first to suggest Buck play elsewhere in the infield. But Buck would be anchored at short for some time to come.

For Buck the 1914 season was both pleasantly memorable and painfully strange. When Buck made his second appearance at the plate on April 16, the game was interrupted to present him with a nearly life-size silver bat and ball emblematic of his winning the batting title of the White Sox the year before. It was a gift offered by a local jeweler.

Just about a month later Callahan named Buck field captain. The previous field leader, veteran third baseman Harry Lord, suddenly left the ball club on the night of May 13. He told his roommate, Hal Chase, that he was quitting baseball for good and going home to Maine. Later in the summer he would show up with Buffalo in the Federal League. Callahan's move to make Buck captain may have been surprising. It was only his third year on the team. But already he was one of the veterans and the spark plug of the White Sox. Callahan may have recalled young Weaver's brashness in telling battle-tested pitcher Tex Russell how to go about pitching in a tight situation.

At the same time Buck was named captain, he started to become a victim of injuries and illnesses that would force him out of games all summer. In his first day as captain he was already limping around the diamond. Buck had been knocked out of action with a leg injury but hobbled on the field as a coach. Two days later he was back in the lineup but somehow hurt a finger on his left hand while trying to throw a runner out at third. Again he was forced to the sidelines. The next day he wrenched his bum foot sliding into second for a stolen base and again left the field for an early shower.

Back in the lineup two days later Buck gave evidence why he became one of the most successful and feared baserunners on the ball club. In a scoreless game in New York he raced for the plate on a short fly to left field. The throw beat him by a couple of steps but the catcher muffed the ball and the Sox went on to win, 1 to 0. At Cleveland he tripled to right and "scored on Chase's fly to short right" by surprising Joe Jackson "who lobbed the ball home, expecting Weaver to stay on third."

Buck's exuberance and daring on the bases sometimes backfired. "Cap Weaver had a hunch he could steal home and give the large assemblage a bunch of thrills. He tried it," . . . but the pitcher threw "to the third base side of the pan and Capt. George was a dead one." Faber shut out the Yankees that day, 4 to 0, so no harm done.

Buck was asserting his leadership as team captain, too, wrote Sanborn: "Weaver, the Sox mouthpiece, always cautions his players 'take your time' so as to steady them." And he was scratching and clawing on every play in his direction. One day first baseman Chick Gandil of Washington "stole second base by a margin so close that Weaver argued himself into the clubhouse over it."

Buck spent most of July off the diamond. On July 1 he was knocked out of the lineup in Detroit with a "severe case of tonsillitis which kept him in bed all morning." While the White Sox headed for St. Louis, Weaver stayed in Detroit with coach Gleason to see a doctor. Then the two of them returned to Chicago to see another physician. Gleason had become more than a coach and assistant manager on the playing field; he was a mother hen guarding its brood. It had become customary for the coach to take players in tow, especially the younger ones, when they needed special help or an extra pat on the back. It was Gleason who was teaching Buck to become a wily baserunner. Callahan may have been the boss on the field, but it was the "Kid" who kept "in close touch with the players from breakfast to bedtime." If a player had performed poorly that day or was in some kind of slump, Gleason was most likely to join him for dinner or invite him to a movie or engage him in a game of billiards. By the end of the evening the ballplayer was usually in a happier frame of mind, hopefully with regained confidence to face the next day.

Buck missed the next seven games. Even though he wasn't ready to play, Callahan inserted Buck in the coaching box just "to ginger up the players . . ." The "gingered" players won all seven games Buck missed and they skyrocketed into second place.

When the White Sox opened a series in New York, Buck persuaded Callahan to put him back into the lineup. Ray Schalk, who also was sidelined with a badly puffed finger on his throwing hand, talked himself back behind the plate.

"Weaver celebrated his return to the fray by cracking the first ball pitched for a double." However, the "convalescent couple" had a rough day in the field. Weaver dropped a pop fly back of second and then threw low to first allowing two runs to score. Schalk made a home run heave to the fence when he tried to catch the runner at second who reached base when Buck dropped his pop up.

Yet in the clubhouse after the game manager Callahan didn't criticize either player even though Schalk's three throwing errors led to four runs, and Buck's two errors had put the game out of reach. Instead of scolding his shortstop for dropping the Texas Leaguer in short left center field, Callahan said left fielder Ray Demmitt or center fielder Ping Bodie should have made the play easily. Still he didn't fling harsh words at his two outfielders, either. All he did was point "out that a little of the fighting spirit of Weaver to either of them would have driven Buck from the play entirely and left the chance for one of them to handle."

Once again Buck became a casualty on July 16 in Philadelphia when he collided with Demmitt. The play was reminiscent of the accident in the 1912 city series when he was knocked unconscious. Weaver cruised into short left field to gather in a little pop fly. Demmitt, perhaps inspired by Callahan's pep talk in New York, came charging in and smashed into Buck. Demmitt's "jaw bore a hole in Weaver's forehead just above the nose and the Sox captain was led from the field only partially conscious of his surroundings." When

Weaver went to Quaker hospital the next day at the insistence of two doctors, X-rays "showed a slight dent in the frontal sinus." Though Buck was anxious for action, Callahan rested him a few days. Back on the field, Buck got hit over his eye by a ball thrown by Schalk who had fired wildly trying to nab a runner stealing second. It was more than a week before Buck could pull the patch off his eye and resume play. Two weeks later in New York he fell ill. All he could eat were ". . . soft boiled eggs and toast." In pre-game practice the next day, Buck was so weak he was wobbly. Callahan tried to talk him out of playing, but the team captain insisted on getting into the lineup.

Chicago Tribune sportswriter James Crusinberry observed, "With Buck Weaver or Ray Schalk out of the game, the team is all unbalanced and helpless." He ripped into the struggling ball club, which had won only 2 of 8 games on an eastern road trip in late August, with dripping sarcasm: "Playing baseball that wouldn't get by in Peoria or Kalamazoo, the struggling White Sox took the prize beating of the trip today when Frank Chance's near trailers trounced them by a score of 9 to 0.

"There were no excuses for the mess this time, because all the regulars were in the game, recovered from illnesses and injuries, and one of the star hurlers of the year, Joe Benz, was on the slab. Benz couldn't pitch much, Schalk was a bum pegger, Weaver didn't do much on shortstop, Fournier couldn't hit worth shucks, and most of the others had little difficulties of some kind. Otherwise the team was all right. No mistakes were made by the fellows on the bench.

"It was a horrible exhibition of the national game to give in the beautiful Polo Grounds before a crowd of select fans. The game ought to have been played on the Jersey side in some lonely and uninhabited spot.

"Old King Cole was on the slab for the New Yorkers and he grinned all through the game. He had fellows striking out by swinging at wild ones and striking out by taking good ones. He just zipped the ball through (sic) the catcher and had no fear.

"Joe Benz, our crack hurler of no-hit fame, was awful. He was in there only long enough to retire one man. Two runs had come in and more fellows were on the way in until it seemed doubtful if Joe would ever get another man out, so he was canned and the former Moose, Ed Walsh, was summoned from the distant pen.

"The only thing resembling the Walsh of old was the athletic stride as he made his way over the green to the diamond while the crowd applauded. After he got on the slab, it was quite a different Walsh. He was rapped for two more runs before the side was out and then he went along fooling the Yanks on his reputation and artistic poise until the middle of the fifth, when the manager removed him to prevent humiliation.

"In all the time Walsh was in it didn't seem that he pitched one ball with anything on it. The Yanks finally began taking toe holds and driving the ball against walls and distant fences and the old master was waved to the clubhouse . . ." It was obvious that Walsh was in the twilight of a great career.

Comiskey hadn't been happy with what he saw on the field. Long before the end of the season he kept constant lookout for new talent. On August 9 the *Tribune* headlined: "HARD HITTING BREWER PICKED UP BY WHITE SOX." Comiskey outbid all rivals in buying slugging outfielder Oscar "Happy" Felsch from the Milwaukee ball club. Felsch, only a twenty-year old Milwaukee native, was batting .302 with 16 homers, 24 doubles and 7 triples. He would report to the White Sox the following spring.

The White Sox stumbled along to close the season in seventh place. But they rallied again to beat the Cubs in the city series. Ring Lardner took time to compose a bit of doggerel comparing Cubs and Sox players for each position:

THE SHORTSTOPS

Buck Weaver is the White Sox shortstop,
And naught can make this little sport stop

Smiling even for a day;
His countenance is built that way,
He also talks a lot, this bird,
While Derrick seldom says a word;

Buck played vintage Weaver in the city series. He was ejected in the second inning of the third game when he protested being called out on a close play at first. "Weaver screamed his protest and rushed at the umpire, impressing his point by means of elbows as well as harsh words. He was promptly ordered off the field . . ." After the series was over, Crusinberry wrote: "Buck Weaver's play was even above his usual speed. His stunt of knocking down (Claud) Derrick's base hit in the ninth inning of the final game, thus preventing the tying run from going home from second after two were out was rated as one of the best and most crucial plays of the entire series." Buck surpassed his usual batting skills by lashing 10 hits in 20 at bats in the first five games. Even though he did not notch any hits in the last two games, he finished with a .375 average. He tried to steal home on a passed ball but didn't make it.

Perhaps Buck's "play was even above his usual speed" because of his personal happiness off the diamond. He was getting married. But much as he welcomed the adulation of the crowd when he was in field, he was quiet and reserved out of uniform. He valued his privacy. He discouraged publicity about his upcoming marriage and tried to keep the event out of the press. In fact when a *Tribune* reporter phoned Helen, inquiring about the wedding, Helen acted as if she didn't even know a Buck Weaver. But the *Tribune*, in an exclusive story, bannered on October 13: "WEAVER'S CITY SERIES MONEY WILL BUY FURNITURE." There was a two column picture of Helen huddled in a coat and big hat seated in a box seat at Comiskey Park and in an insert, a portrait of Buck. The head over the picture read: "Sox Hero of City Series Games Who Will Become a Benedict."

Buck was angry. He told one reporter that his getting married was a distinctly private event in which the public had no right to take any interest whatever. Reminded that he was a distinctly public character, Buck said, "Maybe—on the baseball diamond. Off the diamond I'm a private citizen. Get me?"

Helen and Buck were married Saturday, October 17, in a simple, rather bizarre ceremony. Buck didn't invite any of his teammates for some unexplainable reason. Neither did Helen's three sisters attend. Accompanied by Helen's parents, Mr. and Mrs. James Cook, Buck and his fiance eased out of the Cook residence at 6550 S. Lafayette Avenue about 2 o'clock in the afternoon. They walked less than half a block north to 6530 S. Lafayette, the home of Rev. Williard H. Robinson, the pastor of the Presbyterian church of Englewood (one of Chicago's south side communities). In a brief church ceremony with only Helen's folks as witnesses, "the former Miss Cook became the better half of 'half the White Sox team.' "

Back at the Cook residence, Buck later told a reporter, "The boys down at the clubhouse this morning presented us with a big, fat check as a wedding present. They were waiting for me when I came in—Comiskey, Callahan and the rest of the bunch." The honeymoon would be delayed until spring training. Buck's effusiveness with the press after the wedding contrasted sharply with his antagonistic behavior before the ceremony. Perhaps he was a typical nervous bridegroom.

In early December, Comiskey, promising his White Sox fans an early pennant, purchased Eddie Collins, the great second baseman of the Philadelphia A's for $50,000. Connie Mack, the A's manager, was breaking up his magnificent infield after losing the World Series to the upstart Boston Braves, who had been in last place on July 4. The Federal League also was dangling some attractive financial bait before his athletes. Rather than lose his players without any compensation, Mack decided to peddle them off. Collins, voted the most valuable player in the American League, finished second only to Ty Cobb in hitting with a robust .344 average. No one challenged Collins as the best fielding second baseman in baseball. He signed a five year contract calling for $15,000 a year, making him the highest paid White Sox player in history up to that time. But not before Comiskey shelled out $15,000 as a bonus for signing and $5,000 for moving expenses. Comiskey more than met his match in contract negotiations with the Columbia University graduate. Not many players held college degrees as leverage in contract talks with club owners. Weaver, who would be playing alongside Collins, would collect $6,000 a year for the next four years. Buck took note of Collins' skill as a negotiator for future reference.

A day after the deal was made, Comiskey said, "Collins cost a heap of money, but I consider myself lucky to get him at any price. He is a wonderful player and will make my team a winner but I am not through yet. . . .

"For years I have been spending money for players from the minors, and paying high prices for some of them who lacked class. I was tired [of] throwing away coin that way, and made up my mind that if I ever got into the same room with a club owner who could be induced to fix a price on a real ballplayer I would pay the price. That's how I got Collins." Then Comiskey uttered words that must have stuck in Buck Weaver's craw. Collins had not yet put on a Sox uniform but the Old Roman couldn't wait: "Collins will captain the team."

Comiskey shook up the baseball world again only a little more than a week after the Collins' deal. Contrary to his vote of confidence in him during the summer, Comiskey suddenly fired Callahan and appointed a minor league manager, Clarence "Pants" Rowland, as the new pilot. Almost thirty-six years old, Rowland was a long-time friend and frequent guest of Comiskey's at his Camp Jerome lodge in Wisconsin. Rowland had been managing Peoria in the Three-Eye League. There is more than one version of how Rowland acquired his nickname. At least one suggests that as a youngster, Rowland one day wore his father's pants to play ball and they fell to his ankles while he was circling the bases. Onlookers began calling him "Pants."

According to Sanborn, Rowland's "proclivity for picking out promising recruits had as much as anything else to do with Commy's choice of him as Sox pilot." It was Rowland who had tipped Comiskey on "Red" Faber.

Rowland already had a long and varied career in baseball. At sixteen, Clarence quit high school. He took a job as bellhop at a Dubuque hotel and started playing semipro as a catcher. It wasn't long before he showed executive ability and leadership qualities beyond his years when he formed a team called the Rowland Colts. In a neighboring town, Rowland feared he might be aced out of his share of a game's gate receipts. He demanded from the owner of the opposing team, who was also the town's banker, guaranteed payment. He was also to notify Rowland's bank in Dubuque as well. The amused banker granted the youngster his wish.

When a clothing store furnished uniforms as an advertising promotion, Clarence changed the name of the team to the Rowland Models. The young executive rented a local ballpark and as many as 1,000 people would attend weekend games. Each player picked up $4 to $7 a game. That wage was equivalent to or greater than what most jobs paid in a week.

In 1903 the aggressive, determined and imaginative young baseball entrepreneur crashed a meeting of officials of the Three-Eye League in Chicago. He persuaded them to grant him a franchise in Dubuque. Then, according to a *Tribune* story bylined Handy Andy, Rowland "floated out to Comiskey's residence, then in Wabash Avenue, one bright morning between 7 and 7:30 A.M. 'Commy' was so surprised at the nerve that he farmed to Rowland" several players.

Rowland, satisfied with his trimphant visit to Chicago, suddenly discovered he didn't have enough money for train fare back to Dubuque. "He managed to get into a day coach bound in that direction, and by good footwork he succeeded in dodging the conductor all during the trip."

Besides being owner and manager of the Dubuque ball club, Rowland also caught the games. Later he helped Dubuque secure a municipal baseball park, the only one in the country at the time. Eventually, Rowland sold his team and for a couple of years played in Canada. He returned to Dubuque in 1910 and became manager a year later. By the time Rowland left Dubuque in 1913 he also was part-owner.

As soon as Comiskey named Rowland manager, the new skipper wrote an open letter to White Sox fans which appeared in the *Tribune* on December 19. "In Eddie Collins we have the greatest second baseman in the game. There are no better catchers than Schalk. Weaver is without a peer as a shortstop. That is a mighty fine start. I really believe we will open the season with a great ball team."

If Weaver was "without a peer as a shortstop" as Rowland wrote, a casual observer might wonder about Rowland's judgment. Buck tallied 59 errors in 134 games to lead the league for the third year in a row. In his first three years in the majors Weaver racked up exactly 200 miscues. Obviously Rowland thought there was more to Buck's fielding than statistical records.

On December 29, coach and assistant manager Kid Gleason, who was like a father to Buck, was given his unconditional release. The Kid's "well known ability to handle players on or off the field" meant little with the arrival of a new manager.

6

The Federal
League Threat

A bombshell struck the baseball world at the beginning of
the new year. On January 6 the Federal League initiated an
anti-trust suit charging the major leagues with being a monopoly in restraint of trade. Judge Kenesaw Mountain Landis would hear opening arguments in federal district court
in Chicago starting January 20, 1915.

Judge Landis was named for a battle in the Civil War
where his father, Dr. Abraham Landis, a surgeon, lost a leg.
As a youngster in Logansport, Indiana, he delivered Chicago
newspapers and became an ardent lifetime fan of the Chicago National League ball club, originally called the White
Stockings. Although he never graduated from high school—
algebra proved to be the stumbling block—Ken became a
reporter for the Logansport *Journal*, covering the courthouse
beat. He became fascinated by shorthand practiced by court
reporters, taught himself the skill and was drawn to the
study of law. He attended the YMCA Law School in Cincinnati first and then completed his courses at the YMCA
law school in Chicago in 1891.

After practicing for two years in Chicago he was picked
by federal Judge Walter Q. Gresham to be his secretary when
Gresham was named secretary of state by President Cleveland. Landis's skill with shorthand was a big plus, but the

fact that Gresham was Ken's father's commanding officer at Kennesaw Mountain most likely secured the position.

In 1895, following Gresham's death, Landis returned to Chicago and practiced law for ten years. He gained the attention of President Theodore Roosevelt when he directed the Republican campaign for Illinois governor in 1904. Although his candidate lost, Landis impressed Republican leaders with his vigorous effort. A year later, as a reward, Roosevelt named Landis a federal judge for the northern district of Illinois.

The threat posed by the Federal League suit to organized baseball as it had been operating was serious. If Judge Landis decided that the national agreement under which the majors operated was illegal, the contracts of all players would be null and void, and the players declared free agents. The Federal League demanded equal status with the American and National Leagues.

At the opening day hearing, Landis, a baseball fanatic himself, suddenly blurted out, "Do you realize that a decision in this case may tear down the very foundations of this game, so loved by thousands, and do you realize that the decisions must seriously affect both parties?" Before a decision could be handed down, Landis declared there would have to be further proceedings. But he kept postponing taking action. It was thought Landis recognized that the Federal League had a solid case, that the major bone of contention, the reserve clause, which chained a ballplayer to one team for life unless sold, traded or released, was in violation of federal anti-trust laws. Had Landis followed through with an honest and fair decision, it was thought the major leagues would have been thrown into chaos. Star ballplayers would declare themselves free agents and sign contracts with the highest bidders. Ball clubs would be in total disarray. Therefore, he kept his silence, hoping the Federal League would just go away. Eleven months later it collapsed.

Buck became a businessman just before the White Sox headed for spring training. He bought a billiard hall and barbershop on the south side at 306-308 East Garfield Boulevard. For one of the few times in his life, baseball suddenly became a secondary priority. He wanted to stay in Chicago an extra week so he could attend to his new business venture. But Rowland convinced Buck he should let someone else mind the store while he traveled west with the rest of the squad. Said Rowland: "I'm sure Buck figured it out the right way. He realized that he has a great chance this year, working alongside of a fellow like Eddie Collins, and every bit of practice he can get beside his new mate will be of great assistance in getting the team to working together before the season opens. I'm glad he decided to go along now, for I believe he and Collins will make the fastest pair of infielders in the game. One can't win a pennant without having a pair of stars crowd the middle bag." En route to California *Tribune* sportswriter Sam Weller observed, "Collins immediately started a long chat with Buck Weaver, who will be his sidekick around the keystone sack . . ."

Rowland wasted no time the first day in camp at Paso Robles. He ordered a 5 mile hike in the morning and a 5 mile hike in the afternoon. On the second day Rowland called for a 16 mile hike on the sun-baked roads and the "new manager led the way and proved himself a hiker." The ballplayers "started out at 10 o'clock in the morning and returned so late that the dining room was closed. Hot dogs and ice cream from a nearby refreshment place had to do for a substitute for lunch."

Buck captured the first exhibition game headline in the *Tribune* on March 1: "Weaver Leads in 5 to 2 Victory at San Jose with Double and Triple . . ." On that same day, Helen, who had made the spring training trip with a host of other wives, celebrated her twenty-third birthday, serving tea and cakes at the hotel in Paso Robles for all the other women.

No longer the team captain, Weaver may have enjoyed the tug of war between Comiskey and Rowland about having a team captain at all. Comiskey already told the press when he made the deal for the ace second baseman that Collins would captain the team. One day after the first exhibition game, Rowland expressed other ideas: "I never have had a captain on any ball club that I managed. I see no need for a captain. If one is appointed this year it will be a departure from an old custom of mine. I will be responsible for the mistakes made by the boys."

Buck couldn't have cared who was team captain four days after Rowland made his position known. The ex-Sox captain suffered another attack of tonsillitis forcing him to miss one week of games. The infection grew so severe that Buck needed more than rest. He was operated on at a Los Angeles hospital on the morning of March 14 for the removal of his tonsils and adnoids. Buck remained out of action for more than three weeks. Obviously, a tonsillectomy in those days, any operating procedure for that matter, was much more hazardous and physically debilitating than today. Buck bounced back in a game on April 9 when he tripled and singled in a win over Kansas City.

When the White Sox arrived in St. Louis on April 13 to await opening day Buck was well enough to take over as acting manager. Rowland was still out on the exhibition trail with the second team. Whether Buck took command on his own with the approval of the other players or was told by Rowland to supervise practice is not known. He had been, after all, team captain in 1914. In any case, "Weaver put the men through a brief batting and fielding drill, permitting Jim Scott to work on the mound just long enough to give his arm the proper amount of exercise," according to the *Tribune's* James Crusinberry.

On May 8, shortly after the season got underway, the great British luxury liner Lusitania was torpedoed and sunk by a German submarine off the coast of Ireland with a loss of 1,198 lives, including 128 Americans. Five White Sox— Weaver, Benz, Scott, Faber and Daly—must have been especially shaken by the event. They had sailed home from England on the Lusitania on their last leg of the world tour. However, they must also have been relieved that George

Kessler, the American millionaire wine merchant who entertained the world tourists at his home in Paris, survived the sinking.

Back on the playing field, in a pleasant reversal of form, Buck committed only two errors in the first month of the season. Yet he played with that same relaxed, carefree, aggressive spirit that propelled him all over the infield. In one game near the end of May he made two spectacular plays to prevent runs from scoring. In the first instance, the batter "bounced a nasty one far to the left of Weaver. Buck dashed across the diamond, leaped into the air in front of second base, stabbed the ball with his glove hand, and then while still running in the direction of right field, made a perfect shot to the plate" cutting the runner down by three feet. Then, with the speedy Tris Speaker on third, the batter "slashed a hot grounder to right of Weaver. Buck skidded over, dug the ball out of the earth, and once more shot perfectly to the plate, this time getting his man by a hair."

But on July 18 at Comiskey Park, Boston knocked the White Sox out of first place and the next day Buck got involved in a play that would haunt him at Fenway Park the rest of the season. Boston shortstop Jack Barry singled. Only two weeks earlier he had been purchased by the Red Sox from Philadelphia as Connie Mack continued to dismantle his great infield. Barry, starting to steal, was caught off first base. First baseman Jack Fournier fired the ball to Weaver who tagged Barry on the head as he slid in. Barry was sprawled on the diamond for a while before he could "wobble to the bench" with the help of two teammates. He was "too groggy" to return to action.

Before an immediate return series in Boston, the White Sox, and Buck in particular, gained a momentary respite from the baseball wars by playing an exhibition game in Utica, New York against the locals of the New York State League. It gave Buck a chance to entertain the crowd as a baseball clown. Wrote a *Tribune* correspondent: "Buck Weaver appeared in the role of a comedian and kept the fans in good humor despite the one-sidedness of the score. Never before has the Sox shortstop batted so highly as a humorist. Buck kidded the bleachers, put his cap on the home plate when batting, and turned around and hit from both sides. He appeared like a dummy the last time at bat, not moving a muscle or his bat although in a position to hit when called out on strikes."

When the series opened in Boston, the fans booed and hissed Weaver, blaming him for deliberately attempting to knock Barry out with the ball in that play in Chicago. Sanborn wrote that Barry said the incident was his own fault but the Chicago writer observed, "but that makes no difference to a scribe who is looking for a chance for a story that will cause trouble." The Red Sox won the opener but the next day the White Sox edged Boston, 1 to 0, in a game that "kept nearly 20,000 people close to the raving maniac stage." One man died of a heart attack, there were three double plays on each side and pitcher Jim Scott drove in the winning run with a single. "Half the crowd jeered Weaver and the other half cheered him . . . showing that the Hub fans are at least fifty-fifty sportsmen."

The *Sporting News* reported: "Buck Weaver was panned and booed and roasted by a certain element in Boston. . . . Most of the fans of the Hub who attended the game refused to join in the chorus of booing and even went to the other extreme and applauded the Sox shortstop. Some of the bench warmers in the coup at Fenway Park led in the booing probably to disconcert the Sox shortstop. . . . Umpire Evans finally drove these troublemakers off the bench."

On top of the razzing the fans gave him in Boston Buck got word that he was slapped with a fine for getting involved in a fracas during the same game as the Barry incident. In the last of the ninth, with the Sox trailing, 6 to 4, Walter Mayer, a reserve catcher, apparently was hit by a pitched ball and started for first base. Umpire Silk O'Loughlin called Mayer back to the plate, saying that Mayer was to blame for getting hit. Manager Rowland charged the umpire, complaining a bit too energetically. O'Loughlin ordered the Sox skipper off the field. Weaver, standing around the batter's circle, also got his dander up and told the umpire in no uncertain terms that he didn't care for the call either, so he too was invited to an early shower and later fined. Mayer subsequently struck out. According to Buck, however, the fine was not paid out of his pocket. A little more than two years later, while wintering in California, he told a group of Pacific Coast League players that he did not pay any fines. "Why up in the big league none of us ever pay our fines. They want you to get out there and fight, don't they, and do you think that we pay for the privilege? Well, I guess the old club treasury looks after that, all right, all right."

If Comiskey did foot the bills for player fines, it was an exception to his general niggardliness towards the players. The White Sox owner held a tight lid on the treasury when it came to doling out coin to his team. While other teams provided $4-a-day meal money to their players, Comiskey dished out only three. The White Sox gained the unenviable reputation of wearing the dirtiest uniforms in the majors because Comiskey required the players pay 50 cents every time their uniforms were cleaned. If they refused, he raided their lockers, laundered their outfits, and then docked their salaries for the cleaning.

On the other hand, Comiskey, sensing the Sox could still win the pennant (they were only four and a half games out of the lead on August 9) was willing to spend a bundle as he kept prospecting for talented ballplayers. Only a month earlier he missed a chance to land Jack Barry when he was still with Philadelphia because of slow mail delivery from the east coast during the July 4th holiday. Boston learned Barry was on the block before Comiskey did and made an acceptable offer to Connie Mack. Comiskey had been prepared to outbid the Boston offer.

The question arose as to why Comiskey would want Barry when he already had Weaver on the payroll. The fact was, Comiskey sought another starting shortstop so he could move Weaver to third base. By this time, Rowland and Comiskey agreed that Weaver would better serve the White Sox at third. Buck's "sensational mechanical ability" and quick reflexes and his powerful rifle arm left no doubt that he could excel there. But then who would play short? Spring training camp would hopefully reveal a successful candidate.

Undaunted by the failure to land Barry, Comiskey continued to wheel and deal. He purchased left-handed pitcher Claude "Lefty" Williams from Salt Lake City who would not report until the following spring. According to the scouting reports Williams showed "excellent promise."

Then from Cleveland came the startling news from Charles Somers, the owner and president of the Indians, that his slugging outfielder, Joe Jackson, was on the auction block. He would go to the highest bidder. Since joining Cleveland in 1910, Jackson rivaled Ty Cobb and Tris Speaker annually for the batting crown. The Federal League was making a determined drive to lure more major league talent, and Somers faced the possibility of Jackson jumping to the outlaw circut. He just could not afford a bidding war to retain Jackson who held a five year major league batting average of .374. Cleveland had floundered in last place in 1914 and attendance at Indian games in 1915 was meager. So Somers tried to salvage something before he lost it all. He needed money.

Comiskey ordered his team secretary, Harry Grabiner, to Cleveland with the instruction: "Go to Cleveland, watch the bidding for Jackson, raise the highest one made by any club until they all drop out." According to the *Tribune*, Grabiner soon telephoned Comiskey that he was successful in landing Jackson for $15,000 and three forgettable players. Grabiner brought Joe to Chicago on the first available train. That $15,000 figure reported in the *Tribune* August 21 seems suspiciously low, even though the story said Somers rejected a straight cash deal for $25,000. It was said Somers preferred less cash in favor of ballplayers. Other more recent sources indicate Somers picked up more than $15,000 in cash. *The Baseball Trade Register* by John L. Reichler, published in 1984, states Comiskey paid $31,500 plus three ball players. Glenn Dickey in *The History of American League Baseball Since 1901* writes it took $65,000 to bring Jackson to the Windy City.

By late August the White Sox were still trying to match-up a player with third base. By this time Buck must have felt as if he was playing next to a carousel. Four different third basemen were tried and found wanting. The situation at first base was just as frantic. Buck threw to a quartet of first sackers: two primarily played other positions; one could sting the ball but couldn't glove it; and one, named Bunny Brief, whose stay in the majors matched his name.

In Detroit Buck committed four errors in three games. Furthermore, Sanborn sarcastically noted that one scratch hit, "a swift grounder which broke through Weaver's hands for a single . . . would have been copped by several short-stops and which Weaver would have eaten up seven times out of ten, provided there had been nothing depending on his doing so." Buck may have had his mind elsewhere. Back in Chicago the mayor's office had revoked Buck's license for his billiard hall and barbershop. Police had discovered dice games being played on the premises.

When the White Sox returned home Buck went down-town to city hall to try to get the pool hall license restored. He was accompanied by his store manager, a man named Jack Hartford. Buck promised there would be no more dice games in the store. A sympathetic, pleasant exchange occurred between Buck and Chief of Police Healy who was obviously a baseball fan. "You see, Chief, it's sort of getting on my nerves, this place of mine being closed. The Sox leave tonight, too."

"Is that so?" Healy said. "Do you think you could play better ball if you get your license back?"

"Just watch me," Buck replied. "We'll gather in the pennant."

"In that case, wait a minute till I see the mayor."

It wasn't long before Buck and his manager left city hall with the license. Hartford told a reporter, "Oh, I guess it was all arranged in advance. You see Bill Burkhardt is a friend of Buck's." William Burkhardt was the commissioner of public works.

As if Buck didn't have enough of a headache with his billiard hall, the White Sox left town for Boston, hardly one of his favorite cities since he had become the target of verbal abuse from Red Sox fans. Besides, the team was not exactly in a gung-ho mood to play ball after a thirty-four hour sleeper trip from Chicago in a roundabout route through Pittsburgh. The White Sox were now trying to hold on to third place and their task wasn't made any easier by the bush league antics of the Red Sox front office. Boston management placed a bunch of youngsters with fish horns in box seats behind first and third base. Every time they thought they could rile White Sox players they let go on the horns. In a doubleheader defeat Buck went hitless. "Weaver was booed by the crowd at nearly every move, and that . . . with the horning . . . got his goat so completely that he walked up in front of the screen in the second game and started an argument with a flock of real box holders. Eddie Collins finally went out and yanked Weaver away to the bench."

In any case, if third place had been locked up, Rowland would have liked to try Weaver at third base. It was almost the end of the season and the parade of third basemen had still failed to reveal a qualified candidate. But with Washington right behind the White Sox in the standings, Rowland didn't make the move. The Chicagoans didn't clinch third place until September 30, almost the end of the season.

While the White Sox ended the pennant race on a high note by winning eleven games in a row, the Chicago Whales, who didn't know it at the time, were putting the coup de grace on the existence of the Federal League on the north side. But they went out in grand style before a standing room crowd of 34,212. The happy throng saw the Chicago team win the Federal League pennant by beating Pittsburgh 3 to 0.

With their third place finish, the White Sox rolled up their most victories since their pennant winning year of 1906. In their last world championship season they ran up 93 wins against 58 losses. The 1915 White Sox also recorded 93 victories but lost three more games.

Weaver finished the year with a .268 batting average,

22 points higher than his mark in 1914. As for his fielding, The *Sporting News* commented that it was the "worst field-ing Buck Weaver has had since he donned a Sox uniform." Yet statistically Buck improved. In 148 games he committed 49 errors for a .939 average, still not too much to crow about when George McBride of the Washington Senators topped the shortstops in fielding with a .968 average on 25 errors in 146 games. Statistics, anyhow, never captured Buck's virtu-osity on defense.

As usual the White Sox conquered the Cubs in the city series but not without incident. Disgruntled players on both teams were angry with the owners of both ball clubs. Cold weather had held down the crowds for two days. In the last and fifth game, a Sunday throng of 32,666 mobbed Comis-key Park. But since players could only participate in the re-ceipts of the first four games, they could not realize an income from the one big crowd of the series. Of course the players knew this going into post-season play. But they complained the early games should have been postponed.

"Leave it to the big bosses to cop all the dough," one of the White Sox players grumbled after the game. "They have all the say as to whether the games shall be played or post-poned. They never would have considered playing such days as Thursday and Friday if it had been in the regular season. They would have postponed the games in a hurry and booked doubleheaders for later, so as to get more dough."

"They always told me Comiskey was a friend of the ballplayer," a member of the Cubs said. "I understand he was responsible for our playing on the two cold days. Con-sequently he gets the big money from the big Sunday crowd and the ballplayer gets his little mite which came in on the cold days."

However Buck felt about the situation he couldn't lin-ger over it long. He pocketed $420 as his winning share and moved on to other interests. He and his traveling roommate, Jim Scott, were embarking on a show business adventure. Together with Helen and her three sisters, Harriet, Bess and Annetta Marie, Buck and Jim were putting together a song and dance act to tour the vaudeville circuit for the fall and winter.

It was customary at the time for many major leaguers to tour the theatres during the off-season. Usually, they simply talked about their baseball experiences, reminiscing and relating anecdotes. McGraw of the Giants was appearing at the Palace theatre in Chicago when he agreed to make the world tour with the White Sox. Ty Cobb went on the stage during the winter of 1911-12 and he did more than tell stories. He played the leading role in George Ade's comedy, "The College Widow," and toured Detroit, Pittsburgh, New York, Atlanta and a string of small towns.

Before opening in Chicago, the sextet went through a test run for three days in Benton Harbor, Michigan, and three days in Kankakee, Illinois. Then before a friendly and excited crowd of 1,500 people the act debuted at the Empress Theater on Chicago's south side Rialto at 63rd and Halsted streets on Monday night, November 2. With two shows every evening, 3,000 "loyal rooters of the South Side thronged the vaudeville house . . . "

Buck and Jim and the girls talked baseball, danced, sang ballads and ragtime. Buck teamed up with one of the girls and imitated Vernon and Irene Castle, the internationally popular ballroom dancers. The girls first came on stage in "rapturous conversation about their baseball idols." Then they encountered Buck and Jim wearing their baseball uniforms "in front of a drop which resembles the exterior of Comiskey Park. After some flirting they make a date for that evening and the scene shifts to a parlor with the women entertaining Weaver and Scottie, now arrayed in evening duds."

One Chicago newspaper headlined: "SOX STARS BAT COOL THOUSAND IN STAGE DEBUT: Scott and Weaver Go Big in Local Vaudeville Premier at Empress Theater." Wrote the critic: "When one stops to consider the act has been running about a week . . . any seeming nervousness on the part of the elk hunter may readily be forgiven. Weaver fairly radiated stage presence. He was as much at home on the boards as he is on the ball field. He and Scottie first arrayed in White Sox 'unies' and later in the conventional 'soup and fish' worn on the world's tour, cracked merry jest as the plot thickened, danced a bit and generally got clubby with the populace."

In the meantime the *Tribune* headlined on December 19: "BASEBALL WAR ENDED: FEDERAL LEAGUE DIES." There were compromises and tradeoffs. The Federal League powers were taken care of. Charles Weeghman, the Chicago restauranteer and owner of the Whales, was allowed to purchase the Chicago Cubs. He merged both ball clubs with his best personnel. The Cubs moved from West Side Park on Lincoln and Polk streets to the Whales' play lot on the north side at Addison and Clark streets, what is now Wrigley Field. Weeghman retained Joe Tinker, his Whales manager, as the field boss of the Cubs. Joe was shortstop in the legendary Tinker to Evers to Chance infield of the powerful Cubs of earlier years.

Philip Ball of the St. Louis Feds purchased the St. Louis Browns and took over Sportsman's Park which was then rented to the St. Louis Cardinals for many years. Harry Sinclair, the Oklahoma millionaire, notorious for his later role in the Tea Pot Dome scandal during the Harding presidency, held the Federal League Newark franchise. He was paid $100,000 plus the right to sell his team's players back to the American and National leagues. Sinclair also gained the right to sell other players to the majors who were not under contract to Federal League club owners. The estate of brothers Robert and George Ward, owners of the Ward Baking Corp. of Brooklyn and the Brooklyn Feds, was compensated in the amount of $400,000. Prior to his death in October, 1915, Robert Ward had confessed he'd lost more than a million dollars in the Federal League venture. The agreements included that the Federal League drop its anti-trust suit and that all players in the Federal League would be eligible to play in organized ball. Federal League franchises in Baltimore, Buffalo and Newark would be permitted to field teams in the International League. Baltimore, miffed by the settlement, fought it for a while in the federal courts, but eventually succumbed to the inevitable.

7

"The Maddest Race"

Buck Weaver might have wondered at the beginning of 1916 where he would play during the coming season, not only at what position but for which team. There were rumors that Comiskey sought to trade him to Cleveland for shortstop Ray Chapman. But Comiskey issued denials. Then there were attempts to deal for an established major league third baseman which would have anchored Buck at short. Those also failed. More thought was given to shifting Weaver to third base.

As spring training approached, Rowland observed, "Of course if Weaver is moved to third base it will be because either Terry or McMullin makes good as a shortstop." Zeb Terry, a Stanford University graduate, and Fred McMullin were rookies up from Los Angeles.

The *Tribune's* Weller chimed in, "If Buck Weaver plays shortstop there will be no worry over that position either, but there is a possibility that Buck will find himself located at third." Buck didn't care where he was located as long as he was in on the action.

As the end of spring training neared, George S. Robbins, a sportswriter for the Chicago *Daily News* and The *Sporting News* observed: "Weaver has everything to make a great third baseman for the Sox—everything that his predecessors lacked. He has the nerve to ride and tag runners coming into the bag. He isn't afraid of hot liners. He can come in good on a ball, is a dead shot on a fly and has a great throwing arm.

"But if Weaver isn't shifted to third he'll stay at short— of that one may be certain. The anvil chorus is after Buck though, and he'll have to lead the world at his post it seems, to avoid the knockers. Weaver didn't have his best year in 1915, but his work for the most part was brilliant and helpful to pitchers. There isn't a shortstop, take him year in year out, who will field tighter when a pitcher is in a hole and needs help." Robbins called it a "great injustice to knock Weaver when he is cutting off more hits, courting more errors than most shortstops in the major leagues."

Just before the pennant race started Buck sold his poolroom and was now "free from business cares." He took charge of third base when the season opened before 31,000 fans, the largest inaugural crowd in Chicago history. Alongside him at shortstop was the college grad, Zeb Terry from Stanford. He had won a crack at the job with his sharp performance during spring training. Though the White Sox lost to Detroit, Weller could report: "The lone bright spot . . . was the imperviousness of the left side of the Sox diamond to all attacks. Zeb Terry, the kid shortstopper, lived up to his lithographs, and Buck Weaver, the converted third baseman handled with agility and precision all the work that fell to him, which was considerable."

Sanborn percolated optimism over White Sox chances. Said a *Tribune* headline: "SANBORN DECLARES SOX SHOULD BE FAVORITES." Sanborn wrote that Terry "will tighten up the left side of the infield because Weaver plays better at third than he did at short."

But by late April Buck was switched back to shortstop only because Terry collapsed at the plate, hitting a microscopic .152. Rowland inserted McMullin at third. About the same time Rowland named Eddie Collins team captain. That fulfilled the prophecy that Comiskey made when he purchased Collins and shook Rowland's stance that his teams didn't have team captains. One can only imagine how Buck must have felt. He had been the previous field leader, and this was Weaver's fifth year with the White Sox while Eddie was only in his sophomore season with Chicago.

Disappointing performances by others either at short or third added to a string of injuries forced Weaver to shuttle between those two positions all season. He played almost as many games at short as he did at third. Regardless, the "ginger kid" wore his almost perpetual smile. He was just happy to be playing baseball. His bubbly personality on the field belied his aggressive, combative, iron-willed spirit. Buck would give no quarter and scrap like a "fighting wolf-hound" to win. As he matured he became an increasingly crafty player who learned the tricks and nuances that separated victory from defeat.

At Detroit on June 1 Buck, playing third, aroused the anger of the Tigers' heavy hitting outfielder, Harry Heilmann, who years later became the voice of Tiger baseball on radio. Crusinberry described the action: "Buck Weaver and Big Heilmann nearly engaged in a fist fight in the second inning. Heilmann raced all the way home from first when Faber heaved Burns' bunt to the bleachers and Buck made him take a wide turn at third by standing right by the bag. Heilmann gave Weaver a shove as he passed and then ran back after crossing the plate and said something. Whatever he said included fighting words, for Weaver might have mixed if Jimmy Burke (Detroit coach) and Umpire Dineen hadn't rushed between the angered men."

Buck's base running almost caused a free-for-all fight in Chicago several weeks later. Cleveland and the White Sox already were cutting each other up with high flying spikes when Weaver made "a mad dash for second base, slid into the bag as if he intended to claw the entire Cleveland team under ground." Second baseman "Ivan Howard was covering and the two went in a heap and rolled and scrambled and kicked and punched each other like a pair of wildcats.

"Instantly all the other Cleveland players dashed for the spot and every man on the two benches rushed there. If it hadn't been for some gallant policing by Umpire Nallin there undoubtedly would have been an old fashioned free-for-all fight on the diamond. Nallin rushed between the two factions and Umpire Evans, working behind the plate, went out as fast as his legs could carry him."

Years later Buck confessed to an admiring youth, "Young man," he said in a slow raspy voice, "we used to have a file in the dugout and we filed our spikes good and sharp."

Buck's intense desire to win led to heated arguments with umpires that often signaled early dismissals from the diamond. He was thrown out of a game in Boston when he objected to umpire Ollie Chill's call at first base. "Weaver bounded a slow one to Barry, close to second, and almost every one in the press stand thought he beat Barry's throw."

Crusinberry, writing in Buck's defense, observed: "What Weaver said would not go at all in parlor society, but as he wasn't addressing the remark to the umpire or meaning it when he said it, it looked like Chill was hasty in ordering the Sox star out."

A bum call by Chill again led to Buck's ouster at Philadelphia. ". . . Buck rolled a slow one toward first base. The pitcher fielded the ball and threw to first baseman, Stuffy McInnis, "who did not have his foot on first base until after the runner passed it. Weaver kicked a cloud of dust at Chill and disappeared from the picture . . ."

By mid-summer Buck proved himself a top flight third baseman. Robbins, writing in The *Sporting News* on July 24, praised the performance of the indefatigable infielder: "The wonderful playing of Buck Weaver on this last trip of the Sox around the eastern circle was easily the great feature. No chance was too hard for Buck and he was in there fighting every day. There isn't a greater fielding infielder in the world today than Weaver. His playing has kept the Sox in the pennant fight. One fan said the only thing he didn't like about Weaver's playing was his dirty uniform. It becomes dirty through hard playing, and Buck is some tumbler." Buck's uniform was the dirtiest on the team, a team renowned for dirty uniforms, for more than one reason. He had developed one idiosyncrasy, a superstition peculiar to him. Buck couldn't stand playing in a clean outfit. He'd cuff a handful of dirt from the infield and rub it all over the front of his uniform. In the days before players were identified by numbers, Buck could be spotted on the field by his soiled togs. Buck's defensive gyrations played a major role in the White Sox comeback from last place on May 19 into the top spot on August 3. But he could not untrack himself at the plate. He only mustered a .227 average for the season.

The Sox pitching corps proved to be the sturdy backbone of the ball club. Seven regular hurlers shut down the opposition to less than three runs a game. Most effective was Eddie Cicotte who squelched enemy batsmen to 1.78 runs per nine innings. Only George Herman "Babe" Ruth of the Boston Red Sox, with an ERA of 1.75, topped the little Chicago right-hander.

In the "maddest race the American League ever has enjoyed," Boston invaded Chicago trailing by only one-half game on August 5. The Red Sox thumped the White Sox in the last three games of the series and dropped the Chicagoans into third place. After the White Sox lost the finale of the series, 11 to 5, Crusinberry ripped the team: "In one of the worst exhibitions of baseball ever seen in Chicago, the White Sox were humiliated yesterday . . .

"Mentally and physically the Sox were awful. They did everything the wrong way. Manager Rowland didn't make a good guess all afternoon; Eddie Collins played ball as if in a daze; Ray Schalk was on the bum. Reb Russell pitched as if in a dream; Old Dame Fortune cut in and helped the Red Sox, who didn't need any help; the weather man broke into the affair twice at times most injurious to the Sox, and even the batboy did his work recklessly."

Though the White Sox remained in the thick of the pennant race and had been playing an exhausting schedule—five doubleheaders between July 15 and August 1—the front office booked an exhibition game on August 14 at McHenry, Illinois, a small town about forty miles northwest of Chicago. A *Tribune* reporter caught the irony and sarcastically observed: "Now that the pennant is clinched, the Sox can afford to spend their energy on exhibition games." Playing an extra game also meant an increased risk of injury. But the possibility of harm existed off the playing field as well as on it, as Buck nearly discovered. "Buck Weaver was knocked off the back of an automobile returning from the ball park to the hotel." Fortunately, he wasn't injured and later walked to the railroad station. "It is hard to hurt Buck," assured the reporter.

On August 19 William "Kid" Gleason rejoined the White Sox and got a warm welcome from the players. Gleason had accepted Comiskey's call to come out of retirement to help cure the helter-skelter base running that plagued the team all season. The "Kid" would also coach the pitching staff.

Buck was now sizzling at both short and third. Even Detroit fans applauded his brilliant "hair raising catches." At shortstop, "Weaver made a play for the book in the first inning when he ran back and stabbed Cobb's fly" and then threw to first to double Donie Bush off the bag. In Chicago, when he was back at third, "Weaver made a circus catch of a foul bunt . . ." Then when another batter tried to sacrifice in the same inning, "Buck had to dive for the ball, but held it while he slid on his face."

By September 17, Sunday morning, the White Sox had clawed their way into second place only a half game behind Detroit and one half game ahead of Boston. Weaver led the way a day earlier with a homer as the White Sox topped Boston 6 to 4 at Comiskey Park. For his effort Buck received $100 from Dubuque, Iowa, White Sox rooters who offered the cash prize "for every home run made by a Rowland player during the remainder of the season." Especially beaming in the White Sox dugout as Buck circled the bases must have been the third-string catcher, Jack Lapp, who was playing that day. It was Lapp who spotted Buck in Stowe, Pennsylvania, that fall day in 1909 during the exhibition game against major league barnstormers and recommended him to scout Mike Kennedy of the Athletics. Now the veteran receiver was finishing out a major league career with a few backup appearances with the White Sox.

That Sunday afternoon a record overflow crowd of 40,000 fanatics mobbed Comiskey Park, hoping to cheer the White Sox on to first place. In the first inning, "the Rowlands drove the big crowd into paroxysms of insanity by whanging out a lead of two runs. Three solid hits and a wild pitch were responsible for that glad beginning, but the joy was short-lived. The Red Sox forged in front with three runs in the second and from there to the long delayed windup the Rowlands trailed helplessly." Southpaw George Herman Ruth held the White Sox scoreless the rest of the way on a five hitter.

The White Sox never got as close to first place the rest of the season. Their courageous challenge fell two games short as they finished in second place. Even though the White Sox did not make it to the top, they served notice they were back in the upper rung of competition. Comiskey could chortle about one thing: Attendance at Comiskey Park for 1916 ranked first in the major leagues. The Sox drew 679,923 fans while Detroit finished second with 616,772. The Philadelphia Phillies led the National League with 515,365 spectators.

Buck's fielding for the season showed marked improvement despite being forced to hustle back and forth between short and third. In 151 games Buck committed 36 errors, thirteen less than 1915, and he played three more games. He ranked fourth among shortstops with sixteen miscues in 66 games. At third he messed up twenty chances in 85 matches, again placing him in fourth place.

The top fielding shortstop in the American League, Everett Scott of Boston, committed nineteen errors for a .967 average. Buck achieved a .954 mark, his best effort up to that time. Oscar Vitt of Detroit led third basemen in fielding with a .964 average on 22 errors. Weaver fielded .941. By comparison these fielding statistics pale with the records of modern ballplayers. But one must consider the crude, primitive fielding gloves of the day which barely fit over the players' hands and had little if any flexibility. Furthermore, modern diamonds are finely manicured, baseballs are of higher quality, and uniforms are lighter weight and better fitting.

The White Sox swept the city series in four straight. Even though it was only an exhibition series, there lurked in the minds of baseball observers the sinister hand of crooked gamblers and fixed games. Crusinberry wrote about it in the October 8 issue of the *Tribune*: "Besides winning the city championship, the Sox yesterday scored one for the honesty of baseball. If they had lost the game there would have been another game today at Comiskey park, for which about $15,000 . . . would have been taken in at the gate. Some of Chicago's gamblers who don't yet understand baseball were said to have been offering even money on the Cubs yesterday, and a few of them were reported to be offering odds on the Cubs, their reason being that the baseball leaders never would permit the Sox to win the game and thereby end the series and beat the club out of the big Sunday gate."

The concern about the possibility of crooked play in the Chicago city series was not an isolated worry in that fall of 1916. Only days earlier in New York, on the last day of the season, there was suspicion that the Giants might have laid down before the Brooklyn Dodgers.

The Dodgers and the Phillies were in a nip and tuck struggle for first place up to and including the last day of the season. The Dodgers held a narrow lead, but if they lost their final to New York and Philadelphia beat Boston twice, the race would have ended in a tie. The Phillies lost both games of the doubleheader to end any doubt about the pennant winner. But the Dodger-Giant game in Brooklyn did not progress without incident. Manager McGraw stormed out of the dugout at the end of the fifth inning and marched back to the clubhouse. As he left the ballpark, he told reporters: "I simply would not stand for the kind of baseball the team was playing. I do not believe that any of my players deliberately favored Brooklyn, but they simply refused to obey my orders and fooled around in a listless manner."

A wire service reporter commented: "McGraw's hasty

action in leaving his team is to be regretted, as it served only to lend color, as it were, to the charges that the Giants were not trying and seemingly to confirm the suspicion of those who are looking for something crooked."

Two Giant players who were targets for criticism had quick responses. Shortstop Art Fletcher said, "The statement that any one on the team tried to throw the game is a damned lie." Pitcher Poll Perritt said, "If there is any implication that I helped to lose the game, you can give it the lie for me. And giving it the lie you can go as far as you like."

By the end of the 1916 season Buck still was not recognized as the premier fielding third baseman that he was to become. Sanborn, in naming his choices for the All-America nine, picked Larry Gardner of the Red Sox over the Chicago infielder. He wrote,". . . on third Gardner is undoubtedly superior to Weaver in hitting as well as steadier in fielding, although not as active as the White Sox third sacker."

At the beginning of 1916 talk began to circulate about changing the makeup of the three-man national commission. Barney Dreyfus, the wealthy and powerful owner of the Pittsburgh Pirates, spearheaded the drive. He had become violently and bitterly angry with Garry Herrmann, one of the commissioners of baseball and owner of the Cincinnati Reds. A year earlier Herrmann joined Ban Johnson in a 2 to 1 vote awarding collegiate All-American George Sisler of the University of Michigan to the St. Louis Browns. John Tener, president of the National League, voted for the Pirates. The Pirates had purchased the contract Sisler signed when he was a seventeen-year-old high school star in Akron, Ohio. But Johnson called that contract null and void since it was signed by a minor and because Sisler never played for the Akron club. The Browns waited to sign him after his college career ended.

At the National League meeting in New York on December 14, Dreyfus presented a plan for a reorganization of the National Commission. He suggested some person unidentified with baseball replace Herrmann as chairman. That was exactly what American League club owners wanted. Herrmann himself said he would resign, if such action would benefit organized baseball. Other than Dreyfus, however, the National League owners did not relish any change in the "supreme court" of baseball and the matter was dropped.

Buck and Helen wintered in Los Angeles and mingled with some of Hollywood's motion picture celebrities. Will Rogers, the Ziegfeld Follies comedy star who had by now become a silent screen favorite, was taken by Helen's beauty and offered her a part in his upcoming motion picture. Helen and Buck told him they would think it over. That night they discussed it. They concluded movies would never amount to much so Helen turned down Rogers' offer.

When Buck learned that Rowland had been signed to manage the Sox again, he took time to write his skipper an encouraging note which read in part "that the Sox never yet had done for him what they are capable of doing and might do this season." Rowland also received letters from Collins and Jackson. Since Joe couldn't read or write, he probably dictated his message to his wife, Katie. The letters buoyed Rowland's spirit. "It means a lot to have fellows like Eddie Collins and Buck Weaver and Joe Jackson for you. I always have felt positive that these boys were doing all they could to make the White Sox win and I really think they will strive to do still more just to make things easier for me."

8

The Sox Win
a World Series

Along with the sour notes being sounded about the National Commission, another problem challenged baseball in the early days of 1917. The Players' Fraternity called a strike for February 20, the first day of spring training. The fraternity demanded the removal of the no pay provision in contracts for minor leaguers who were out of action due to injuries. It also sought travel allowances for minor leaguers on their way to spring training. Many major league players ignored the strike call, however, and signed contracts. The strike threat collapsed, and so did the union.

During spring training it became obvious to observers that Buck and third base were a perfect match. Sanborn predicted that "Weaver, playing steadily at third, will be a far better defensive man than when he was switched back and forth." The *Sporting News* hailed Buck's transfer to third. "Buck is [a] wonderful third baseman all agree and Manager Rowland has decided to make the shift of this player to the far corner permanent. In stopping men coming around the bases, going after a fly ball, and digging in for hard chances Buck has few equals in the major leagues."

Comiskey had just brought up a fleet-footed infielder named Charles "Swede" Risberg from the Pacific Coast League. He was "filling Weaver's shoes at short in an able manner and giving Buck a chance to shine where he can work to best advantage, on third base."

Pennant hopes skyrocketed for the White Sox soon after spring training began. Comiskey, relentlessly on the prowl to bolster his ball club, purchased Chick Gandil, the fancy fielding first sacker of the Cleveland Indians. Gandil batted only .259 the previous season but he led the league in fielding, the hole in the armor of Sox defense. Ring Lardner observed, "Chick Gandil, who, if his knee doesn't slip, will come mighty near cinching a pennant for Mr. Comiskey's club . . ."

The *Sporting News* saw the White Sox as a sure bet to win the American League pennant when it headlined on March 29: "MIRACLE IF WHITE SOX LOSE THIS TIME." The baseball weekly felt that Comiskey had "corralled a great club."

As the war with Germany drew closer during spring training, American League club owners worked out a tactic with the cooperation with the U.S. Army to put their players through close order drill under the direction of an army drill sergeant for each ball club. They hoped the military charade would help choke off criticism of able-bodied young men continuing in sport while the nation was at war. When the White Sox opened their home season at Comiskey Park, White Sox players marched onto the field before the game, wearing army uniforms and shouldering Springfield rifles. They executed a snappy military drill before 25,000 admiring fans. "There was a roar that fairly drowned the band which was trying to furnish a quickstep for the Sox to march by."

The war closed in on major league baseball in several other ways. The National League club owners vetoed the close order drill of ballplayers, but both leagues set up booths in ballparks where young men could enlist or fans could buy Liberty bonds. The American flag was raised before each game. Even baseball writers were beginning to employ military terms in their accounts of the games: "Weaver was target for a whole case of grape and canister, but knocked down everything he could reach and faced the hottest fire without quailing, converting every missile into a boomerang by retiring somebody on it."

Buck displayed his playful, carefree spirit on June 14 in New York as rain disrupted a doubleheader. After all, the White Sox were in first place and he was playing third base with the virtuosity of a Rubenstein at the piano. Fans had been waiting patiently for a half hour for the rains to stop when Buck took off his shoes and stockings and ran out of the clubhouse. He took off across the outfield barefooted. The crowd cheered. Crusinberry reported, "Away down in deep center, Buck hit a lake of water, his feet shot out, he went up in the air, and then slid about twenty feet, plowing a furrow through the pool, while the crowd screamed with delight."

Why did Buck go out of his way to entertain the crowd? Why did he act like a kid? He was now almost twenty-seven years old. The answer lay in his sheer love of the fans. He thrived on the joyous response of the crowd. He wanted the fans to feel some of the same exhileration he experienced by just being on a baseball field. He was a paradox. On the field Buck was a free-spirited soul with adrenalin overflowing. Away from the ballpark, Weaver was a quiet, reserved individual, often a loner except for the company of his wife, with whom he was deeply in love. His closest friend on the ball club, Jim Scott, who would one day become his brother-in-law, was not even invited to Buck's wedding.

By the time the White Sox hit Boston, they were two and a half games ahead of the Red Sox. Fenway Park had become notorious for heavy betting. Gamblers crowded the right field pavilion for every game and carried "on operation with as much vigor and vim as one would see in the wheat pit of the Chicago board of trade." The sports betters there had been battered by heavy losses as their favored Red Sox spilled eight of twelve games. Ironically, Boston had returned home running up a nine game winning streak on the road.

Chicago won the opening game of the series, and on June 16, it looked as if the White Sox were on their way to making it two in a row. The Red Sox trailed, 2 to 0, in the fourth. Then while the visitors were still at bat in the inning, a mild mist which had been falling turned into a light rain, though not troublesome enough to stop play. Suddenly, though, the fans in the unprotected bleachers leaped onto the field and dashed across right field, heading for the covered pavilion. Umpire Bill McCormick stopped play until the field was cleared.

The game moved into the top of the fifth with the Red Sox stalling as much as they could. They eyed threatening skies with hopes of a heavier downpour to stop the game before it became official. With two outs in the inning, a disturbance broke out in the right field pavilion where the gamblers nested. Crusinberry described the scene: ". . . a tall man in a long rain coat took comand. Waving his comrades to follow, he boldly leaped out upon the field. In ten seconds he must have had 500 followers. They didn't rush at the players or umpires. The latter stood gazing in amazement. The grand stand crowd became absolutely still. But instead of fighting the mob simply surged out upon the field, clear to the diamond, and stood around."

Boston players and the umpires warned the leaders of the crowd if they didn't get off the field, the game would be forfeited to Chicago. The mob cleared the field but they didn't go back to the pavilion. They took over box seats.

"Just when play was about to begin again new leaders and recruits came from the gamblers' stand. Some of them came from the left pavilion, then the first crowd piled out of the boxes again. This time the mob was riotous. Officers, five all told, came forth. They were helpless and didn't try very hard." Later Umpire Connelly told Harry Frazee, owner of the Red Sox, that "the lack of officers was an outrage and that had he been in charge of the game it would have been forfeited."

As the mob swirled over the field, the players and umpires hurried off, seeking the security of the clubhouse. Weaver and McMullin were grabbed by some fans and had to fight to get through to the exit. Warrants would be sworn out by a fan who claimed he was slugged by Weaver and McMullin.

After a 45 minute delay, the game was resumed with Buck slapping a homer in the ninth to spark a four run outburst in a 7 to 2 victory. But the trouble wasn't over yet. Buck got hit with a pop bottle as he was leaving the field. Fortunately he wasn't hurt.

Crusinberry called it "the boldest piece of business ever perpetrated by a baseball crowd, and back of it all . . . was the gambling crowd which is allowed to operate freely here in the right field pavilion."

Reviewing the problem in Boston and the gambling situation in the major leagues in general, Crusinberry wrote, "The same condition prevails at the National League park, and although gambling may take place more or less in all big league parks, there is no other city where it is allowed to flourish so openly. . . .

"Just why this betting ring is allowed in Boston and not tolerated in other cities, never has been explained by the baseball magnates, but it is supposed to carry a political angle which has the hands of the magnates tied. The attention of major league presidents has been called to it in the past and even has brought forth statements from the baseball heads that there was no open gambling. Any one present, however, can see the transactions and hear them plainly."

Ban Johnson reacted to the Boston riot immediately: "Gambling never has been tolerated by our league. There was an attempt to introduce it on a large scale in New York early this year and we went after the guilty parties immediately. We nailed the effort before it was well started, and we will stop gambling in Boston, too, regardless of what measures are necessary.

"President Frazee of the Boston club is new to baseball. There are many angles with which he is not entirely familiar. This constant effort of the gambling element to wedge into baseball is something new to him. Old baseball men have known for years that gambling and baseball cannot survive together, and they have fought the gambling tendency with every possible means.

"Friendly wagers, with often a dinner or a cigar as the stake, do no harm. Those we are after are the men who try to make a business of establishing themselves at the daily games and taking bets from all comers."

Then Johnson turned his thoughts to the obvious lack of security at the Boston ballpark: "I cannot understand the report that there was not sufficient police in the park to handle the trouble at Boston. This spring Frazee advised me he had installed special police in the pavilion where the gamblers congregate. They were put there solely to break up the practice."

Weaver and McMullin were served with warrants for arrest while the White Sox were still in Boston. The warrants, charging the two players with assault, were sworn out by one Augustin J. McNally, who admitted being in the mob, and as Crusinberry wrote with tongue in cheek, "is supposed to have bumped McMullin's fist with his eye. Also he is supposed to have had his fingers on the railing just when Weaver let his bat fall."

Weaver and McMullin were to appear in court the next day, but since the White Sox would be headed back to Chicago, the district attorney of Middlesex County, Nathan Tufts, scheduled his house and lot as security for the appearance of the players when they returned to Boston. The case didn't go to court until near the end of September, when the judge dismissed the assault charges against them. Afterwards he talked baseball with the players until it was time for the next case.

Despite all the distractions Buck had played a terrific series according to Crusinberry. "One of the features of the whole trip was the third basing of Buck Weaver during the Boston series. Some old fans and experts declared they never had seen anything better, even though much of the time Buck was being roasted and jeered by the crowd . . ."

Midst his great play at third, Buck took time to gripe

about calls umpires were making against him. The occasion was another one of his collisions with Ty Cobb, this time in Chicago on June 28. Weaver complained to Crusinberry: "I have Cobb out easy at third and Connelly calls him safe. Why, look at my hand where his spikes hit. How could he get in and be safe and still spike me? I tell you any time Cobb slides he's safe. You know the umpire may come around after the game—after you've been licked and says 'Well, Buck, I might have missed that one.' I never get the decision when it's close at first and I'm running. They beat me out of three on that last day in Boston and the next time I saw Connelly he says: 'Well, here comes the victim of three close ones. Ain't it awful?'"

Personal encounters between Buck and Cobb usually accelerated the ferocity with which the two men played the game. At least that was the case with Weaver. Cobb was ferocious most of the time anyway. In one situation when the two men collided in a game in Detroit on July 5, Buck let his pleasant disposition get the better of him. Wrote Crusinberry: "Cobb and Weaver staged some side play in the eighth when the Tigers were on a rampage. Ty went from first to third on Veach's single to center. Felsch's throw to third was perfect and there away ahead of Ty, but he made a wonderful fall away slide and got in. It looked as if he might have been six feet out of line, but the umpires let him get away with it. Weaver was so mad that he rolled the ball twenty feet back of third and dared Ty to go home. Finally Ty did make a break from the base and a break to get back and Weaver took a dive for him. It looked as if Ty was blocked off this time, but the umpires refused to see it that way. But this time Weaver was laughing, but he let the umpires know what he thought of them."

In Chicago Crusinberry noticed that the tide was turning in Buck's favor on close calls at first: "Umpires are beginning to realize that Buck Weaver can run. Buck has been the victim of many a close decision at first in the past. Yesterday he got two hits by getting the decision in his favor twice, and the ump was right each time."

The White Sox journeyed up to Ft. Sheridan, just a few miles north of Chicago, for a Sunday morning exhibition game against Philadelphia on July 8. Both teams would play a regularly scheduled game at Comiskey Park that afternoon. But baseball was seeking to win favor as a morale booster, and playing exhibition games for the troops, the moguls hoped, would score some points in Washington. The crowd included not only the soldiers but their wives, children, sweethearts, parents and friends. Buck, as usual in these circumstances, came to the rescue of a dull game when the crowd yelled for more "ginger." He staged a mock fight with umpire Brick Owens. "Buck kicked furiously on a decision and pulled the ump's coat sleeve and cut up generally just as if it was regular combat. Owens kept his mask on to hide his smiles." Crusinberry called it "one of the features" of the game.

By now Buck was playing the greatest baseball of his career. He was leading the club in hitting and fielding like a whirling dervish. By mid-July the White Sox "looked and acted like champions. . . . There was superb fielding, superlative pitching, timely and driving base hits and general all round efficiency."

But the Red Sox were in hot pursuit and clung close with bulldog tenacity. In the middle of July Boston charged into Chicago, trailing by two and a half games. They limped out of town four games behind. In one of the skirmishes which ended in a fifteen inning 5 to 5 tie, Buck showed more of his "fighting wolfhound" character and crowd-pleasing comedic flair. In the tenth inning Jimmy Walsh, Boston's scrappy little left fielder, "bumped Buck rather hard as he was tagged out at third." Buck and Walsh started throwing punches but the fight was quickly broken up and both players stayed in the game. For the rest of the afternoon, Walsh had to duck bottles "pegged from the left field bleachers." In the fifteenth inning, as oncoming darkness shrouded the field, Buck knocked off so many foul balls the umpire had to stop the contest and search for more baseballs. "Buck sat down on the ground to rest. . . . For a time it looked as if darkness would stop the game before Buck could get out." Weaver fouled off seventeen pitches before he flied out.

During the Boston series, it was learned that Weaver had drawn a low number in the draft but it was expected that Buck would claim exemption not only because he was married but he was the sole support of his father. But if the draft spared Weaver, combat on the diamond did not. On August 10 in Washington, Buck broke the index finger on his left hand on a play at third base. Catcher Ed Ainsmith "lumbered" towards third on a single to right. Jackson's throw had the big catcher out by "a couple of parasings [each parasing is equal to 3½ miles in ancient Persian], but he hurled himself feet first at Weaver and the bag. Buck tagged Ainsmith a yard from the base but the force of the collision broke . . . the finger . . . and knocked the ball out of [his glove]. Ainsmith, of course, was called safe, and Weaver contracted an error in addition to his injury." When Buck was knocked out of action, he had hiked his batting average to a solid .280, the second highest on the team. Fortunately for the White Sox, utility infielder Fred McMullin took over third base and proved to be a sensation on defense. And he boosted his batting mark from .217 to .246 by the time Weaver returned to the lineup on September 19.

In the meantime the White Sox grudgingly surrendered the lead to Boston for one day on August 17 by one percentage point. That proved to be the crest of the Red Sox challenge. The White Sox went back on top the next day and stayed there the rest of the way.

As the White Sox surged towards a pennant, they blasted the Detroit Tigers in back to back doubleheaders on Labor Day weekend, September 2 and 3, at Comiskey Park. It was a bewilderingly strange and wild series. In the second game Sunday, Detroit manager Hughie Jennings allowed his shaky pitcher to endure an extra inning struggle even though he was navigating completely out of control. He walked six batters, hit another and heaved a wild pitch. Maybe Jennings figured Sox hitters would be a bit shy about taking a toe hold at the plate. In that same game, the usually highly dependable outfielder Harry Heilmann failed to run out an infield grounder. Jennings wasted no time yanking him out of the game. Another oddity on both Sunday and Monday was the ease with which the White Sox swiped bases. They stole two in the morning game and came back to heist six more in the afternoon. On Labor Day the Sox ran wild with thirteen stolen bases, eight in the first game and five more in the nightcap. Sanborn concluded after the Labor Day doubleheader, "It's doubtful if ever such a day of wild pitching was staged in a major league before yesterday . . ."

Near the end of the second game even Buck Weaver was warming up in the bullpen. "He was about all the pitching Rowland had left," Sanborn wrote. Several days later Weaver could be seen coaching at first base and warming up a pitcher in the bullpen.

Those two days of strange baseball were to be heard of again. Exactly a decade later, in 1927, those games would be reviewed in a special hearing of Sox and Tiger players by commissioner of baseball Kenesaw Mountain Landis because of charges alleging dishonest play by Detroit.

When Buck finally returned to action after an almost six week layoff, he trotted out to his former post at shortstop. Rowland liked McMullin's efforts at third, but Risberg had been a disappointment at the plate. Buck would remain at shortstop through the World Series while McMullin filled the gap at third.

Finally the magic moment, elusive for so long, arrived. All the obstacles that the White Sox had faced on and off the field during the hectic and trying season, were now joyously swept away. On Saturday morning, September 22, the *Tribune* bannered: "HURRAH FOR THE SOX! WORLD'S SERIES NEXT! Crusinberry couldn't resist writing in the style of a war correspondent: "Chicago's gallant White Sox are champions at last. Led by Manager Rowland, the boys from the Windy City went 'over the top' today and captured the Boston Red Sox who held the last rampart between Chicago and a pennant."

Back in Chicago Charles Comiskey waited anxiously in

his office for the results of the game coming by telephone from the sports editor of an afternoon newspaper. When word came, "It was too much for the Old Roman," wrote a *Tribune* reporter on the scene. "His hand shook so that safety required he hang up the telephone receiver. But he turned to his son, Commy Lou, and said, 'Better tell your mother.' Big Lou had Mrs. Comiskey on the phone in a minute or so and the whole family was rejoicing long before Chicago fandom knew the glad news . . .

"After the first excitement subsided, Comiskey was almost as cool as the Comiskey most folks know. He went back as far as 1908 recalling other championships that were within his grasp. 'Twice I had the pennant all ready to nail to the pole, and both times they snatched it from my hands,' he said.

" 'This one is mine though. And after eleven years.' "

Comiskey sent off a telegram to Pants Rowland at the Brunswick Hotel in Boston: "The fondest hopes of all Chicago and the wonderful legion of White Sox fans as well as myself have come true—after eleven long years of patient waiting. Our heartiest congratulations are due your team and self for winning the American league pennant, and we are all wishing you Godspeed and good luck in the coming world's series. Give the club and party as fine a dinner as you can with my compliments. Charles A. Comiskey."

Before the season started, Comiskey had promised each player a bonus if they won a pennant. On the train ride back to Chicago, the players got their bonus. They were presented with a case of cheap champagne. Ring Lardner, still with the *Tribune* and covering the triumphant journey home, said it tasted "like stale horse piss."

Comiskey's cavalier treatment of his ballplayers is difficult to understand. Certainly he couldn't plead poverty. The White Sox franchise was one of the most profitable in the majors with tremendous support from the fans. White Sox attendance led the majors in 1916 and 1917. With no other business interests except for a few real estate holdings, Comiskey became a millionaire strictly on his investment in baseball. He was the only owner who was once a major league ballplayer, yet he doled out salaries far below the going rate for comparable talent on other ball clubs. His niggardliness in giving his players meal money and his peculiar demand that players pay for the cleaning of their uniforms defies ordinary explanation.

On the other hand Comiskey did not hesitate to spend large sums of money to buy ballplayers in order to make his Sox pennant contenders. He shelled out big bucks for his private deluxe train that escorted the White Sox entourage to spring training sites with first class accommodations. He was generous to a fault—or calculatingly courting favor—in treating friends, politicians, sportswriters, celebrities and sundry members of the Chicago power elite to his lodge in Wisconsin and to his Bard's room, the private deluxe dining room at the ballpark. While the White Sox were winning the 1917 American League pennant, Comiskey spent $25,000 to remodel and enlarge the exclusive restaurant which he still declared off limits to his ballplayers.

Comiskey's ballplayers reached the pinnacle of the American League with 100 victories and 54 defeats. Boston limped into second place with 90 wins and 62 losses, nine games behind. No White Sox team since has hit 100 triumphs in one season. The 1983 Western Division champions came closest with 99 wins.

In the prime of his playing career at age twenty-seven, Buck turned in his finest performance playing professional baseball to date. He scorched enemy pitching for a tidy .284 average in 118 games. After five years of volatile up and down defensive antics, Weaver finally climbed to the top of the league as a fielder, matching Yankees third baseman Frank Baker's .949 fielding mark on 20 errors. In only 10 games at shortstop, Buck led the fielders with an average of .983, making only 1 error in 59 chances.

White Sox pitching spearheaded the team's success. Phenomenal earned run averages were turned in by the entire staff. Cicotte led the American League with a 1.53 record as he soared to 28 victories. Lefty Williams compiled the highest ERA on the team—a remarkable 2.97—while winning 17 games.

By now Buck had become recognized as a genuine star. He and Jackson were invited to play on an all-star major league team playing the Red Sox in Boston on September 27. The exhibition game was a fund-raiser for the family of a recently deceased reporter named T. H. Murnane, regarded to be the dean of the country's sportswriters. Buck's teammates on the all-star team included, besides Jackson, Ty Cobb, Tris Speaker, Stuffy McInnis, Rabbit Maranville, Ray Chapman, Steve O'Neill, Wally Shang, Urban Shocker, Howard Ehmke and Walter Johnson. About 13,000 fans saw the Red Sox top the all-stars, 2 to 0, with Ruth pitching the first five innings for the winners.

The newspapers were full of stories of how much or how little money was being bet on the World Series. Crusinberry observed, ". . . that all this betting, or at least talk of betting, is doing the game no good." He reported that on one occasion, Rowland, Secretary O'Neil and a couple of Sox players were headed back to the hotel in a cab after a doubleheader with the Yankees at the Polo Grounds. The cabbie, who had seen the first game, overheard them talking baseball and chimed in without realizing who they were. "Say, those White Sox can play better ball than they did today. Do you know what I think? I think they kicked that ball around and acted like a lot of bums just to get the odds to favor the Giants for the world 's series."

Two days before the Series opened the *Tribune* headlined: "Betting Booms . . ." in New York but in the Windy City there appeared to be less betting than in any recent World Series. There seemed to be, according to Sanborn, too many uncertainties for the big betters.

The press seemed unmindful of the role it played in encouraging the urge to gamble by publishing betting odds. The wagering fan could place a bet by visiting his local bookmaker. Even the comic strips were not immune to the gambling fever. In the *Chicago Tribune*, October 8, "The Gumps" strip, entitled, "MIN IS A GAMBLER ALL RIGHT,"

showed Min and her husband, Andy, sitting in the grand-
stand at the World Series. In the first panel a man is sitting
in front of Min and Andy. In the balloon caption he says,
"I'LL BET ANYONE FIVE THEY DON'T MAKE A RUN."
Second panel Min says to Andy, "GO ON ANDY BET HIM.
I'VE GOT SOME MONEY." Man says, "FIVE THEY DON'T
GET TO FIRST." Third panel Min looks in her purse: "WAIT.
IT'S RIGHT HERE IN MY PURSE." Andy addresses the
man: "I'LL TAKE YOU UP ON THAT OLD TOP. PUT UP
YOUR FIVE." Fourth panel the man says: "YOU'RE ON"
(holding up a $5 bill). Min pulls a nickle out of her purse.

Gambling was not the only unfavorable sidelight to the
Series. Scalpers were extorting $50 for a box seat for three
games. The legal face value was $15. Though the first radio
broadcast was still three years away (the first broadcast of
a major league game was Aug. 30, 1921, KDKA Pittsburgh,
Pirates vs. Phillies), fans who couldn't be part of the capacity crowd of 32,000 at Comiskey Park could still keep up
with the progress of the games. They could "see" the action
on electric scoreboards in a number of locations. The operator would get a telegraphic report from the ballpark, then
indicate with electric lights the progress of the game on a
painted diamond. South of the Loop on Wabash Avenue, the
Coliseum, which was the site of national presidential con-
ventions, could hold thousands. Seats ranged from a $1 to
50 cents. The newspaper advertisement claimed that the play
by play report would describe the action two minutes after
it happened on the field. "This is the nearest thing to the
real article showing in Chicago," said the ad. The Dexter
Pavilion in the Chicago Stockyards chortled in its advertisement: "YOU DON'T MISS A THRILL AND YOU GET IT
TEN SECONDS LATER THAN THE CROWD AT THE
BALL GROUNDS." There was room for 15,000 spectators,
the ad claimed. Arcadia Hall on Broadway and Wilson avenues cautioned the men folk in its ad: "BE SURE TO BRING
THE LADIES." The Chicago *Inter-Ocean* at 57 W. Monroe
could accommodate another 1,000 in its auditorium.

On the morning of the first game in Chicago on Saturday, October 6, the *Tribune* forecast that more than 300 reporters would jam the press section, eighty more than ever covered a World Series before. Five writers would come from Havana, Cuba. The *Tribune* banner headline on the sports page trumpeted: "OVER THE TOP FOR WHITE SOX TODAY!"

As the capacity crowd milled around the ballpark, they were entertained by a band and a male quartet situated in the right field pavilion. One half hour before game time, 1,500 officer candidates from Ft. Sheridan marched around the field and then everyone joined in the playing and singing of the "Star Spangled Banner." All the fans, mainly men, were attired in some kind of headgear such as fedoras, caps and derbies and just about everyone wore an outercoat. It would have been difficult to find a bareheaded spectator in the entire ballpark even though the temperature was a comfortable 58 degrees at game time.

The White Sox charged on the field at 2 o'clock bedecked in their new uniforms with "patriotic stockings," probably red, white and blue like those worn on the World Tour. Taking their positions in the outfield were Joe Jackson in left, one of the greatest hitters of all time, who had just come off his worst year at the plate with a .301 average; Oscar "Happy" Felsch in center, often mentioned in the same breath with Tris Speaker as a fleet-footed, sure-handed fly chaser; and ever dependable John "Shano" Collins, who had joined the Comiskeys in 1910, in right field. In the infield, Fred McMullin, who impressed everyone with his sharp performance during Buck's hand injury, hustled out to third base. Irrepressible Buck scooted out to shortstop while the incomparable Eddie Collins took command of second base. Arnold "Chick" Gandil took his post at first base, ready to dispense his defensive magic. On the mound little right-hander Eddie Cicotte strolled to the hill to take his warm up tosses with the number one defensive catcher in baseball, the diminutive hustler Ray Schalk.

Mixing up his "shine ball" and knuckle ball, Cicotte disposed of the Giants in only 1 hour and 48 minutes as Happy Felsch blasted "one of the longest hits ever made at Comiskey Park" to make the difference in a nerve-tingling 2 to 1 Sox victory. Sanborn described the moment: "Hap Felsch chiseled his name into baseball's hall of fame . . . with a home run wallop into the bleachers at Comiskey park, good for a run which gave the White Sox a brilliantly earned victory over New York's Giants in the opening game of the world's greatest world's series.

"Felsch made his famous blow in the fourth. Jackson was stowed away before Hap came up and waited til he saw one coming across that he fancied. He met it squarely with every ounce of power in his muscles, backed by the full swing of his body. If he had missed it, he might have broken his back but he didn't. The crash was unmistakable, and there was not an instant's doubt about the ultimate destination of the ball.

"It started for the bleachers and it landed there. Burns took one look at the flying sphere and instinctively raced along under it for a few steps, then stopped and watched it fall among the faithful two bit fans, some of whom had spent all night in line for the sake of seeing that blow."

Buck had a mediocre day. He tapped to the pitcher in the second, "lifted a long fly" to left in the fourth and struck out in the seventh. In the field he faced only four chances, making 2 putouts and 1 assist and committing the only Sox error. In the eighth Buck stopped a hard smash by Benny Kauff, the Giant center fielder, but threw wildly to first. Only moments later Cicotte picked Kauff off first.

The *Tribune's* society editor noticed Helen watching the game: "Mrs. Weaver is very pretty and wore a sealskin coat and a jolly bright red turban. She said she and her husband are planning to go west to the mountains and live in a hunter's cabin as soon as these big games are over." The Weavers did go west to California every winter in those years, spending some time with Oscar Vitt and his wife in their mountain retreat.

Several unusual statistics and peculiar plays on the base

paths marked the action of the 1917 World Series. Faber got credit for winning three of the four White Sox victories. McGraw persisted in throwing three left-handed pitchers at the Sox although the American Leaguers had only two left-handed hitters, albeit powerful ones, in Jackson and Collins. Slim Sallee, Rube Benton and Ferdie Schupp all pegged from the south side of the mound and they started every game for the Giants, despite the fact that McGraw had right-hander Bill "Poll" Perritt, a 17 game winner during the season, available to start.

McGraw's strange pitching strategy failed as the White Sox steam-rollered the Giants in the second game, 7 to 2. Buck and Jackson each hammered out three hits. Buck had a busy day on defense as well. "Things came Weaver's way all day, and he piled up the big total of seven putouts and six assists," reported Sanborn. At the plate Buck singled to left in the second, scoring Felsch. In the fourth he beat out a drag bunt to second baseman Buck Herzog and later scored on a single to center. In the seventh he beat out a smash to deep short but was wiped out stealing.

It was shortstop Artie Fletcher's fumble of Weaver's roller in the fifth that led to the first of two rare and peculiar plays in the World Series. Buck moved to second on Schalk's infield out. Faber then singled to right but Gleason flagged down Weaver at third as the right fielder fired hurriedly to the plate. Faber raced to second on the throw home.

Sanborn described the hectic scene. "Red was so certain Weaver had registered he never looked to see. Perritt started his long windup on the slab and Red apparently thought he was crazy, for he broke for third base and stole it easily . . ." Catcher Bill Raridan zipped the ball to third to nab Faber. Buck, thinking Raridan was out to get him, slid back to third. Faber and Weaver "were flat on the ground facing each other, with their feet hooked to the base. Weaver in his astonishment at finding Red there, exclaimed, 'Where the hell are you going?'

"Without an instant's hesitation, Faber responded, 'I'm going to pitch.' "

Comiskey laid out a cold cut buffet for all sportswriters

in the Bard's room. "Although considerably disheartened, the squad of New York scribes declared Charles Comiskey the greatest of magnates. Each day Commy has put on a spread of sliced turkey, cold ham, cold tongue, cold roast beef, potato salad and green onions for the hard working boys."

White Sox bats hibernated in New York as Rube Benton and Ferdy Schupp silenced them in a double dose of shutouts, 2 to 0 and 5 to 0. Now it looked as if McGraw's strategy of flinging left-handers at the Sox was a masterful stroke of genius after all. Buck tried to awake his slumbering teammates by getting two of their five hits against Benton. In the second inning he singled to center with two out. Then he stole second with a "desperate slide." Schalk ended the threat when he lined out to left field. Weaver opened the eighth by swatting a low fly ball back of short out of reach of Fletcher and Burns and he legged it all the way to second. But the prospective rally fizzled when Schalk smashed the ball back to Benton who started a rundown on Weaver caught between second and third. Cicotte struck out and Schalk was doubled up as he tried to steal second. Buck joined the rest of the somnambulant Sox in their 5 to 0 setback. He didn't get any hits and fielded only one bouncing ball.

A subdued bunch of White Sox ballplayers returned to Chicago after two straight defeats in New York. On the train, Crusinberry observed: "Looking out of the window of one's bunk early yesterday morning somewhere in Ohio, one wasn't even surprised to see the ground white with snow and a regular blizzard raging. It coincided with the coldness inside the train."

That gloomy atmosphere engulfed the ballpark soon after the fifth game started. Tex Russell persuaded Rowland to give him a chance to start but the Texas left-hander couldn't survive a single putout. After a walk, single and double, Rowland hooked Russell off the mound and handed the ball to Cicotte. By the end of the inning the Giants had eased ahead, 2 to 0.

Going into the last half of the seventh inning, the White

Sox trailed, 5 to 2. The crowd sat silent and sullen. The inning started somberly as Eddie Collins popped to short. Even though Jackson followed with a single to left and Felsch singled to center, the crowd remained subdued. But Gandil then brought the crowd alive with a double to right center, scoring Jackson and Felsch. Gandil now represented the tying run. Buck stepped into the batter's box, digging in, swinging right-handed against Slim Sallee. Weaver had already singled against him in the sixth and later scored. His first time up in the second he hit a hard smash to short but was thrown out. The crowd now was "shouting, screaming, pleading, they begged their favorites to carry on the charge." Buck fouled one, then another, and another and one more. Then on a 2 and 2 count he tapped an easy roller to shortstop Art Fletcher who could only nab Weaver at first while Gandil legged it to third. The bugs were in a frenzy as they saw Gandil ready to spring for the plate. Schalk coaxed a walk from the obviously tired Sallee but McGraw, for whatever reason, refused to rescue his moundsman. Second-string catcher Byrd Lynn batted for Lefty Williams who had replaced Cicotte. Suddenly Schalk bolted for second, stunning everyone in the park except the Sox strategy board. Catcher Bill Raridan winged the ball through the infield towards second baseman Buck Herzog, but the ball tumbled away from him and Gandil streaked home with the tying run. The ecstatic throng went wild. "Pandemonium broke loose."

Buck became one with the fans. His uncontrollable enthusiasm burst forth like a raging flood. No fan could have matched his sheer boyish joy, his unsophisticated, delirious delight. "All we can remember," wrote Crusinberry, "except the din of noise from the throng present was the capers of Buck Weaver in front of the White Sox bench. He danced around in a manner which indicated he had completely lost himself. He tossed his cap into the air and followed with his sweater and a dozen bats and three or four hats that belonged to the spectators, and if there had been anything within reach it, too, would have gone into the air. Every body was in the air figuratively speaking, because the Sox had come from behind and tied the score in a ball game that looked impossible to win.

"The scene was repeated in the eighth when the Sox went out and put over three runs to win the game. . . . When the White Sox tied the score the game really was won." McGraw must have shared the same thoughts. For otherwise why did he stubbornly stay with Sallee when he obviously had run out of gas in the seventh? He continued to allow Slim to take his lumps in the eighth as the poor unfortunate pitcher absorbed four more hits and three more runs before McGraw lifted him for a relief pitcher. It was very odd managing.

On Tuesday, October 16, the *Chicago Tribune* bannered the ultimate White Sox triumph in New York against the reeling Giants: "SOX WIN WORLD'S TITLE, 4 to 2."

Trivia buffs still relish the most memorable play of the entire Series. It came in the fourth inning of the final game. Giant third baseman Heinie Zimmerman has gone down in baseball lore as pulling off one of the most enduring "bonehead" plays in history, but it wasn't completely his fault. He did, however, initiate the whole fiasco when, on the first play of the inning he snared a sharply hit grounder off the bat of Eddie Collins and then heaved the ball all the way to the box seats. Right fielder Dave Robertson then dropped Jackson's lazy fly ball, allowing Collins to scoot from second to third. McGraw must have been fuming in the dugout. Nicknamed "Little Napoleon," he probably was ready to send some of his troops to the firing squad. But it only got worse for him. Felsch grounded to pitcher Benton who threw to Zimmerman, hanging up Collins between third and the plate. Quick thinking Collins jockeyed between the bases until he noticed that catcher Raridan had charged up the third base line, leaving home plate unprotected. Collins then raced past Raridan heading for home. When Heinie saw that no one backed up the play at the plate, he futilely chased Collins home. When asked later why he didn't throw the ball, he said, "Who was I going to throw the ball to, the umpire?" The worst of it, however, was that Jackson and Felsch moved up to second and third during the Zimmerman / Collins foot race. They then scored on Gandil's single. This is the real reason Zimmerman's play was considered boneheaded. He should have held the ball to check the runners. Although McGraw exonerated Heinie at the time, two years later he accused Zimmerman of trying to throw the game!

As the final game was winding down towards a White Sox world championship Buck got in a few more pleasant licks. In the bottom of the eighth Zimmerman "hit one that looked like a single, but Weaver skidded over toward second and nabbed it in time for the throw." Buck led off the ninth "with a poke over shortstop for one base." Faber bunted him to second. Then "Leibold slammed a low fly over second for a single, sending Weaver home."

Back in Chicago, Judge Landis kept tabs on the baseball action while holding court. He stationed his faithful aide, Benny Stern, at a telephone in his chambers. Benny took reports from Associated Press every half inning and then promptly relayed the score to Landis. After every inning Landis sent a "Landisgram" to the press table giving the reporters the latest score. When Benny flashed the Sox had won, Landis sent down his final "gram" to newspapermen waiting eagerly for the tally. Over the whole page was scrawled "WHITE SOX, 4," and in one corner, in as small letters as the judge could write, "Giants, 2." When Landis adjourned court, he remarked: "Well, we did a good day's work today, anyway. We disposed of the Giants."

Buck emerged as the second highest hitter for the White Sox in the Series with a robust .333 average, getting 7 hits in 21 at bats. Only Eddie Collins topped him with a booming .409 mark. Jackson, having the worst offensive year of his career, still batted a respectable .304, three points over his season's average. Leading all the hitters was New York right fielder Dave Robertson, who exploded with 11 hits in 22 tries for a towering .500 average.

In the field Buck suffered one horrendous afternoon in the fifth game when he committed 3 errors. That reduced his fielding average for the series to .871. His counterpart on the Giants, Art Fletcher, batted an anemic .200 and didn't field much better than Buck with a .897 mark.

Before returning to Chicago, the White Sox played the Giants in an exhibition game a day after the Series was over for the soldiers stationed at Camp Mills, Long Island, and the Sox won that one too, 6 to 3.

Helen and Buck again sojourned to the West Coast for the winter. While there Buck and his teammate, Swede Risberg, were asked to play in an exhibition game in San Francisco. Since there was a rule against participants in a World Series playing post-season exhibitions, the players had to obtain the consent of the White Sox owner. Comiskey wired his approval so Buck and Swede could play in a game for the benefit of families of firemen who lost their lives in saving others in a recent fire. All the players donated their talent for the game. While in San Francisco, Buck gained a new brother-in-law when his former roomie and close buddy, vaudeville partner, and erstwhile White Sox pitcher, Jim Scott, married Helen's sister Hattie on November 17.

Manpower demands of World War I became more insistent after the 1917 season. Owners grew apprehensive about the security of their investments in the national pastime. They feared President Wilson might call the game off for the duration of the war. They talked about a shortened season, pooling receipts and reducing rosters. Ban Johnson suggested that eighteen players from each team be exempted. That idea drew hostile fire immediately from the head of the draft, General Enoch Crowder: "That must be a pipe dream," he retorted angrily on November 18. "There is certainly no warrant in the law for exempting ballplayers from the draft, and there is nothing in the regulations to warrant making exceptional rulings for men liable for service who make baseball their means of livelihood."

Another high draft official observed sarcastically, "I suppose tennis players and leaders in other sports also should be exempted with baseball players. Baseball players are exactly the sort of men the country needs as fighters, they make the best bomb throwers."

Comiskey, vacationing in Excelsior Springs, Missouri, in late November postured patriotically: "Anything the United States government asks of me or my ball club it can have. It is the duty of every citizen to help the government to the limit of his capacity, and I'm not in accord with any suggestion to ask special favors, either personally or for baseball.

"If it takes all my ballplayers it can do so. I have no desire that any of them be exempted. If they are drafted I will try to get along with what is left and either get new players or close the gates of my ball park." Johnson had offered to close the gates of the American League ballparks during the previous summer but President Wilson rejected the idea.

Hot stove baseball, when fans, young and old, loved to talk baseball almost anywhere in relaxing moments, took over in the fall and winter months. Discussions were devoted to the relative merits of players and teams. Sportswriters and the various publications were only too delighted to feed them their baseball dope. *Baseball Magazine* in its December 1917 issue, named Buck to its American League All-Star team. Weaver was described as an "active and dangerous element in the Sox offense, and fielded with all the snap and energy of a dynamo." Four of his teammates joined him on the squad: Eddie Collins, Felsch, Schalk and Cicotte. In the same issue that *Baseball Magazine* named Buck and his four teammates to the all-star team, the magazine called Comiskey, "Prince of Magnates."

9

Casualties of War

Buck signed his 1918 contract on January 31 in Comiskey's office at the ballpark. Both he and his long-time teammate, pitcher Joe Benz, were called into the owner's office at the same time. Red Faber and Ray Schalk were also on the premises. Buck signed for $6,000, the same figure he received for three previous seasons. His 1917 World Series check alone came to more than half that at $3,528.13.

Buck was unhappy about the contract. For the fourth year in a row, Comiskey dished out the same pay, this time even after a World Series triumph and after attaining the highest attendance in the majors for the previous two years. It was a bitter pill for Buck to swallow, especially after lifting his batting average to .284, the best of his career. Buck also had tied Frank Baker of the Yankees for the best fielding average at third base. Weaver signed reluctantly after Comiskey expressed doubts that the club would make money during the coming season because of the war. Buck commented that he hoped the Sox owner would reciprocate when things got better.

Comiskey's payroll starkly belied the success of the White Sox at the gate and on the field. Only Eddie Collins, at $15,000 a year, was accorded the star status salary to which he was entitled. From Collins to the next highest paid player, Ray Schalk, was a steep drop of more than half to

$7,083.33. Jackson only equaled Weaver's salary. The rest of the team signed below that figure.

Buck's disappointment about Comiskey freezing his salary again at $6,000 was compounded when he learned Rowland planned to switch him back to shortstop. Buck felt more comfortable playing third, admitting that for him shortstop was a tougher position. Earlier he told *Baseball Magazine*: "When Rowland was worried at the beginning of the season about the lack of a good third baseman I felt sure I could play the position and would like to try. So he shifted me over to the hot corner and I will say I appreciated the change. Anybody who says third base is as hard a position to cover as shortstop never played both positions. If he had he would be glad to change his berth at short any day. I like third base first rate and was hoping to be on that bag through the series. But Rowland wanted me to shift once more back to short so I played that position to the best of my ability. Still I was a little rusty and feel I could have done myself more justice at third base."

Rowland planned to return McMullin to third base because of his gallant performance there the last six weeks of the previous season. The Sox manager said Risberg, who would "have to bat far above his mark of last season" when he struggled with the lowest average among the regulars at .203, would be held in reserve.

Eerie and strange accidents marred Sox spring training in 1918. Most of the incidents happened off the field, but if one were superstitious, and baseball players were and are, it would certainly bode ominous things for the coming season. At least it must have cast some gloom and doom around spring training camp. First of all, as the White Sox headed for Mineral Wells, Texas, the Pullmans almost telescoped when the emergency break stopped the train after the tender of the engine left the track. At camp one day Schalk, Jackson, Cicotte and Gandil were riding back to the hotel from the golf course when they were hit by another car coming out of a side street. Fortunately, no one was hurt, but Rowland ordered no more golf. Apparently the cliques that were to split the ball club had not yet formed. How else could one explain Schalk associating on the golf course with fellows who would be in the opposite camp as inner conflict grew on the team?

The worst of the accidents was only indirectly related to the White Sox. A seventeen year old girl, staying at the same hotel as the ball club, was killed when she fell out of her bedroom window while trying to adjust curtains.

The accident jinx finally caught up with the Sox on the field when rookie pitcher Ed Corey fractured an ankle when he started to slide into home plate and changed his mind. His spikes caught and his ankle doubled under him. That injury would be the first in a long parade of injuries that would plague Chicago all year long.

None of the unfortunate incidents during spring training hurt the White Sox as much as the departure of Kid Gleason. The Kid angrily turned down Comiskey's contract offer and quit the team. Another familiar face missing from camp was that of old "Doc" Buckner, the "Ethiopian expert" trainer, who had been a fixture with the White Sox since 1912. He was fired and replaced by Harry M. Stephenson, the trainer for the Union League club.

Despite everything, Buck would have fun. Even in the rain he kidded with the crowd watching the Sox play Southwestern University at Georgetown, Texas. Some pretty girls seated in an automobile made some sort of bet with Buck that he wouldn't get a hit. Buck got the hit "but gave the young girls a baseball anyway" which amused the crowd.

Buck's effervescence was dampened when he received a telegram on April 4 telling him that his father was dying. He left the ball club immediately for Pottstown, Pennsylvania. Following the funeral, he returned in time for the season opener.

While Buck was gone more trouble hounded the Sox. While playing exhibition games in small Kansas towns, they spent two nights in sleepers in railroad yards "entirely without heat of any kind, all blankets insufficient to keep the athletes warm." Eddie Collins had caught cold before leaving Texas and it was aggravated by the hardships of the trip. He went to see a doctor and fainted during the examination. The doctor ordered him back to Chicago to rest.

Sanborn told his *Tribune* readers, "The White Sox are in the worst shape a major league team ever was at the opening of a race." Soon after leaving the starting gate their condition grew worse. Both injuries and demands of war disabled the world champions. Eddie Collins injured a knee and was forced out of the lineup for the first time in 477 games. Cicotte tripped over first base running out a key single and hobbled around with a cane for several days. Gandil ate something that "did not agree with his department of the interior. He was too wobbly to put on a uniform" on May 10. That same day Felsch left the team to go looking for his injured brother stationed with the army in Brownsville, Texas. He would return in ten days satisfied that his brother was safe.

Buck joined the crippled corps after playing in an 18 inning cliffhanger against Washington on May 14. The Sox lost it on a wild pitch by Lefty Williams. In his unbounded enthusiasm Weaver unwisely slid into first baseman Joe Judge in the first inning and "suffered torn cartilages in the top of his right foot . . ." As usual Buck played with such intensity he didn't realize he was hurt until 18 innings had been played and the game was over. As soon as he took off his shoes, his foot began to swell and "he could hardly limp to the street car." After resting for three days and receiving treatment from the Sox trainer, Buck came off the bench in a 13 inning game and singled to help beat Washington.

The Chicagoans were so banged up that Rowland refused to fulfill an exhibition game commitment at Camp Meade, Maryland, "for fear of absolutely wrecking his crippled team."

The dismantling of the White Sox began in earnest on May 13 when Jackson left the ball club in Philadelphia. Classified 1A in the draft, Joe went into draft-exempt war production work as a painter in the shipyards owned by Bethlehem Steel Corporation in nearby Wilmington, Delaware. Joe would play in the Bethlehem Steel baseball league that had teams in Pennsylvania, Delaware, Maryland and Massachusetts. Comiskey postured before the public and threatened not to rehire his ballplayers who chose essential war production work. He blustered: "There is no room on my club for players who wish to evade the army draft by entering the employ of shipbuilders."

Newspaper editorials and sportswriters found it sport to criticize Joe for his decision. They ignored the fact that other players preceded him into essential war production work. Joe had three brothers in service already and was the sole support for his wife, mother, brother and a sister.

Manager Rowland took another tack. He said as far as the White Sox were concerned Joe was free to take any action he pleased in his choice of serving his country and he "wished him all the good luck in the world." Corporate executives looked upon baseball as a healthy way of providing leisure time activity and amusement for war workers. Otherwise they might have spent too many hours in bars getting drunk and disorderly. Thousands of workers let off steam as they watched games in a league that was considered one of the strongest outside of organized baseball.

In the meantime the war was closing in on baseball. Congress passed an amendment to the draft law that ordered men between twenty-one and thirty who were engaged in "games, sports, and amusements except concerts, opera or theatrical performances" to be ready to "work or fight" after July 1. Eligible men would either get a job in essential industry or don Uncle Sam's uniform.

Baseball owners were flabbergasted that theatrical performers were considered vital to bolster morale while ballplayers were not. However, in a matter of days the actors, singers and dancers were swept up in the same net with the ballplayers.

Baseball executives voiced assurances that they would cooperate fully with the demands of government. After all the July 1 deadline was still more than a month away. Perhaps there was still time to convince the government that baseball was a morale booster for the country and should be exempted from the draft.

Unfortunately for Comiskey, several key White Sox players weren't waiting to be exempted or drafted. Jackson already was painting warships. In early June Red Faber enlisted in the navy and was assigned to the Great Lakes Naval Training Station just north of Chicago. But he wasn't entirely lost to the White Sox. He would come in on weekend passes and pitch when the Sox were in town. Tuesday, June 11, should have been a jubilant and joyful day for the White Sox as the world championship flag was raised over Comiskey Park. But Comiskey chose to charge it with turmoil and anger that overshadowed the celebration. That morning Lefty Williams and second-string catcher, Byrd Lynn, announced they planned to go to work in the shipyards. Comiskey immediately stripped them of their uniforms and put them under suspension. He said, "I don't consider them fit to play on my ball club. I would gladly lose my whole team if the players wished to do their duty to their country . . . but I hate to see any ballplayers, particularly my own, go [to] the shipyards to escape military service."

Only three weeks later, Happy Felsch abandoned Comiskey Park. He wasn't repairing to the shipyards or marching into military service. On July 1 he turned in his uniform and departed for Milwaukee to take a job with the gas company for $125 a month. He also would play ball for the company team on Sundays. There was some question in the press about the gas company job being essential. In any case, Felsch remained out of the draft.

In a last ditch effort to stave off the impending doom of baseball for the rest of the war, the National Commission presented a brief to draft chief General Enoch Crowder and Secretary of War Newton D. Baker: "[A] work or fight order to baseball players at this time would deprive the big leagues of such a large percentage of their ballplayers that immediate suspension for the remainder of the season will be imperative and that resumption of play next season will be a matter of serious doubt." The brief concluded that the owners and players would "be saved financial embarrassment" if the work or fight order would not be applied to baseball until the end of the season.

The baseball moguls didn't have to hold their breath long for an answer. Two days after presenting their case on July 24, they got the clear message from Washington to wind up the season by September 1. Permission was granted to extend the season only for the playing of the World Series.

The White Sox' ranks continued to hemorrhage. By the middle of August Swede Risberg had enlisted in the army, Fred McMullin joined the navy and Eddie Collins signed up with the marines. The team was in tatters. In one series in Philadelphia only sixteen players were in uniform. And many of them were plugging holes in unfamiliar positions.

But in the long run the worst stroke of luck for the White Sox and Comiskey was the unfortunate loss of pitcher Jack Quinn. With the early close of the Pacific Coast League in July, Comiskey obtained permission from the National Commission to negotiate directly with Quinn, a member of the Los Angeles Angels. Quinn accepted a White Sox contract and by August 25 had won four straight games. About the same time the New York Yankees negotiated directly for Quinn's contract with Los Angeles. The Angels accepted the New York offer for Quinn's services. In the ensuing dilemma with both Chicago and New York claiming Quinn and Quinn already pitching and winning for the White Sox, the National Commission declared that both teams were right in the action they took. Then it declared the situation "peculiar and unfortunate" and awarded the player to New York. Evidence showed that Ban Johnson's vote was the determining factor in awarding Quinn to the Yankees.

Comiskey exploded. His anger and hate for Johnson now knew no bounds. There had been earlier spats between the two strong-willed, proud personalities but they always reconciled. The Jack Quinn affair, however, would only lead to greater conflict and bitterness between the one-time close associates. Both men first became drinking buddies when Comiskey was manager of the Cincinnati Reds and Johnson was the young sports editor of the Cincinnati *Commericial Gazette* in 1892. Johnson had joined the newspaper as a general reporter after dropping out of law school in Cincinnati at the age of 21 in 1884. Earlier he had attended Oberlin and Marietta colleges in Ohio but did not graduate from either even though both his parents were successful educators. Johnson became sports editor in 1887. Comiskey had recommended to club owners of the newly formed Western League, which he helped organize, to appoint Johnson as president in late 1893. A year later, Comiskey, ending a three year contract with the Reds, obtained the Sioux City, Iowa, franchise of the Western League and shifted it to St. Paul. Comiskey and Johnson then marched together to form the American League in 1900 with Johnson as president and Comiskey going back home to Chicago as owner of the White Sox. Together they challenged the National League major leaguers in a bitterly fought baseball war that ended with the senior circuit recognizing the American League as its equal in 1903.

No two men could have been much closer than Comiskey and Johnson for more than a decade. Chicago sportswriter, Hugh Fullerton, described them as inseparable. "They worked, hunted, fished and played together." A frivolous incident seems to have been the spark that started to unravel the warm relationship. The story goes that Comiskey, who invited Johnson and other friends to go hunting and fishing at his lodge in northern Wisconsin, kidded Johnson about his poor shooting one day. Johnson discovered someone had removed the bullets from his new gun and replaced them with wadding. Johnson had been blaming his gun for his inaccurate marksmanship. Now the irate Johnson, a rather humorless man, felt it was Comiskey who played the trick and wouldn't talk to him for months.

Next it was Comiskey's turn to take umbrage because of a tactic taken by the American League president. Ironically, the situation was made worse by a gesture of friendship shown by Johnson. Early in June, 1905, James "Ducky" Holmes, a White Sox outfielder, was booted out of a game in Chicago by umpire Silk O'Laughlin for using foul language. It happened on a Saturday afternoon. O'Laughlin immediately sent a report to Johnson at his Chicago downtown office. On Sunday, Johnson took extra pains to send a personal messenger to the ballpark to tell Comiskey that Holmes, who was suited up to play, was suspended for three days. Comiskey already had another outfielder sitting out the last day of a suspension. Had Johnson sent word of Holmes's suspension through regular channels Comiskey would have received the message on Monday in time to play the other outfielder in place of Holmes. Earlier that Sunday morning Comiskey had been elated by a shipment of bass expressed to the ballpark by Johnson while he was still on vacation. Comiskey, beaming, told a friend, "Look what Beebee sent me." The White Sox owner then posed for pictures as he proudly held up the fish. But when Comiskey got word of Holmes's suspension, he erupted: "What does that fat so and so expect me to do? Play this string of bass in left field?" Manager Fielder Jones sent in a pitcher to play left field that day.

Although their friendship was strained at times, Comiskey and Johnson managed to continue a close relationship. They still hunted and fished together. When Comiskey returned from the world tour in 1914, he invited Johnson to his Woodlands Bards retreat in Wisconsin. They were in each other's company, together with their wives, when they took mineral baths at Hot Springs, Arkansas and Excelsior Springs, Missouri. Comiskey had Johnson as his guest on his houseboat, the "White Sox," as it cruised the Mississippi River. The two men spent time together at Dover Hall in Georgia, an enormous rural estate where baseball executives could hunt and fish. Owned jointly by the top baseball brass and one extraordinary ballplayer, Ty Cobb, it was originally envisioned as a giant training camp for all major league teams. That plan was never realized.

As late as 1916 Comiskey and Johnson must have been on somewhat friendly terms. Ban sent Commy a wristwatch and golf bag for Christmas. What Comiskey sent Johnson, if anything, is not known.

Despite the wartime disintegration of the ball club, Buck continued to play with his patented zest. Against Philadelphia one day Buck was the centerpiece of a defensive gem. The baserunner, caught between second and third, ". . . tried to pull an Eddie Collins - Zimmerman race on Weaver, but Buck proved too fast for him. Weaver took a throw from McMullin close to second and started after Kopp, tagging him a yard before he slid into third base. The chase was so hot that Buck turned a somersault after making the out but held the ball." In late June he was forced out of the opening lineup because he had strained the muscles in his groin and could not stoop without pain. But before the afternoon was over, he grabbed a bat to pinch hit. On a rainy afternoon in Chicago, ". . . Weaver skidded and fell in the mud in going after a pop foul in the ninth, but without getting fussed he arose and caught the ball just the same."

Sometimes Buck's "fighting wolfhound" spirit backfired. Amid constant injuries and wartime departures, Buck aggravated the situation by getting thumbed out of a couple of games. Buck protested a call by umpire Billy Evans on a close play at first base in the ninth inning of a first game of a doubleheader on July 2. It was a foolish complaint since the Sox were way ahead and it cost Buck the right to play the second game. Then in New York as 24,000 fans "howled from start to finish," Buck exploded in a fit of fury over an umpire's call. "The big row came . . . when Weaver poled a terrific line drive to left field. Bodie tore in, got the ball at his feet and held up his hand, claiming a fair catch. It looked like a trapped ball but Ump Owens called Buck out. There was a terrific protest by a half dozen Sox, but Weaver, storming louder than ever, was the only one banished. After being put out, he tossed cap and glove into the air and pawed up dust most of the way to the distant gate."

Buck's eruption on the field earned him some chiding from Crusinberry. The headline cautioned: "WHITE SOX

NEED SOME TRAINING IN DISCIPLINE; Face Hard Time if Buck Weaver Is Suspended for Row with Ump." Crusinberry observed: "If the White Sox wish to remain in the fight for the American League pennant this year it seems a little practice in discipline would aid them about as much as a little batting practice or an additional pitcher or two.

"While they are in fifth place at present, they are by no means out of the race, for the season is less than half gone and they are only six games behind the Boston Red Sox." Crusinberry was forgetting the threat of a shortened season.

"Six game leads often have been overcome in two or three weeks. With several star men already gone, either into the government service, shipyards, or gas houses, it does seem that there is little excuse for any of those remaining to be out of the game because of disorderly conduct on the ball field. . . .

"Even if Weaver had a good kick coming, and it looked as if he had, there is no reason he should carry it so far as to be put out. The Sox need every ounce of their strength in the game every inning of every day, and they need Buck Weaver in there perhaps more than any other man, with the possible exception of Eddie Collins."

Happily Weaver was not suspended. Crusinberry conceded, "It looks as if the umps must have realized he had a kick coming." Buck kind of evened the score with Ping later in the series. Bodie was up to his old tricks when he clouted one to the fence in right-center and then tried to circle the bases "but a rattling relay to the plate by Buck Weaver, who had run away over in that direction, cut him down."

But Buck couldn't avoid another injury. He suffered a torn thumb nail on his throwing hand in a game with Boston and was out of action for a week. In the meantime he coached at third base.

Back in the lineup Buck busted out with his greatest hitting binge of his major league career. On the last day of the season, Labor Day, September 2, Buck exploded with 5 hits in 5 trips in the first game and rattled Detroit pitchers for 3 more safeties in the nightcap in 5 at bats. Weaver registered the highest number of hits by an individual batter in a doubleheader for the 1918 season. Buck hiked his batting average to .300 to top all American League shortstops. He ranked third in fielding with a .941 average on 32 errors. Everett Scott of Boston committed the fewest errors with 17, holding a .976 average, but he could only produce a .221 batting mark.

The White Sox managed to hang on in the first division until August 20. But in the end constant injuries and losses of players to the war effort took their toll. The team utterly collapsed, dropping eight straight games to end the season in sixth place.

On paper it looked as if Eddie Cicotte had lost all his skill and guile when he lost nineteen games. However, anyone who watched the White Sox knew otherwise. Early in the season he lost four 1 to 0 games in a row. After 7 successive defeats, Cicotte captured his first victory on May 31 and still managed to win 12 games. The spunky little right-hander achieved a 2.64 earned run average, ranking him twelfth in the league, hardly a slump as some writers would have it.

The Chicago Cubs won the National League pennant in 1918 and played their World Series games at Comiskey Park against the Boston Red Sox. Apparently the Cubs and their fans were not so emotionally attached to the friendly confines of Weeghman Park as they would be years later when the same ballpark would be called Wrigley Field. Comiskey donated his ballpark to the National Leaguers so more fans could see the World Series.

Unfortunately the fans stayed home. Perhaps it was the effects of the war. Among other things, the quality of play had obviously deteriorated. Only 19,274 bugs bothered to attend the opener. The next two games at Comiskey Park drew 20,040 and 27,054, far from the capacity of 32,000. Attendance wasn't any better at Fenway Park for the fourth game which attracted only 22,000 spectators.

That spare attendance led to a threatened walkout by the players before the fifth game when the owners, forced by poor gate receipts, proposed to cut the players' share of the money for the first four games. When the players heard about the cut they refused to don their uniforms for the game. Representatives of the players, the owners and the National Commission met in the umpires' room beneath the stands. The game was delayed for one hour as they haggled over the division of the receipts. The owners and commission refused to budge. The players finally caved in saying they were going to play for the good of baseball and so as not to disappoint the fans.

The Red Sox won in six games with the winners' share coming to $1,108 while the losers' each received $574.62. The players also objected to the division of the receipts which gave the second place finishers almost as much as the Cubs' share. The owners promised to use their influence with the National Commission and league officials to increase the players' pool to near what the players expected. The players had anticipated a winner's kitty of $2,000 while the loser's take would be $1,400. That had been originally agreed to by the owners and the National Commission. However, no more money would be forthcoming.

Since the regular season had been cut short, all the major league club owners mutually agreed to "fire" all their players. Then they wouldn't be liable to pay their employees their contracts for the full season. All the players received their ten day notices, informing them that no salaries would be paid after September 2. At the same time all the owners agreed not to tamper with any ballplayers on other clubs. They would be offered new contracts at the appropriate time. Meanwhile, the players were free to sign up with semi-pro and shipyard teams, keeping in mind the work or fight order.

10

Holdout

With the work or fight order in force, Buck immediately signed a contract to play with the Fairbanks-Morse Corporation semipro baseball team and work as a mechanic in the factory. Fairbanks-Morse, a stationary engine manufacturing plant, is located in Beloit, Wisconsin, about 114 miles northwest of Chicago on the Illinois-Wisconsin border. The company now is a subsidiary of Colt Industries.

Helen accompanied Buck to Beloit where he teamed up with pitchers Bunny Hearn, who had just finished the season with the Boston Braves, and George "Zip" Zabel, formerly of the Chicago Cubs. A young pitcher named Dick Kerr, who was still the property of the Milwaukee Brewers, joined Beloit. He would soon become Buck's teammate on the White Sox.

In becoming an employee of Fairbanks-Morse, Weaver joined a work force of one of the most progressive and benevolent corporations in the country, especially considering it was a time when capital-labor antagonisms were brewing violent new battles. The year 1919 would usher in a wave of colossal strikes in the coal and steel industries. Even the Boston police would strike.

Fairbanks-Morse philosophy centered on maintaining a contented and satisfied group of workers by affording them entertainment and recreational opportunities. On Labor Day,

September 2, Fairbanks-Morse sponsored a company picnic at their ballpark.

About 2,500 employees and their families, friends and guests attended but rain abruptly halted the festivities. Quickly, within a half hour, company executives contacted the manager of a local theatre who opened its doors. Company officials somehow managed to line up three genuine vaudeville acts. To go along with the acts, the Fairbanks-Morse Athletic Association band performed a short concert. A motion picture, "My Own United States," guaranteed to stir up patriotic fervor, opened a program which had to be presented three times to accommodate the picnic crowd. The biggest hit of the day proved to be Ackerman and his trained horse.

Although the picnic had been canceled, the athletic events for the holiday had only been postponed. The company rescheduled the contests for a Saturday afternoon, two weeks later. Reported the Beloit *News* on that Saturday, September 14: "Every employee of the big 'hill' factory will be admitted to the park for the athletic events free." Besides the foot races and novelty races for men and women, the special feature of the afternoon would be a softball game between women of the office and the women's shop team. "The men in charge of the afternoon events say the girls will wear honest to goodness baseball uniforms—regular uniforms, and not camouflage ones." As a climax of the afternoon's activities, the Fairbanks-Morse baseball team would battle an aggregation from Great Lakes Naval Training station.

Buck and his Fairbanks-Morse teammates competed in Chicago almost every weekend until the baseball season closed in the middle of October. On Sunday, September 22, "before one of the biggest crowds that has ever seen a semipro combat in the Windy City," Fairbanks beat the Negro Chicago American Giants, then known as the "black wizards" in both ends of a doubleheader. In several previous meetings they had attracted at least 8,000 fans. Several weeks later the Beloit *News* didn't equivocate at all about the size of the crowd when it reported that the Fairies beat a team called the Normals twice (both nicknames carried a sexual connotation in 1918) "before the biggest crowd that ever saw a semi-pro battle in Chicago." Bunny Hearn out-duelled Jack Quinn in a 2 to 1 thriller. Dick Kerr won the second game, 5 to 1, against a pitcher who hid his identity as the "mysterious masked marvel." He had held the Fairies to a couple of runs until the ninth inning. A "sensational play by Buck Weaver at third base prevented Normals from tying the contest up." An overflow crowd jammed the ballpark in Chicago's suburban Cicero on October 13 to watch the Fairies, behind Kerr, squeeze out a 2 to 1 victory over Red Faber, who pitched for another semipro team while on weekend furlough from his naval post at Great Lakes.

The huge, enthusiastic crowds attending semipro games proved that baseball was still popular among the fans even though the war still raged on. There didn't appear to be any significant illwill towards the athletes who hadn't shouldered a rifle. The game certainly provided a chance for those fans to escape the concerns and worries of war. With major league baseball shut down, the fans gladly seized the opportunity to see baseball of any kind. Since so many major leaguers stocked semipro teams they were watching a high level of professional baseball.

Americans had other worries than the war and baseball that fall. An epidemic of flu swept the country (and the world) causing the deaths of millions. Beloit was not spared, reaching a peak of 114 new cases in one day. For weeks, the Beloit *News* carried a spate of death notices every day. Victims of all ages fell to the scourge. Finally, by early November the epidemic subsided and the quarantine lifted. Beloit theatre owners quickly placed a full page ad in the *News* on November 8: "THEATERS OPEN TOMORROW. . . . The danger part has been passed and our city returns to normal again.

"During those days that the theaters have been closed they have been thoroughly cleaned, purged with disinfectants and each one will be fumigated Under the Direction of the Health Department which has lifted the present closing ban.

"In Times of Public Anguish the well regulated theater has been the hand maiden of the Church in upholding the people's morale. WILSON—FOX—STRAND."

The theater owners didn't have to worry about the people's morale for long. Three days after they had placed their advertisement, the war ended.

Though peace had returned, Buck and Helen didn't rush home to Chicago. They enjoyed small town life in Beloit. Buck's brother-in-law, Jim Scott, and his wife, Hattie, joined the Weavers after Scott's discharge from the army. Buck probably arranged for Jim's employment at Fairbanks. Buck seemed to thrive on his job at the foundry and he was taking special classes in mechanics provided by the company. With the baseball season over, Buck turned his athletic attention to bowling. He joined the foundry team in the Fairbanks-Morse bowling league. He also bowled occasionally as a member of the Fairbanks-Morse team that competed against other company teams in Beloit and neighboring towns. When Lee's All-Stars beat Fairbanks-Morse in early November, Buck bowled a 177, 178 and 161 series. In a doubles match in the middle of January at Watertown, Wisconsin, Weaver bowled a 147-204-187 series and in singles he finished with a 176-180-118 record. In one other match of record in February, Buck bowled a 168-184-182 series for his foundry team.

Fairbanks-Morse also sponsored a basketball team but that was one sport Buck seemed to have shied away from. He did attend the home games though. One of his baseball teammates, "Zip" Zabel, played guard. Buck was still "rooting" for the Fairbanks-Morse basketball team as late as March 16, "amusing the kids by tossing shekels of various denominations into the crowd of youngsters." Buck still had not signed his contract and it was only a few days before the White Sox would leave for spring training with a new manager at the helm. On the last day of 1918, Pants Rowland said he knew nothing about plans for 1919 so he must have been as surprised as everyone else by the *Tribune*

headline on January 1: "KID GLEASON APPOINTED MAN-
AGER OF THE WHITE SOX." Suddenly Gleason took over
the field reins of the White Sox after refusing to rejoin the
Sox as a coach in 1918. It was "generally supposed that
Comy [sic] and Gleason were not even on speaking terms."
Comiskey gave no reason for dismissing Rowland. Perhaps
Comiskey soured on Rowland early in the season when the
manager said Joe Jackson was free to take any action he
pleased in his choice of serving his country after Comiskey
had postured that "there is no room on my club for players
who wish to evade the army draft by entering the employ of
shipbuilders."

Buck and Helen came in from Beloit on the first weekend of the new year, making the rounds of theatres and restaurants. Crusinberry caught the couple for an interview.
Buck told the *Tribune* reporter that he and Helen like the
quiet, small town life. Buck said, "You see they made us fellows go to work last fall. Well, I never knew before that
working was so easy. It's much easier than playing ball. I
got a regular job, too, something a lot of fellows would call
hard work, but say, it isn't hard. Why, I don't have to work
any harder than you do here.

"I never knew much about business before I got in with
those fellows but now I am getting interested. I can see the
possibilities for a young fellow in such a thing. It has never
been a grind for me. I like it, and we like the small town to
live in."

As for being back playing for the White Sox, Buck said:
"Oh, I suppose, but then again I don't know. It looks pretty
good to me up there and might look better in ten or twenty
years from now. Of course I like to play ball, but I don't
know. This here work stuff is pretty nice."

Buck had some thoughts about Gleason becoming manager: "You know what I think about the 'Kid'. He was there
when I broke in the big show. You can't beat him I tell you.
Comiskey got an ace when he got the 'Kid' to manage the
team next year. Well, maybe I'll be out there playing for

him, but I don't know." Buck was playing it cool. He had learned years earlier on the world tour how to be a shrewd negotiator.

Buck had returned his contract unsigned. He asked for an increase in salary and a three year contract. Comiskey had offered Weaver a contract "practically the same as 1918." Buck personally told Comiskey he wanted about $2,000 a year more. Comiskey said that was out of the question. To friends Weaver confided, "I've outhit and outfielded Collins for three seasons. The records show this. So I contend that at least I am as valuable a player as Eddie. But when the 1st and 15th has (sic) rolled around it's Eddie who has carried off almost three times as much money as I have received. Now, I'm not asking that I be paid any $15,000 for a year's work, but I think I'm entitled to the salary that I've named the Sox and I'm determined not to sign for less."

Buck was off base if he told his friends that he had outhit and outfielded Eddie Collins for three seasons. The records didn't show that at all. Buck did outhit Eddie in 1918 when he climbed to .300 for the first time while Collins slipped to a .276 mark. In the field Collins maintained a statistical superiority over his teammate for three years. But comparisons muddied the waters, especially since both infielders operated at different positions and Weaver was constantly being moved between short and third. Buck would have been on higher ground if he simply said his improvement merited a substantial boost in salary since he had been getting the same $6,000 a year for the last four years. Certainly Buck was worth more than less than half of Collins' salary. In any case, Buck had a legitimate gripe.

Beloit baseball enthusiasts continued to hope that Weaver would stick with the Fairies. Reported the Beloit *News* on February 19: "Semi-pros are offering bigger money than they ever have. . . . Buck Weaver is still with the Fairy aggregation at the big plant on the hill and Jim Scott swears he will work in a Fairy suit."

Buck remained steadfast in his salary squabble with Comiskey. "BUCK WEAVER SAYS COMMY MUST SUB-

MIT," headlined the Beloit *News* on February 21. The story revealed how determined Buck had become in his demand for what he thought was fair compensation: "If Commy wants Buck he needs to pay him $2000 a year raise before midnight tonight. That's what Buck told his pals at the hill plant.

"Buck figures Commy has another guess coming if he counts on a compromise at the last minute."

The raise was not forthcoming before midnight or after.

Helen and Buck visited Chicago in early March but Buck didn't make any effort to see Comiskey about a contract. The couple took care of personal business, attended several theatres and returned to Beloit. Buck told the press he hadn't changed his mind about salary. It was up to Comiskey whether he played on the south side or with the Beloit team where he could also hold down a job in the plant.

The general manager of Fairbanks-Morse corporation, Walter E. Seymour, took a great liking to Buck. He offered Weaver not only an attractive salary for playing baseball, but to continue the financial aid for his studies in advanced mechanics. Seymour sympathized with Buck in his salary stalemate with Comiskey and pulled for Weaver to remain with his firm and team.

"I hope Comiskey stands pat and doesn't give you more money Buck," said Seymour, "for the simple reason that I want you up here. Guess I'll write Comiskey and tell him you won't come back."

Even the *Sporting News* recognized the powerful hand held by the baseball lover who had become a crafty bargainer. It observed on March 13: "This firm wants Buck as an employee, also as an entertainer, and the lucrative employment he is receiving at Beloit makes his holdout case assume an entirely different aspect from what it would otherwise appear."

Weaver laid down the challenge: "I am absolutely through with the club if Comiskey doesn't come to terms with me by the time the team leaves Chicago on the spring training jaunt. Perhaps the owner of the Sox imagines I'm

bluffing and that I will come around to his terms if he holds
out too, but this time I'm in earnest and I've made full arrangements to play ball in Beloit and continue to study mechanics if Comiskey fails to talk turkey with me.

"It was in the spring of 1918 that I talked with President Comiskey about a contract for that year. He told me
about the bad war conditions. He said his club would do
well to make money owing to unsettled conditions. I signed
a contract calling for the same amount of money I was receiving the previous season, when I helped win the world's
championship, although I felt I deserved a boost.

" 'There will be a time when I'll ask you for the benefit
of the doubt,' I said to Comiskey as I signed that contract.
Last year I had the best season of my life, beating my record
of 1917, when we copped the flag. I outbatted and outplayed
Eddie Collins."

It was certain that Weaver, envious, frustrated and rankled by the size of Collins' salary as compared to his, may
have had a distorted view of the matter when he said he
outplayed Collins. He was talking about one of the greatest
second basemen in the history of the game. Perhaps some
observers may have agreed with Buck, but again, the figures simply didn't show it. Collins fielded for a .974 average
while Buck trailed at .941. Collins participated in 231 putouts and 285 assists, making 14 errors. Buck handled 191
putouts and 319 assists, committing 32 errors. Collins was
involved in 53 double plays while Weaver was in 50 twin
killings. Each player had 5.5 chances per game. Of course,
one could argue that all this was irrelevant since they played
different positions.

Knowledgeable baseball people understand that statistics alone never measure the value of a ballplayer to his
club. Perhaps Buck did outplay Collins in the field. He
seemed convinced of it. On baseball statistics, Branch
Rickey, the great baseball executive who invented the farm
system as general manager of the St. Louis Cardinals, had
this to say in 1951 in hearings before a subcommittee on the
study of monopoly power in the House of Representatives:

"On the ability of the player to earn, that involves his record. It involves the mathematics of his work. It involves an understanding between the club and the player as to the meaning of runs batted in, which is almost a complete fallacy in the evaluation of a player's service. The public likes it. But it is almost meaningless. . . . It involves his health, it involves his domestic relations, it involves his team spirit, his morals, and his contributions, apart from the physical."

Buck needed to argue only the merits of his own case. He finished up by telling the *Sporting News*: "I did Comiskey a good turn when conditions were bad, and now that the game is coming back I'm simply asking him to return the favor."

On March 17, Weaver came into Chicago and met Gleason and Harry Grabiner at the ballpark. Comiskey was out of town. In a discussion that lasted about thirty minutes both parties compromised. Buck, who had insisted that he would never take anything less than a $2,000 raise, signed a three year contract at $7,250 a year, an increase of $1,250 over his salary the previous four years.

To wean Weaver away from Beloit, Gleason and Grabiner made the point that the White Sox would be playing baseball almost every day while the Fairies would be playing mainly on weekends. Then too, there was the strong possibility that the White Sox would make the World Series. As Sanborn concluded: "If there is one thing Weaver would rather do than eat, it is play baseball."

Buck's brother-in-law, pitcher Jim Scott, decided to stay in Beloit and was given his unconditional release by the White Sox. He had been with the team since 1909.

Buck, of course, loved the game but had developed into a bright businessman as well. He had leverage over Comiskey that most ballplayers never had. Comiskey's usual cry with a disgruntled ballplayer at contract time, one echoed by Harry Grabiner, his faithful lieutenant, was "take it or leave it." Since most of those talented athletes could only go back to toil in the mills, mines and factories, they meekly accepted whatever Comiskey doled out to them. But Buck's ace in the hole was Fairbanks-Morse. It made him the second highest paid player on the team next to Eddie Collins. Yet he was still getting half Collins' salary.

In its farewell story, reporting on Buck's new contract with the White Sox, the Beloit *News* reflected on the future and the past: "Beloit fans expect to see Buck back here next fall to do his barnstorming stunt in a Fairy uniform. The Sox star has made a big hit here. He likes Beloit and the Fairy fans like him. His career during the coming season will be closely followed in this city."

11

1919

While Buck and Helen enjoyed their interlude in Beloit, the major leagues were buffeted by a stormy winter of discontent. Late in December, the worried owners voted to reduce the playing season to 140 games. They hoped to cut their anticipated revenue losses because they expected the fans . . . would not be psychologically ready to flock to ballparks in the aftermath of war. The owners had taken a bad beating at the turnstiles in 1917 and 1918. The White Sox, who led the majors with almost 700,000 fans in 1917, could only attract 195,081 customers in 1918. Even on the north side of town, the Cubs, who had won the National League pennant, could only collar 337,257 viewers into the ballpark. The early shutdown of the season on September 2 obviously affected the gate. But the owners must have taken that into account. Nevertheless, they felt attendance had shown too much slippage, so they deemed it wiser to curtail the schedule for 1919.

With the schedule hurdle out of the way, the major league executives met in joint session in New York at the end of January. They appointed a search committee to scour the country to find a neutral chairman for the National Commission to replace Herrmann. Herrmann, in the meantime, would continue in the position until a new head was found. The *Sporting News* of January 30 reported that there was even talk at the meetings about finding one man to head baseball.

More critical to the integrity of baseball were the corkscrew antics of Hal Chase who again was being charged with gambling and fixing games. This was already old hat for the fancy fielding first baseman who had been accused by two New York managers of throwing games years earlier. On January 30, 1919, Chase was in New York, submitting to a five hour hearing before National League president John H. Heydler. In early August 1918, Cincinnati Reds manager Christy Mathewson suspended Chase for "indifferent play." Herrmann then called Chase into his office: "I wish to tell you Mr. Chase that charges have been brought against you affecting your integrity as a ball player. These charges will be submitted to the National League for due consideration and till the league has acted your suspension will have to stand. I sincerely trust that all charges will prove baseless and unfounded both for your sake and the honor of the game."

Almost six months passed before the National League took action, the expressed reason being that John Tener, the National League president, had resigned shortly before the Chase problem had surfaced. It was months before the league's secretary, Heydler, was named to head the league.

Four ballplayers, three with Cincinnati—Greasy Neale, Jimmy Ring and Mike Regan—and Pol Perritt of the Giants, testified that Chase offered them money for throwing games. Mathewson, having since joined the army and still stationed in France mailed his deposition. McGraw also spoke against Chase but offered the first baseman a job with the Giants if he escaped punishment.

The verdict was announced on February 5. Reported the *Tribune*: "Hal Chase . . . was cleared today of the charge of 'throwing' games preferred against him by the Cincinnati club." He was declared "not guilty" by the president of the National League. Heydler announced: "It is nowhere established that the accused was interested in any pool or wages that caused any game to result otherwise than on its merits."

As related in *Baseball: As I Have Known It,* by New York sportswriter Fred Lieb, Heydler later confessed in an off the record interview that he thought Chase was guilty. "But I have no proof that will stand up in a court of law." Then Heydler expressed his dismay with McGraw over his ill-timed offer to Chase: "Here I am trying to prove charges that Mathewson, McGraw's close friend, has made against this man, and McGraw already is offering him a job."

After the hearing, Chase did find a job with the Giants and one of his new coaches was none other than Christy Mathewson. Lieb made an incisive observation: "How many good young ball players may have said, 'Chase gets by with it, year after year, so why shouldn't we pick up a little extra money when the chance is offered us?' And how many, when tempted, fell?"

In Chicago, Comiskey, despite his earlier tirades against his ballplayers who quit the team to go into essential war work rather than fight, mailed new contracts to Jackson, Felsch, Williams and Lynn. He was now telling the press that the fans will again "be as strong as ever for Joe after he poles a few hits to the fences and drives in a few winning runs." Comiskey chose to forget that it wasn't the fans who called Joe a "draft dodger" and "slacker."

Soon after Weaver signed his White Sox contract, the *Sporting News* on March 27 reacted most favorably to Buck's return: "Since professional ball players as a class lost much public sympathy because of their actions in the Federal League war, the general inclination has been to denounce and berate the athlete who announced himself a holdout. But there are holdouts, and holdouts and now and then circumstances alter cases. It was so with the refusal of Buck Weaver of the Chicago White Sox to sign up for the terms originally offered him this spring.

"The followers of the club evidently felt he was entitled to some consideration because of his great value to the team and the result was that President Comiskey, sensing this feeling among his patrons, made a liberal compromise with the shortstop." In fact, however, the compromise was fash-

ioned by Grabiner and Gleason. The *Sporting News* continued: "Now everything is lovely, Weaver is signed and in
training camp, prepared to again demonstrate that he is
about the most valuable man on Commy's ball club, bar
none. And the fans too, are happy, for whatever his rating
in the 'galaxy' of stars, Buck is their big favorite ranked on
real delivery of the goods."

Not only had Buck become a star baseball performer,
by this time he had cultivated a taste for fine clothes. He
dressed splashily to reflect his high jinks spirit on the field.
His clothes even merited a headline: "Weaver's Shirts Distinguish Our White Sox." Sanborn was noticeably impressed: "Weaver waited until he reached Mineral Wells before springing his sensations at the first dinner dance given
by the guests of the Sox hotel. Buck appeared in a silk shirt
that caused a gasp of envy or dismay, it was not certain
which. It was a blue shirt of . . . iridescent, incandescent,
and inflammable hue. . . .

"Those who congratulated Weaver on his taste were informed that the inaugural display was the most modest shirt
of a half dozen which he purchased last fall on the last trip
to New York. He said he began with that one so as to make
it easier for the eyes. No one believed it possible to create a
shirt more strikingly stylish than the first one until Buck
sprang the second of the series.

"This baffled all description. It was a cross between gold
cloth shirred over a 100 candle power arc light and the
shimmering of the midnight sun on the top of Mount Mc-
Kinley with decorations resembling the kind of wall paper
one finds in a Halsted Street tenement."

Buck's fondness for colorful and attractive shirts went
back at least to his early days with the Sox. One time during a home stand, Buck's younger brother, Luther, came in
from Pottstown, Pennsylvania, for a visit. While Buck was
at the ballpark, Luther went to his hotel, told the clerk who
he was and gained entry into Buck's room. He spied Buck's
collection of beautiful pure silk shirts and put one on. He

then went out to the ballpark. When Buck saw Luther all he said was "Kid, that's a good looking shirt you have on."

Buck gained another vote of confidence when Hugh Fullerton of the *Tribune* wrote one day after the dinner dance that "In the American league Buck Weaver figures at the top of them all . . ." Fullerton, however, had devised his own point system in evaluating players on offense and defense and gave the nod in overall superiority in the major leagues to Heinie Groh, third baseman of the Cincinnati Reds, by a point total of 1,063 to 1,056, a virtual tie. "Groh, of course," Fullerton wrote, "is the leader of the third basemen, and no torturing of figures can take the lead away from him . . ." It seemed Buck had to keep proving himself.

In light of later developments Chicago interestingly finished the exhibition tour by beating Cincinnati twice at Redland Field. In so doing they discovered a future pitching star in Dick Kerr who "worked the first game against major league swatsmen and pitched brilliantly."

The White Sox then blasted their way into the new campaign on April 23 by pulverizing St. Louis pitching for 24 hits and breezing to a 13 to 4 victory. Every player in the lineup racked up at least one hit. Buck feasted on Brownie pitching for 4 hits including a triple. For the game the White Sox were attired in new uniforms but you'd never know it looking at Buck by the end of the game. Wrote Sanborn: "The White Sox were resplendent in new suits of steel gray, with blue trimmings, and the traditional white stockings. Buck Weaver kept his new unie clean for half of the preliminary practice. After that it looked natural on him." Buck couldn't resist his habit of scooping up dirt from the infield and rubbing it all over the front of his uniform. Even a brand new one.

One week into the season the *Tribune* proclaimed: "Just Like 1917! Sox . . . Lead League." By the end of May, with the White Sox holding a four game lead, Buck was blasting the ball at a .356 clip and the *Sporting News* said he was pulling off "miraculous" plays at third base.

New York and Cleveland kept nipping at the heels of the White Sox who led by only one game by June 10. The next morning in Boston some of the White Sox players sought temporary relief from the pressure of the red hot pennant race. Buck, Eddie Collins, right fielder Nemo Leibold and third-string catcher Joe Jenkins motored out to the Brae Burn Country Club to watch Walter Hagen and Mike Brady tie for the open golf championship at 301 for 72 holes. What is particularly interesting about this outing is that Collins and Weaver reputedly were not talking with each other on the playing field, yet here they were voluntarily spending their free time together. If they were at odds, they had a strange way of showing it. The next morning half of the White Sox team, including Gleason, drove out to the golf course to watch Hagen beat Brady for the open title.

Near the end of June Gleason had seen enough of Risberg at shortstop. Swede had been wobbly in the field and puny at the plate. Buck returned to his original position and McMullin again took over at third. By now the White Sox had slipped into third place.

Buck contributed some lusty hitting as the Pale Hose parlayed 9 victories in 10 games to climb to the pinnacle in the American League on July 10. The White Sox remained perched in first place the rest of the race but it was a rather precarious roost. There was a growing concern about the health of the pitching staff. The Sox were down to a reliable two man starting pitching corps with Cicotte and Williams carrying the heavy load. Red Faber mysteriously had lost his stuff. Crusinberry noted: ". . . Red hasn't won many games this year and if he doesn't start pretty soon, Cascade, Iowa, is liable to drop off the map again." Cascade was Red's home town. Dick Kerr, whom Gleason planned to use mainly in relief, began getting some starting calls in addition to his fireman duties. Gleason had hesitated putting Kerr in the starting rotation because he thought that at his height of 5 feet 7 inches, he was too small to be effective.

Nifty relief work by Kerr saved both games of a doubleheader against the Yankees at Comiskey Park on July 21 as the Sox pulled out to a six game lead. Williams and Faber were both driven from the mound. Buck went 4 for 5 in the first game.

But the afternoon was marred by tragedy that struck in downtown Chicago. A hydrogen filled blimp, flying over the Loop just before 5 o'clock, suddenly exploded and crashed in flames through the skylight of a bank building. Fiery gasoline sprayed on bank employees and customers, killing ten and injuring twenty-eight. Two passengers and one crew member were killed while the pilot and a mechanic parachuted to safety. The blimp, called the "Wing Foot," had been aloft for several hours when it plummeted to earth on top of the now Illinois Continental National Bank Building at Jackson Boulevard and La Salle Street. The aircraft was sponsored by Goodyear Tire and Rubber Co.

Almost everyone at the ballpark caught sight of the ill-fated dirigible and thousands screamed the instant it caught fire. "It seemed the entire thing burned up in about a half minute." Action on the field came to an abrupt halt as stunned fans and players watched the catastrophe. "After that, there wasn't much enjoyment felt over the ball game." Ironically, a twenty-seven year old mechanic from Warren, Ohio, named Carl "Buck" Weaver, was aboard the blimp and died of injuries sustained in the crash. Reaction to the crash in the city council went as far as one alderman suggesting an ordinance that would forbid aircraft flying over the city of Chicago.

Before the shock of the air crash inferno could wear off, Chicagoans underwent the trauma of another human tragedy. Within a week, bloody racial violence broke out on the south side only a few blocks from Comiskey Park. The flare-up had been smoldering for several years. World war had increased the demand for black unskilled workers in factories. The black population of Chicago had more than doubled from 50,000 in 1916 to about 125,000 in 1919. Racial bigotry and prejudice restricted housing for the new arrivals to the so-called black belt on the south side and the smaller black neighborhood on the near west side. As blacks moved into adjacent neighborhoods, probing and pushing for more living space, tensions mounted. For two years, from July 1917 to July 1919, twenty-four bombings ripped black residences. Not one person was arrested for any of the explosions.

Then on Sunday, July 27, while the White Sox were being whipped by St. Louis, 11 to 5, the temperature hit a searing 95 degrees and weary Chicagoans flocked to the beaches for relief. The spark was ignited at the 29th Street beach along the shore of Lake Michigan. A seventeen year old black youth swam across an imaginary line that separated white and black swimmers. White boys started throwing rocks at the youngster who had climbed aboard a raft. He got frightened, fell off and drowned.

Police couldn't control the fighting, stabbings, shootings, looting and brick throwing. A street car and "el" strike called at midnight the next day only made matters worse as some workers, attempting to walk to their jobs, were attacked by persons of the opposite race. Finally, 5,000 state militia arrived Wednesday to gain control of the situation and end the violence. A rain storm then broke the intense heat and helped calm roused tempers. By the time the race riot was over, twenty blacks and fourteen whites were dead. Many more had been hurt.

Comiskey Park found itself right up against a growing black belt neighborhood. After the race riots, some white fans would hesitate going to Sox games. July 27 marked the end of the White Sox home stand. It was a good time to get out of town.

The White Sox were in the driver's seat but they weren't always steering with authority. In the St. Louis series Crusinberry wrote of a victory over the Browns: "If a stranger had watched the game, he might have wondered how it could be possible that two such teams were actually in the race for a major league pennant."

In the same series, the Browns pounded Faber into defeat but there was something more disconcerting and threatening than Faber's ineffectiveness or the loss of a ball game. Though protestations had been made frequently by baseball's top brass that professional gamblers would not be tolerated in the ballparks and sporadic raids had been staged to clear them out, the betters still plied their trade in the open, unmolested. Crusinberry told how he discovered Schalk would not play that day because of a "strained muscle in his left leg."

"A half hour before game, the reporter was standing in the lower part of the grand stand. A bunch of five or six well dressers were there. One of them said, 'Who do you like?' Another said, 'I like St. Louis.' 'So do I,' said another. And it was followed with: 'I can get all your money covered in box—if you offer 11 to 10, and of course you know Schalk is not in the game.' A few minutes later the reporter verified the words of the well dressers that Schalk was out."

About two weeks later towards the bottom of a *Tribune* sports page was a small one column story, dateline New York, headed: "JUDGE LANDIS MAY BE NAMED 'COMMISH' CHIEF." The text said in part: "Charley Comiskey, owner of the Chicago White Sox, is said to have suggested Judge Landis as the new chairman of the commission." If there had been any doubt about the break between Comiskey and Johnson, it was totally erased by Comiskey's action. Johnson had been not only the president of the American League but in reality the czar of baseball. The chairman of the national commission, Garry Herrmann, almost always deferred to Johnson's wishes. Johnson wasn't about to relinquish any of his power to some Johnny-come-lately outsider.

Buck shuttled back to third base on August 10 with McMullin ailing. A couple of days later McMullin felt ready to play but Gleason decided to keep Buck at third recognizing that Weaver was "even a greater player there than at short." Besides, Buck preferred third base. Risberg stayed in at short.

Though the White Sox were in the midst of a 10 game winning streak when they trimmed Boston, 7 to 6, on August 16 in Chicago, it was Babe Ruth who gave them and their fans something to remember. Crusinberry witnessed the Herculean blast: "Big Babe Ruth . . . hit one up into some white floating clouds and out over the right field bleacher into the soccer football field . . .

"All the Sox players stood in their tracks transfixed with the splendor of it. Players and fans craned their necks as if watching an aeroplane until it fell out over the back of the bleachers. . . .

"Ruth's homer . . . was even a bit toward right center, away over in the middle of the bleacher, and it wasn't a drive. It was simply one of Ruth's flies."

Ruth astonished the baseball world with his gargantuan drives. In his last season as a regular pitcher, he walloped 29 homers to establish a new major league record that he alone would break.

Two days later, on August 18, Buck's twenty-ninth birthday, he received a box of American beauties while he sat in the dugout before the game. He celebrated with two hits that day as the Sox romped over the A's, 11 to 6. On the following day, the Sox, after trailing 7 to 2, scrambled back to win 8 to 7 as Buck's rousing spirit ignited the whole team. Crusinberry witnessed the extraordinary exuberance of the "ginger kid." "When a ball team is five runs behind the usual thing is to give up. Gleason's fellows never gave up. And to a close observer, it looked as if Buck Weaver simply wouldn't let them give up. Chicago's third baseman is nothing but a bundle of vitality when he's in the ball game. When it's over he's the quietest fellow in town but while the fight is on, he's filled with the old pep that makes not only himself, but those associated with him, do extraordinary things.

"Buck was stomping the earth, beating the ground with a ball bat, yelling on his mates and never was idle for a moment yesterday until the ball game was finished.

"When the winning run was finally pushed over the plate—and it was Weaver himself who scored it—he grabbed Happy Felsch, standing nearby waiting for his turn to hit, and simply hugged him right in front of the crowd. This is the kind of ball player Weaver is, and he imparts the same sort of enthusiasm to his mates." Buck stroked 4 hits in 5 tries in that game.

Buck showed more of his puckish nature on the field as the White Sox 10 game winning streak was stopped by New York on August 25. Weaver's former teammate, outfielder Ping Bodie, was in Yankee togs. It was a windy day at Comiskey Park. Every time Ping came to the plate, Buck purposely kept kicking up dirt around third base which flew right into Ping's face. Apparently it didn't disturb Bodie because he came through with 3 hits.

As the month of August was fading, the *Sporting News* commented on the White Sox determination to stay on top of the pennant race: "The Sox simply refuse to crack under the terrific strain of their pennant fight and are literally playing their heads off to win. The Sox are great money players. Show that gang a bunch of coin and they'll do almost anything except commit murder . . . Probably not in the history of baseball has there been a greater money team than the White Sox."

For the White Sox the long hot summer battle ground to a close when they beat St. Louis in Chicago to win the American League pennant on September 24. "Beyond the power of the ultimate mathematical or mundane mishap to thwart them," Sanborn rhapsodized, "Chicago's White Sox made themselves immutably and eternally champions of the American League for 1919 by trimming the Browns. . . . Risberg and Weaver have been performing feats that have astonished the natives of towns in which they have played, and more than one of their miraculous plays have been due to the brilliant first base work of Gandil . . ."

Buck Weaver was now showered by accolades from all directions. No greater praise for Buck could have come to surpass the glowing admiration that Gleason showed for his third baseman: ". . . Buck Weaver, by many experts, is declared to be as great a third baseman as any of the old stars . . .

"No one ever had as much pep and fighting spirit as Buck Weaver. You know when he's in the game of ball he's a regular firebrand. He's never still. He can talk a steady stream from start to finish and no matter what happens, he wouldn't blow up. He might kick four of them in a row, but when the fifth was coming at him, he'd be smiling as confidently as ever. Every ounce of vitality he has is used in every game. And when the last man is out he simply relaxes into the mildest and quietest fellow of them all. Actually, sometimes he doesn't seem to have enough strength left at the end of a game to drag himself to the clubhouse."

Hughie Jennings, manager of Detroit, was singing the praises of Heinie Groh, the Cincinnati Reds third baseman. "However," he said, "those who say there is no other third sacker in his class are certainly overlooking Buck Weaver. It is my belief that Groh and Weaver are the two greatest third sackers."

Sanborn also compared the two leading third basemen: "Heinie Groh, if he is able to play at his regular gait after his long layoff, will give Buck Weaver a battle for the third base honors, because of his superiority at bat. He has it on Weaver by a fair margin with the stick and is the more reliable batsman of the two when it comes to a pinch, but on the defense, Weaver will get more hard chances, and convert them into outs, than Groh can unless he corrects his fault of stumbling and falling down on slow hit balls."

Harvey T. Woodruff, the sports editor of the *Tribune* wrote: "Groh probably will be ranked above Weaver by 'experts' on the dope, yet our Buck is one of the greatest third basemen in the game."

George S. Robbins, the Chicago *Daily News* reporter covering the White Sox for the *Sporting News*, wrote in the September 25 issue: "We can never recall a period in which Buck Weaver has played the kind of ball he has shown the fans this year. Buck has been a wizard around third and has batted in keeping with his play in the field."

As the baseball season drew to a close, the major league magnates turned their attention to gate receipts. They now regretted that they had cut the schedule to only 140 games. They had feared financial red ink in the wake of the war, but they'd guessed wrong. White Sox turnstiles clicked merrily to the tune of 627,186 fans as compared to only 195,081 in 1918. The New York Giants attracted the most customers in the first postwar year with 708,857.

With baseball back in favor the National Commission voted for a best of nine games World Series. That would recoup a small amount of the money lost because of the reduced schedule. Publicly the National Commission announced that the World Series was extended "because of the unprecedented demand for tickets . . ." The majority of owners ratified the recommendation. Comiskey voted no.

At a meeting on September 16 in Chicago, the American League board of directors, seeking to find a successor to Herrmann as commission chairman, mentioned that they "may offer" the job to Kenesaw Mountain Landis. At the same time the board took up the issue of gambling. Johnson had publicly charged that betting was going on in some American League ballparks. The owners replied that they had done everything possible "to stamp out the evil," and condemned Johnson for not producing any evidence that gambling existed.

As the White Sox and the Cincinnati Reds moved closer to their World Series showdown, the betting odds emerged with the Chicagoans heavy favorites. But thoughtful baseball observers, analyzing the two teams closely, weren't so sure that should be the case. Probably no one was a keener judge of the situation than American League umpire Billy Evans. Evans, who originally pursued a law career, dropped out of Cornell University in his junior year when his father died. He found a job as a reporter on his hometown newspaper, the Youngstown, Ohio, *Vindicator*. When an umpire failed to appear for a game in the Ohio-Pennsylvania League, Billy was asked to fill in. In a short time Evans was umpiring in the National League in 1906 at the age of twenty-two. Articulate, well-dressed, polished in manner, Evans combined his career on the field with his interest in the press box. By 1919 he was not only officiating the World Series, but as sports editor of the Newspaper Enterprise Association, a national syndicate, he was writing a column about the World Series. In later years he would become a baseball executive in the American League with Cleveland, Detroit and Boston.

On September 23 Evans observed: "Ball teams do not always run true to form in a short series. In a season's campaign class will tell and the best team will invariably win unless disaster over takes it.

"In a short series some freak situation, some unusual play, may prove to be the turning point. In a number of world's series the final result has been greatly influenced by some one situation that was not reckoned with as even a probability." Two days later Evans contributed a prophetic comment, even considering the circumstances that followed: "If the Cincinnati Reds are able to stop Eddie Collins in the big show, then the National leaguers need not worry about the outcome of the baseball classic." Evans offered his most discerning commentary for September 30, one day before the World Series would open in Cincinnati: "National League's Best Chance to Win, Evans," headlined the *Tribune.* Wrote Evans: "If Red Faber of the Sox were pitching in 1917 form, I would say without any hesitation that I would lean strongly to the chances of the White Sox. But Faber during the season has not shown 1917 form, therefore, I am much in doubt as to Chicago's chances. It is a pretty big task to ask two pitchers, Eddie Cicotte and Lefty Williams to carry the burden of a nine game series.

"It is possible that Dick Kerr, the midget southpaw of the Sox, may prove to be Gleason's ace in the hole. Lefthanders, they say, make lots of trouble for the Reds, and Kerr is a pretty pert southpaw, despite the fact that this is his first year in the big show. Cincinnati, on the other hand, has a surplus of pitching, and in a short series pitching strength is of untold value.

"It is my opinion that no National league club that has met the American league entry in the big Series in the last ten years entered the classic with a better chance to win than the Reds. On paper the Reds do not shine, but on the field they perform most brilliantly, and it is on the field that ball games are won. It wouldn't surprise me if the Series went at least seven games."

One day before the Series opened, the *Tribune* headlined: "DOPE ON SOX VS. REDS DOESN'T JUSTIFY DEMAND FOR ODDS; PITCHING STAFF GIVES MORANS AN EVEN CHANCE." Sanborn opined: "Collectively there is apparently no such difference between the White Sox and Reds as the betting odds demanded by the Ohioans would indicate. Chicago is admittedly superior in eight positions, outside the slab, considering them as a whole, but Cincinnati has a better balanced pitching staff, according to all the dope available.

"Pitching has always been the determining factor in world's series, yet the Red fans cannily looking for bargains when it comes to backing their pets with the inflated coin of our realm."

Even a Cincinnati sportswriter, Jack Ryder of the *Enquirer*, expressed confidence in the Reds: ". . . the Reds have at least an even chance, if not a little better than even, to come through in the nine game series.

"This opinion is based principally on two things. One of these is the strength of the Red pitching staff, while the other is the well known ability of the entire club to rise to the occasion in pinches and play its best ball in its most important engagements."

Evans quoted Hughie Jennings in one of his columns: "I regard Cicotte and Williams on par with the best the Reds can offer but I have my doubts as to whether or not these two great pitchers can carry the burden, that probably will be alloted to four of the Reds' staff. The pitching staff is the one vulnerable point in the Sox defense."

If the White Sox pitching staff was not its long suit, the ball club certainly had one of the league's foremost pitching aces in Eddie Cicotte. By the end of the season Cicotte posted a remarkable record of twenty-nine wins and only seven defeats. He shut down opposing hitters on a 1.82 earned run average. Eddie had been taking extra turns on the mound to help capture the pennant. During September he took a two week rest, giving rise to suspicions that he had an ailing right arm. But he came back after the layoff to beat Boston, 3 to 2, on September 19 to win his 29th game.

Eliot Asinof suggests in *Eight Men Out* that Comiskey ordered Gleason to bench Cicotte in 1917 to prevent him from winning 30 games and collecting a $10,000 bonus for attaining that rarified milestone. The movie version of Asinof's book places this alleged occurrence in 1919. Not only is evidence of such a promise by Comiskey scarce, if not nonexistent (Asinof doesn't cite his source), the newspaper accounts clearly show that Cicotte's place in the rotation was not interrupted in 1917. Furthermore, such a bonus offer seems inconsistent with Comiskey's penny-pinching tendencies.

Cicotte *was* benched for two weeks prior to his September 19, 1919, victory, reportedly for an ailing right arm. On September 24, the Chicago *Daily News* headlined: "Manager Gleason May Call on Cicotte to Hurl Against Browns—A Victory Would Be His Thirtieth." Cicotte did pitch that day and St. Louis blasted him for 10 hits in seven complete innings. He surrendered 3 runs and 4 hits in the first inning, a run in the third, and got slugged for 2 triples and a run in the seventh. Cicotte left the game trailing, 5 to 4. The White Sox, needing a victory to clinch the pennant, sent Dickie Kerr in to pitch the eighth and ninth innings. The White Sox rallied for two runs in the last of the ninth to win the game and the 1919 pennant. On Sept. 28, as planned, Cicotte hurled the first two innings against Detroit as a warmup for the World Series.

In any event, neither Asinof nor any other researcher to date has suggested that a bonus had been offered to Cicotte in 1919. Thus, the story of Comiskey interfering in the rotation to cheat his ace right-hander of $10,000 seems apocryphal.

Lefty Williams ended the campaign with an impressive mark of 23 victories. But he got slapped with 11 defeats. Four of his losses came in the last month of the season. In two of his setbacks he was knocked out in early innings. In another he allowed 3 runs in the first but survived to go the route in a 4 to 3 loss to Boston. In that skirmish on Saturday, September 20, the first game of a doubleheader on "Babe Ruth Day" at Fenway Park, the White Sox knocked Ruth off the mound after clubbing him for 9 hits in 5⅓ innings. Ruth shifted to left field and in the ninth inning he smashed a spectacular home run over the left field fence off Williams to win the game. It was such a towering drive even the players were awed by the blow. For a left-handed hitter to whack the ball over the left field fence against a southpaw of Williams' caliber was unheard of. Between games Buck visited the Red Sox dugout and told the Beantowners, "That was the most unbelievable poke I ever saw."

Ruth finished his last year as a pitcher with a 9-5 mark and a 2.97 earned run average. Not bad for a slugger who startled the baseball world by clouting 29 homers for a new major league record.

As for Williams, in that last month he admittedly didn't look too often like one of the stoppers on the Sox pitching staff, except that sandwiched between his less than mediocre starts, he hurled 2 shutouts, one a two-hitter.

The most severe blow to the White Sox was the sudden and mysterious failure of Red Faber to be a big winner. He came up with a weak arm in spring training. For the season he struggled to win 11 games while absorbing 9 defeats. To fill the gap left by Faber's reversal of form, Gleason tapped rookie Dick Kerr. The little southpaw came through with 13 wins while losing 8. Newcomer Bill James helped in the home stretch drive. Picked up on waivers from Boston, he pitched 2 shutouts, even beating Walter Johnson. He also held New York to 2 runs for his third victory. The rest of the staff included such luminaries as Grover Lowdermilk, 5-5; Roy Wilkinson, 1-1; Erskine Mayer, 1-3; and Lefty Sullivan, 0-1. Mayer, one of the first Jewish ballplayers in the big leagues, was coming to the end of the trail after 8 seasons. He had been a big gun for the Philadelphia Phillies, winning 21 games in 1914 and then repeating the same number of victories for the pennant winning Phillies in 1915.

Pitching for both the Phillies and Pittsburgh in 1918, he racked up his best year percentage-wise with 16 wins and 7 losses. Before coming to the White Sox earlier in the year, he posted a 5-3 record with the Pirates.

By contrast the Cincinnati Reds boasted a pitching staff with six starters with victories in double figures. Slim Sallee, whom the White Sox defeated twice in the 1917 World Series, headed the staff with 21 wins and only 7 losses. Walter "Dutch" Ruether collected 19 triumphs against 6 setbacks. Hod Eller, who the White Sox discarded years earlier, also notched 19 wins while dropping 9. Hod had pitched a no-hitter against St. Louis during the season. It was the first no-hitter by a Red hurler before the home crowd since 1900. Like Cicotte, Hod's most powerful weapon was the "shine ball." Ray Fisher, later to become an outstanding baseball coach at the University of Michigan, contributed 14 wins while losing only 5 games. Adolph Luque, a brilliant young Cuban find, brought in 10 triumphs, while losing only 3 games. For some reason, Luque was seldom used in the second half of the season. The worst record belonged to Jimmy Ring and he had 10 games to his credit while getting tattooed with 9 defeats.

As for offense the White Sox possessed superior credentials with a team batting mark of .287 to lead the major leagues. Joe Jackson, returning to form, soared over all his competitors but one with a resounding .351 average. But it still wasn't high enough to win the league batting title because his arch rival, Ty Cobb, rattled enemy pitchers for a .384 mark. Eddie Collins followed with .319 and Weaver came in third at .296. In Buck's wake were Chick Gandil at .290, Ray Schalk at .282, Happy Felsch at .275 and Swede Risberg at .256. Only one third baseman barely outhit Buck. Cleveland's Larry Gardner reached an even .300.

A team batting average of .263 earned the Reds second place behind the New York Giants who led the National League with a mark of .269. In the vanguard of the Red attack was Edd Roush, who had developed into a sensational center fielder as well as a solid hitter. Ironically, Edd was

another player let loose by the Sox when he was rookie outfielder on the grounds that he had a pop gun throwing arm.
In 1919 Edd won the National League batting title with a
.321 average. The Reds, like the White Sox, finished the year
with only two hitters in the .300 class. Besides Roush, third
baseman Heinie Groh hit a handsome .310. Heinie swung a
peculiarly shaped bat. The extraordinarily thick end of the
bat suddenly tapered off at the handle like the neck of a
milk bottle. Other respectable batters in the Cincinnati lineup
included first baseman Jack Daubert at .276, catcher Ivy
Wingo who hit .273 and shortstop Larry Kopf at .270.

The Reds led the National League in fielding with a mark
of .974, five points higher than the White Sox who finished
second in the American League. "The averages, however,"
Woodruff of the *Tribune* wrote, "do not show the hits cut off
by Eddie Collins and Swede Risberg, the hard chances accepted as well as missed by Buck Weaver, the wide throws
which Gandil pulls out of the atmosphere."

Even though Buck by the end of the 1919 season was
popularly considered as the outstanding third baseman in
the American League, considered by many the best in baseball, he still put in a lot of time at shortstop. As a third
baseman in 97 games, Buck fielded for a percentage of .963,
committing twelve errors. Only his old buddy from San
Francisco, Oscar Vitt, now holding down third base for Boston, did better with .967. With 8 miscues in 43 games at
shortstop, Weaver fielded three points higher there than he
did at third. Again another Boston player, Everett Scott,
blocked him from the top spot with a record of .975.

The Cincinnati Reds were hardly pushovers. Managed
for the first time by "Whiskey Face" Pat Moran, who led the
Phillies to their first pennant in 1915, the Reds had learned
to play under pressure. They had just outclassed the pugna-
cious New York Giants by 10 games. Back in the middle of
August, the Reds and Giants tangled in 3 consecutive doubleheaders in a tension-filled, fight-to-the-death series. The
rancor and animosity between the ball clubs and among the
fans ran so high that the Reds brought their own bottled

drinking water for fear of being poisoned by rabid New York fans. Midst an unruly crowd that hurled not only verbal abuse but bottles on the field, the Reds swept the first and third double bills. The Giants took both ends of the middle set. From New York the Reds raced on to 10 straight victories and clinched the National League flag one week before the White Sox wrapped it up in the American League.

Just before the World Series the major league owners still expressed their discomfort with Herrmann as chairman of the national commission. New York Yankee owner Jake Ruppert said Herrmann should resign immediately, declaring it would be "open to objection from every point of view to have the president of one of the contending clubs also serving on the commission during the world's series." No action was taken and the situation would eventually prove embarrassing to Comiskey.

Buck Weaver as a young man.
(Courtesy of Bette Scanlan)

Charles A. Comiskey as a young ball-player.
(Courtesy of George Brace)

Ban Johnson, founder and first president of the American League.
(Courtesy of George Brace)

The brilliant pitcher Eddie Cicotte who became a ring leader of the Black Sox.
(Courtesy of George Brace)

Hall of Famer Ray "Cracker" Schalk, fire-brand catcher of the White Sox.
(Courtesy of George Brace)

Buck—seated, with his usual big smile—and fellow tourists in front of the Sphinx in
early 1914.
(Courtesy of Bette Scanlan)

The world tourists pose in front of the Vatican. Buck is the second from the left in the
top row. The children are the son and daughter of White Sox manager Jimmy Callahan
who, along with Mrs. Callahan, also made the trip. John J. McGraw is seventh from the
left in the front row. *(Courtesy of Bette Scanlan)*

The American ballplayers line up to be presented to King George V before the game in London. Buck is the fifth player from the left, arms folded and sporting his habitual grin.
(Courtesy of Bette Scanlan)

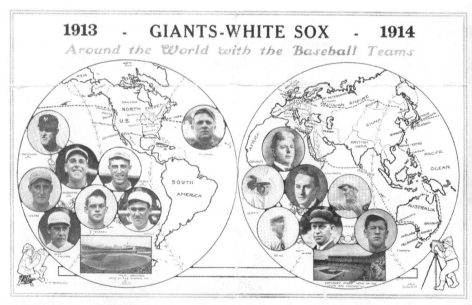

Publicity souvenir card issued by the teams after the World Tour. Several of the players pictured failed to make the actual tour.
(Courtesy of Bette Scanlan)

White Sox pitcher Jim Scott, Buck's brother-in-law by late 1917. *(Courtesy of Bette Scanlan)*

Compared favorably to Tris Speaker as a ballhawk, Oscar "Happy" Felsch, White Sox center fielder, became a Black Sox. *(Courtesy of George Brace)*

Original Hall of Famer Eddie Collins, White Sox second baseman. *(Courtesy of George Brace)*

White Sox manager Clarence "Pants" Rowland who guided the White Sox to the 1917 World Championship. *(Courtesy of George Brace)*

Judge Kenesaw Mountain Landis, the first sole commissioner of baseball.
(Courtesy of George Brace)

"The Grey Eagle" Tris Speaker, an original Hall of Famer, patrolled center field for Cleveland.
(Courtesy of George Brace)

Claude "Lefty" Williams of the Black Sox got bombed in the eighth game of the 1919 World Series.
(Courtesy of George Brace)

Harry Grabiner, Charles A. Comiskey's secretary and loyal lieutenant.
(Courtesy of George Brace)

The inimitable "Shoeless" Joe Jackson, illiterate off the field but a genius on it. He
wanted out of the Black Sox fix.
(Courtesy of George Brace)

Buck and Jim Scott join the American
Girl Quartet in a vaudeville act after the
close of the 1915 season. The Cook sis-
ters (left to right) are Harriet, Annette
Marie, Vesta and Helen.
(Courtesy of Bette Scanlan)

"The greatest third sacker in White Sox
history," 1916.
(Courtesy of George Brace)

Fred McMullin, reserve White Sox infielder who got in on the fix.
(Courtesy of George Brace)

Shortstop Charles "Swede" Risberg, another White Sox turned Black Sox.
(Courtesy of George Brace)

Charles "Chick" Gandil, slick fielding firs baseman, led the way for the Black So× perfidy.
(Courtesy of George Brace)

The Ginger Kid on the road, 1916.
(Courtesy of George Brace)

Ray Chapman, Cleveland shortstop, th only major leaguer fatally wounded o the diamond.
(Courtesy of George Brace)

Buck Weaver, Will Rogers and Helen Weaver in California, probably 1916. *(Courtesy of Bette Scanlan)*

The Chicago White Sox World's Champions

WORLD'S CHAMPION WHITE SOX. Upper row, left to right: Harry Grabiner, Sec'y.; Charles Comiskey, Pres.; J. L. Comiskey, Treas.; Lower Row: Jordan, McMullen, Williams, Jenkins, Jackson, Scott, Russell, Faber, Gandil, Lynn, Danforth, Felsch, Schalk, Rowland, Mgr.; Gleason, E. Collins, Liebold, Cicotte, Risberg, Weaver, Benz, Byrne, Wolfgang, J. Collins, Murphy.

HARRY GRABINER   CHAPLES COMISKEY   J. L. COMISKEY

JORDAN McMULLEN WILLIAMS JENKINS JACKSON, SCOTT RUSSELL FABER GANDIL LYNN DANFORTH FELSCH SCHALK ROWLAND GLEASON E.COLLINS LIEBOLD CICOTTE RISBERG
WEAVER BENZ BYRNE WOLFGANG J.COLLINS MURPHY.

The 1917 World Champion Chicago White Sox. *(Courtesy of George Brace)*

Buck and his brother Luther during World War I.
(Courtesy of Bette Scanlan)

Dickie Kerr, the little left-hander who shut out the Reds 3–0 in Game Three of the 1919 World Series.
(Courtesy of George Brace)

Kid Gleason, White Sox manager, 1919. *(Courtesy of the National Baseball Library, Cooperstown, NY)*

The Chicago White Sox of 1919.
(Courtesy of George Brace)

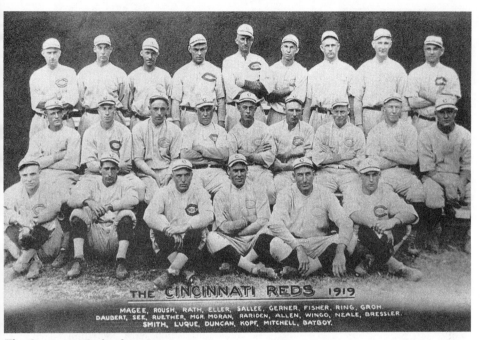

THE CINCINNATI REDS 1919

MAGEE, ROUSH, RATH, ELLER, SALLEE, GERNER, FISHER, RING, GROH.
DAUBERT, SEE, RUETHER, MGR. MORAN, RARIDEN, ALLEN, WINGO, NEALE, BRESSLER.
SMITH, LUQUE, DUNCAN, KOPF, MITCHELL, BATBOY.

The Cincinnati Reds of 1919.
(Courtesy of the National Baseball Library, Cooperstown, NY)

Cincinnati third baseman Heinie Groh
and his well-known "milk bottle" bat.
(Courtesy of George Brace)

Grantland Rice, nationally respected
sportswriter, knew of the fix but did not
report it.
(Courtesy of George Brace)

The Babe and Buck enjoy a visit with Douglas Fairbanks in California during the winter of 1919–20. *(Courtesy of Bette Scanlan)*

"The two Bucks get together." Screen cowboy Buck Jones and Buck Weaver tussle in California in 1920. *(Courtesy of Bette Scanlan)*

Buck and Helen with comedian Al St. John in Hollywood circa 1920. *(Courtesy of Bette Scanlan)*

Buck (second from the left) visits the Chicago Cubs in spring training in California in 1920. Third from the right is popular western movie star Buck Jones. Weaver reported to the Sox camp a little late. Note the uniform formality of the fans' dress. *(Courtesy of Bette Scanlan)*

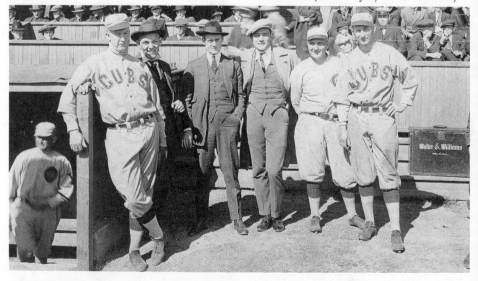

The Babe. (*Courtesy of George Brace*)

Buck and his two nieces, Pat and Bette, about 1933.
(Courtesy of Bette Scanlan)

Buck and Helen Weaver, 1945.
(Courtesy of Bette Scanlan)

Patricia and Bette Scanlan, 1945. Buck was their surrogate father.
(Courtesy of Bette Scanlan)

Buck in his later years, with his Irish setter, "Sandy."
(Courtesy of Bette Scanlan)

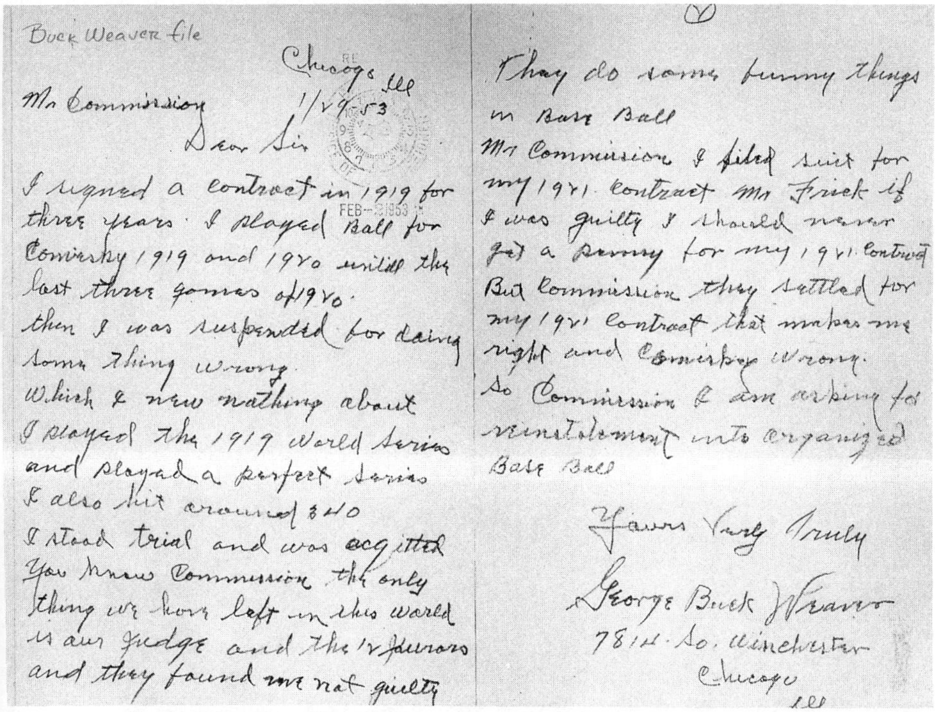

Chicago Ill
1/x 9 53

Mr Commission
Dear Sir

I signed a contract in 1919 for
three years. I played Ball for
Comiskey 1919 and 1920 unless the
last three games of 1920.
then I was suspended for doing
some thing wrong.
Which I new nothing about
I played the 1919 World Series
and played a perfect Series
I also hit around 340
I stood trial and was acquitted
You know Commission the only
thing we have left in this world
is our Judge and the 12 Jurors
and they found me not guilty

They do some funny things
in Base Ball
Mr Commission I filed suit for
my 1921 contract Mr Frick if
I was guilty I should never
get a penny for my 1921 contract
But Commission they settled for
my 1921 contract that makes me
right and Comiskey wrong.
So Commission I am asking for
reinstatement into organized
Base Ball

Yours Very Truly

George Buck Weaver
7811 So. Winchester
Chicago
Ill

Buck's appeal to Commissioner Ford Frick for reinstatement in 1953.
(Courtesy of the National Baseball Library, Cooperstown, NY)

The Ginger Kid in a rare moment—without his ready smile.
(Courtesy of George Brace)

12

Rumblings

On the morning of the day before the World Series started, the White Sox worked out at the ballpark and then motored over the Ohio River in the afternoon to see the horses run at Latonia race track, a pretty oval set in the Kentucky hills in suburban Covington. Many of the wives of the ballplayers accompanied them. Most likely Helen was at Buck's side.

During the season Helen occupied a box near the White Sox dugout during most of the home games. Whenever Buck lashed a key hit she rose to her feet to cheer. If Buck was mired in a slump, Helen "coached her husband to extend himself."

Helen's beauty caught the eye of a woman reporter of the Cincinnati *Times-Star* as Helen entered the hotel lobby that Tuesday morning. The reporter noticed the electricity that sparked among her observers: "When Mrs. George Weaver walked into the Sinton lobby . . . heads turned and eyebrows went up, while whispered questions from man to man wanted to know 'Who is she?' And of course, the women gave that appraising glance that they never waste on just a moderately handsome person.

"For Mrs. Weaver, from the top of her small red feather turban to the tip of her well-shod foot, is stunning. More than that, she is pretty and vivacious."

A *Times-Star* photographer pleaded for a moment to

take her picture. "Make it snappy," she said. "I'm hungry as a bear." Hungry as a bear and all she ordered was half a grapefruit and a cup of coffee. Helen claimed she wasn't reducing. "I wouldn't let her. She's all right just as she is," beamed Buck. Helen looked forward to the financial rewards of the World Series. She told a Chicago *Journal-Transcript* reporter, "You see a new dress or a stylish suit costs more money nowadays. Then besides the house rent and other incidentals run up into more money than they did a few years back. But Buck is ambitious. He's the kind of ball player who is always in the game to win and is what they call a scrappy ball player.

"I can't say that my husband is entitled to any more credit than the other players on Mr. Gleason's team. They all share the glory alike."

A holiday atmosphere pervaded the Queen City in the Ohio Valley. For the first time in National League history, the Cincinnati Reds had ascended to World Series heights. Baseball fanatics, tourists, national celebrities and, less welcome, a host of gamblers, jammed the hotels and restaurants. The hotels could not accommodate all the visitors. Private homes were thrown open to out-of-town strangers. The home owners were warned by the chamber of commerce not to charge more than $1.50 per night. City officials declared benches in the park were available for sleeping since the weather was unseasonably sultry and hot. The city assigned extra police to patrol the parks. Governor James Cox and Senator Warren G. Harding made their appearances. Harding, an avid baseball fan, owned his hometown team, Marion, in the Ohio State League. Harding and his entourage occupied the bridal suite at the Sinton. Also in residence at the Sinton was songwriter-entertainer George M. Cohan. At the Gibson, right across the street, the popular race track driver, Barney Oldfield, held sway. He took over the bridal suite of that hotel. Governors from the nearby states of Indiana, Kentucky and West Virginia joined the festive throng. About 250 Woodlands Bards, directed by chief White Sox rooter Joe Farrell, hired a special train to be on hand with their new chant, "Oh, Sox bring home the rocks, no hostile knocks; no dreadful shocks shall scare you, Sox; bring home the rocks."

Cincinnati was in a frenzy. Most big stores shut their doors. The business section was bedecked with flags. With traffic blocked off, people congregated in the streets already celebrating the Reds' entry into the World Series. Now they were mulling over the Reds' chances to win. These chances, according to the odds makers, were steadily improving. The day before the game, the White Sox were heavy favorites at 7-10. But by game time the Reds surged ahead in the betting. Most of the doubt expressed about the Sox centered on the uncertainty over the condition of Eddie Cicotte's pitching arm, though manager Gleason had publicly assured the fans that his ace was ready to go. The White Sox already had one of their star flingers on the shelf. Red Faber wouldn't even attempt to pitch during the Series because of a weak arm.

Word circulated in Cincinnati, however, of more disturbing and far more sinister developments than the mere incapacity of a couple of ballplayers. Ugly rumors surfaced and quickly spread around town that the World Series had been fixed. The alarming story was out that the highly vaunted White Sox were going to take a dive. Such stories had been pandered before in baseball prior to big games. Games had been fixed since the beginning of the National League. In 1877, four Louisville players threw games and were banished for life. In the early years of the National League, an umpire told gamblers how to bet on games he worked. But fix a World Series? Never. Too many players would have to be in on the plot. There were too many chances for loose talk. It couldn't be done! Yet more betting money poured in favoring the Reds. In New York betting boss Jack Doyle became suspicious of the sudden shift in the odds.

That the White Sox may be in the tank had become an open secret on the evening before the first game. Nationally known sportswriters were conscious of it. Hugh Fullerton, then of the Chicago *Herald and Examiner*, wired all papers taking his column. "Advise All Not to Bet On This Series. Ugly

Rumors Afloat." With the advice of Christy Mathewson, who was covering the series for the New York *World*, Fullerton would pencil in every suspicious play. Grantland Rice, one of the most popular and respected sportswriters, admitted in later years he knew of it. Rice, in his autobiography, *The Tumult and the Shouting*, published in 1954, said a friend of his had come to his hotel room the night before the Series opened. He was Champ Pickins, who in later years would organize the annual Blue-Grey football game at Montgomery, Alabama. Plainly upset, he told Rice, "I've just been offered five to four on Cincinnati by a professional gambler."

"How much did you take?" Rice asked.

"Take hell! The series is fixed," replied Pickins, tossing his ticket on the bed. "You can have it. I'm going to the race track."

A clerk in a stationery store, not recognizing Chick Gandil, confided to him, "I have it first hand that the Series is in the bag." Waitresses and bellhops were talking the same way, said Gandil, who offered his version of the White Sox scandal in a *Sports Illustrated* article in 1956.

Everyone who was suspicious had good reason to be. The rumors were supported by fact. The World Series would not be kosher. Crooked gamblers and a number of disgruntled White Sox ballplayers had found each other. Eliot Asinof, in his painstakingly detailed story, *Eight Men Out*, traces the intricate maze of the conspiracy. The ringleaders among the ballplayers were Chick Gandil and Eddie Cicotte who met at one time or other with a host of crooked gamblers. The gamblers looking for a sure thing included Joseph "Sport" Sullivan of Boston; "Sleepy Bill" Burns, ironically an ex-Red and White Sox pitcher of little note who gained his nickname catching catnaps in the dugout and who was then in the Texas oil business; Billy Maharg, an ex-boxer, now a Philadelphia auto mechanic; and Abe Attel, a former featherweight boxing champion who consorted with the kingpin of New York gamblers, Arnold Rothstein.

Rothstein at first declined to get involved when first approached by Attel and Burns at different times. He said,

"It couldn't be done. It was too big. Somebody would talk." At first Rothstein planned to sit on the sidelines, betting his money appropriately. Why get implicated? Later evidence, however, showed that Rothstein emerged as the brains of the fix and supplied most of the bankroll for the bribery.

Rothstein wasn't an ordinary run-of-the-mill gambler. Before the days of Mafia control of gambling, Rothstein circulated among the upper echelons of baseball as well as the upper crust of New York society. He owned the Brook, an exclusive resort at Saratoga, New York, and he was a majority stockholder in the Havre-de-Grace race track, located about 80 miles older in the northeast of Baltimore. He often was seen seated with Horace Stoneham, the new owner of the Giants, at the Polo Grounds. Stoneham owned a race track in Havana, Cuba. At one time, Rothstein was in partnership with John McGraw in the ownership of a pool hall in New York City.

The tentacles of the fix first reached out to Buck Weaver when Cicotte cautiously approached him while the team was on its second road trip to Boston. He sounded Buck out about whether he "wanted to get in on something good—fixing the World Series."

"You're crazy," exploded Buck. "That can't be done."

Near the end of the season Cicotte again talked with Buck and invited him to meet with some of his teammates at the Warner Hotel on Chicago's south side where some of the players stayed. Then, on the night before the Series opened, Weaver went to a second meeting at the Sinton.

It had finally come down to this. Angered, embittered, resentful ballplayers, frustrated by Comiskey's feudalistic treatment, especially his piddling salary checks, were willing to chance throwing a World Series before the eyes of thousands of witnesses—fans, ballplayers, former baseball players, sportswriters and others who could observe everything out in the open. There were no shadows or dark recesses in which to hide. The drama of a fix had to be enacted in public.

But baseball was a game of inches. Who could tell about

a deliberately poor pitch? Who could distinguish a purposely missed ground ball or fly ball from a failed attempt? Who could decipher a phony error from an honest mistake? These players were counting on the uncertainties of the game to camouflage their compromised efforts. Huddled together listening to the enticements of the gamblers were players who made up the backbone and heart of the team: Cicotte, Williams, Felsch, Gandil, Risberg and Weaver. McMullin, the top-flight utility infielder, overheard the discussions and demanded to be included in. Jackson remained absent from the meetings.

Even though Joe later confessed his involvement in the fix, his role as a true participant in the affair seems rather nebulous. An eloquent defense of Jackson's involvement is found in *Say It Ain't So, Joe* by Donald Gropman.

As the meeting broke up at the Sinton, the players walked away not knowing for sure who was in and who was out. Details of the defection seemed fuzzy even to the ballplayers. There was no master plan as to how to go about blowing the games. Only Cicotte and Williams knew what they had to do. Gandil would handle negotiations off the diamond. In their personal dealings with each other they were tight-lipped about the matter. One thing for certain, however, was that Buck Weaver must be counted out. There is little doubt he listened to the blandishments of the gamblers and then decided not to get involved. In the end he advised them "to go screw themselves."

Obviously, Buck had been tempted. He thought about it. The Ginger Kid had become, like the others, embittered, soured and frustrated by his relationship with Comiskey. In fact, he may have had more motives for getting even with Comiskey than some of the others who became entangled in the plot to throw the World Series. After the world tour with the Giants, when there was evidence that Comiskey had realized a profit, Buck, the only everyday player to make the trip, expected some kind of bonus. He got nothing. Later when Harry Lord abandoned the White Sox, manager Callahan named him captain only to have Comiskey give

Eddie Collins the honor soon after he came over from Philadelphia. Like the other players, he must have bristled when
Comiskey gave them his promised bonus for winning the
1917 pennant—a case of cheap champagne. Then there was
Buck's salary hassle with Comiskey during the previous winter when he threatened to leave the club and stay in Beloit,
working and playing ball for Fairbanks-Morse. Above all,
Weaver, like the other players, must have rankled at the
penny-pinching salary checks meted out by Comiskey over
the years. By 1919, Buck, by dint of his determined, tough
salary stance, was getting $7,250 a year in the first year of a
three year contract. It was the second highest salary on the
team, only surpassed by Eddie Collins' salary of $15,000. It
was $2,000 less than his counterpart, Heinie Groh, was get-
ting on the Reds. By this time Weaver was recognized as
either the top third baseman in all of baseball or at least the
peer of Groh.

Buck probably didn't know the salaries of the other players unless they vented their spleen in bitter moments. But
that likely happened with some regularity so he may have
known the plight of some of the others. Even though the
White Sox supposedly had split into two antagonistic cliques,
they agreed that their salaries, with one exception, did not
match their successful accomplishments. During the pennant
race they became so disgruntled that they threatened to
strike. In a clubhouse meeting, Gleason convinced them to
retreat. Instead, Gleason agreed to present the players' griev-
ances to Comiskey and request salary boosts. He came back
empty handed.

Exact figures of players' salaries are not available. Players and club owners often were too embarrassed by the figures to make them public. But over the years there has developed enough general agreement about some salaries to
make a point. Comiskey's wage scale was dramatically lower
than those of other club owners. Not that the others were
big spenders, but they appeared munificent in their salary
outlays when compared to the offerings of the Old Roman.
For example, a few figures reveal the inequality between

the remuneration of Chicago and Cincinnati players. Cicotte, a thirty-five year old, thirteen year veteran of the big show received $5,500 base salary in 1919 plus a $300 bonus for winning a whopping 29 games. By contrast, Cincinnati pitcher Dutch Ruether, only twenty-six years old and in his third season in the majors, received twice as much. He had 19 victories. While Reds first baseman Jack Daubert pulled down $9,000 a year, slick fielding, clutch hitting Chick Gandil was paid $4,000. Fleet-footed Happy Felsch, no slouch as a hitter, squeezed out $4,000, but somehow Comiskey must have become conscience stricken. He presented Hap with a $3,000 bonus for 1919. Felsch's opposite number in center field for Cincinnati, Edd Roush, entertained the folks for $10,000 a year. Lefty Williams, a 23 game winner, wasn't as fortunate. He labored on the mound for a mere $3,000 plus a $500 bonus. Comiskey honed the practice of handing out bonuses rather than salary raises. The players, contending for salary hikes in their new contracts, would have to start from their base pay, not including bonuses. Of all the salaries begrudgingly doled out by Comiskey, the most disgraceful was the $6,000 a year contract he foisted upon Joe Jackson, the illiterate South Carolinian, whom Cobb and Ruth agreed had the most beautiful swing in baseball. Ruth admitted patterning his swing after Jackson's. Joe would finish his thirteen year major league career in 1920 with the third highest lifetime batting average in history. Only Cobb with an astronomical .367 and Rogers Hornsby with his towering .358 outranked Jackson's phenomenal .356.

As for the wherewithal of the two teams in the 1919 World Series, the White Sox far outdistanced their National League rivals. Most of the team's revenue came from ticket sales, and the White Sox from 1917 through 1919 outdrew the Reds by more than a half million fans.

Despite what the others may have intended to do, however, Buck was going to play it straight all the way. To hell with Comiskey, Gandil, Cicotte and the rest. Buck loved baseball. It was as vital to him as the air he breathed. Life and baseball were coupled in his psyche. He would remain faithful. But he couldn't bring himself to inform on the others. Since childhood he was taught, like millions of other American youngsters, not to peach on your friends. He had played alongside these guys for years. They were fellow ballplayers who had endured, as he had, the worst of Comiskey's character, his penuriousness. Perhaps Buck remembered how George Stallings, manager of the Yankees, complained to the owners that his first baseman, Hal Chase, was throwing games. For a thank you the owners, after Stallings quit or was fired, promoted Chase to manager. Late in the 1918 season Christy Mathewson, as manager of the Reds, tried to get Chase kicked out of baseball for fixing and attempting to fix games while a member of his team. Many months later National League president John Heydler let Chase off the hook after a special hearing, despite the incriminating testimony of fellow ballplayers.

Buck made his ultimate decision. What the other players did—and he couldn't be sure what they *were* going to do—was their business. Buck's business was to hustle on the field and play ball with his usual intensity and make total commitment to win. He couldn't disgrace the game he loved so much, and he couldn't disgrace himself.

Only a few days before the World Series started Sanborn asked a Sox player why Gleason, a natural born "kidder" could command "such perfect respect as a manager." The player answered: "Respect hell! We love him and there isn't a man on the team who wouldn't break a leg for him to win a ball game."

Comiskey told his biographer, Gus Axelson, in 1919: "To me baseball is as honorable as any other business. It is the most honest pastime in the world. It has to be or it could not last a season out. Crookedness and baseball do not mix. It has become immeasurably more popular as the years have gone by. It will be greater yet. This year, 1919, is the greatest season of them all."

13

The Series is Lost

The eyes of the baseball world were concentrated on Cincinnati. The telegraph ticker would relay the action only seconds after it occurred on the field to hundreds of cities and towns from Canada to Cuba, where the scores would be posted on giant scoreboards for eager fans to see. In the big cities like Chicago and New York, electric scoreboards with moving mannequins and blinking electric lights reported every detail.

In Chicago, the *Tribune* set up two scoreboards, 15 feet by 12 feet. One was mounted in front of the Colonnade building at 724 South Michigan Ave., opposite Grant Park. Passersby could "see" the game from the immediate sidewalk below or from the open spaces in the park across the avenue. Another scoreboard was placed in Orchestra Hall, the home of the Chicago Symphony Orchestra, where one could "watch" the game in a comfortable seat for 50 cents. The proceeds, the *Tribune* announced, would be donated to the family of a railroad flagman who had lost his life vainly trying to save a couple from an onrushing train. Before the game, Miss Mildred Fitzpatrick, the organist for Orchestra Hall, would entertain the crowd. Other sites advertising for fans' patronage were the Coliseum, the Auditorium theatre, and the Morrison Hotel as well as a number of other places around the city. Tickets were going for 50 cents to a dollar and many of the ads advised to "Bring the Ladies."

In Cincinnati scoreboards were set up in front of newspaper offices and a half dozen halls and theatres. One leading hotel placed a scoreboard in its ballroom.

Of course there were other diversions than baseball to occupy the attention of the populace. In downtown Chicago movie theatres, the silent screen featured Mary Pickford in "The Hoodlum" at the Randolph; Will Rogers could be seen at the Castle in "Almost a Husband" and the great Houdini was in view in "The Grim Game" at the Rose.

On the national scene, a violent steel strike was just about ready to explode across the country. In the White House, President Wilson was resting after his collapse on his western swing across the country trying to convince the American people to encourage their senators to support his League of Nations plan, a part of the Versailles Treaty to end World War I. Whatever the crisis, however, nothing would stop the playing of the World Series. Perhaps someone or something should have.

A hot, sultry August-like day greeted the players as they took the field for their pre-game practice on Wednesday, October 1. When the White Sox made their initial appearance a brass band welcomed them by playing "Hail, Hail, the Gang's All Here." As they smoothly went through their drill, the band struck up "I'm Forever Blowing Bubbles," a popular song of the moment that soon would be twisted by a famous baseball writer into reproach of the White Sox. When the two managers, Gleason and Moran, both of Irish extraction, shook hands, the band broke in with "The Wearing of the Green."

Shortly before the game, the march king, John Philip Sousa, attired sharply in a U.S. naval lieutenant's uniform, emerged from his box seat near the White Sox dugout and walked briskly towards the brass band. As he approached he was greeted by the playing of the "Star Spangled Banner." Then he took over the direction of the band in a rendition of his stirring "Stars and Stripes Forever."

The crowd of 30,511 roared its approval. Redland Field normally held 22,000 but temporary stands and standing room offered space for more delirious baseball bugs.

The umpires moved into their positions. Charley Rigler and Ernie Quigley of the National League joined Billy Evans and Dick Nallin of the American League. No matter what rumors and plots swirled about Cincinnati, it was 2 o'clock, temperature 83 degrees. It was game time.

To the accompaniment of the cheering fans, the Reds hustled to their positions. New faces had propped up most of the inner defense. Around the infield it was Jack Daubert at first, obtained in a trade with Brooklyn; Morrie Rath ran out to second base, the same Morrie Rath who joined the White Sox along with Buck Weaver in 1912. He had been rescued from the minors for another brief taste of major league cuisine and hostelry. At shortstop the dependable Larry Kopf, brought back to Cincinnati in another trade with Brooklyn, was unlimbering, while at third base Buck Weaver's only rival for premier third sacker in the major leagues, Heinie Groh, was getting in his practice throws to first. Heinie was concerned about those throws. He would be playing under a handicap since he had broken the second finger on his throwing hand several weeks earlier. He was now just getting back into action and was playing with his finger taped up.

Out in left field, the Reds stationed a rookie, Pat Duncan. He was brought up in the later half of the season. The incomparable Edd Roush was ready to spring into action in center field. Right field would be patrolled by Greasy Neale, who in a later generation would gain greater fame as head coach of the Philadelphia Eagles in the National Football League.

Starting on the mound for Cincinnati was 19 game winner Walter "Dutch" Ruether. Some fans may have remembered that as a collegiate six years earlier, Dutch beat the Sox, holding them to two hits in a spring training game. One of the hits was a disputed home run in the tenth inning. Buck was familiar with Ivy Wingo, the Reds' starting catcher, who made the world tour with him as a member of the Giants.

The White Sox went into action with a lineup of Shano Collins in right field; Eddie Collins at second; Buck Weaver at third base; Joe Jackson in left field; Hap Felsch in center field; Chick Gandil at first base; Swede Risberg at shortstop; Ray Schalk catching and Eddie Cicotte on the hill.

An invisible tenth man crowded into the Cincinnati lineup. Before the season ended, Cincinnati dispatched point men to survey the potential enemy. As early as September 9, two weeks before the Sox clinched the pennant, the old Chicago Cub star second baseman, Johnny Evers, was seen watching the Sox play Washington in the nation's capital. The White Sox were suspicious that he was spying for Cincinnati and they were right. The Reds had hired Evers, Cubs manager Fred Mitchell and Cubs pitcher Grover Cleveland "Pete" Alexander to discover the strengths and weaknesses of the Chicago ball club. When the series got underway, the Reds knew much more about the Sox than the Sox knew about them. Only a haphazard attempt was made by the White Sox to gain information on the condition of the Reds. Fred McMullin had been sent out near the season's end to gather intelligence on the condition of their World Series opponent. McMullin was a member of the sellout conspiracy.

With the game underway, Buck sought to put as much distance between himself and the defectors. In the first inning he smashed a drive which soared into deep left-center field. It looked like a sure triple, but Roush, "who seemed to have the legs of a gazelle and the arms of a gibbon, committed a one handed act of robbery . . ." by racing back and snaring the ball near the fence. He would repeat such fielding gems throughout the series. Buck led off the fourth inning by laying down a picture bunt along the third base line, but Groh played it perfectly and nipped him by a step. In the sixth, the Sox tried to come alive, trailing 6 to 1. Shano Collins opened the inning by smashing a long drive to deep left-center, but Roush made another "swell catch" to rob Shano of an extra base hit. Eddie Collins caromed a liner off

Ruether's glove and hustled to first before Rath's throw. Buck then followed with a Texas Leaguer into right field, pushing Collins to second base. The rally fizzled as Jackson grounded to Daubert on the first pitch and Felsch flied to Neale. In his last appearance at the plate in the eighth with the Sox behind 9 to 1, Weaver ended the inning by lining deep to Roush.

The first critical play to cast suspicion on Cicotte and Risberg came in the fourth inning. [The *Tribune* picked it up immediately.] Wrote Sanborn: "That fourth inning rally could have been averted, or, at least postponed, if the Sox had pulled a cinch double play that would have retired the side." The inning opened with Felsch, one of the conspirators, racing to deep left-center to make a circus catch of Roush's long smash. Watching that play, Weaver must have wondered if Hap had also backed out of the crooked deal. Only supreme extra effort made that catch possible. Then Duncan dropped a Texas Leaguer into right field.

Sanborn again: "Kopf slammed a fast one back to Cicotte, who scooped it and forced Duncan at second. Risberg, who pivoted in the play, caught the ball low, then had to straighten up before the relay. He paused too long and let Kopf beat the play to first by a toenail. On that toenail hung the game."

In a special boxed story in the *Tribune* headed "BREAK OF THE GAME" came another view of the play: "Kopf hit sharply to Cicotte who wheeled and then held his throw until Risberg could cover the bag.

"Risberg stumbled after receiving throw, which slowed his relay to first just enough for Kopf to get the decision. A double play would have retired the side scoreless."

Then Neale bounced one back of second base that Risberg raced over for but could only knock down. Again the side could have been retired without a run had Swede made the play. It was scored as a hit. Sanborn reported it without comment: "Neale singled . . ." Four more hits followed including a triple by Ruether into left-center field. Gleason stubbornly allowed Cicotte to get pounded even after Ruether's smash. Rath, a notoriously weak hitter, doubled over Weaver's head and Daubert singled. Finally Gleason rescued the beleaguered Cicotte after 5 runs had crossed the plate.

Buck had only one defensive opportunity and it was rather undistinguished. In the seventh inning Roush laid down a sacrifice bunt that Buck threw badly to first, pulling Gandil off the bag. No error was charged on the play.

Much ado would be made about that mishandled double play in the fourth, but it didn't cost the ball game. The Sox only scored 1 run, an unearned tally in the second inning. Jackson grounded to Kopf, who fumbled and then threw wildly to first, Jackson reaching second. Felsch sacrificed Joe to third, and Jackson scored when Gandil dropped a Texas Leaguer into short left out of the reach of Roush, who made a sensational attempt to reach the ball. The names of the three players involved in the only scoring of the game for the White Sox are noteworthy. Of the 6 hits made by the Sox, two were recorded by Gandil, one by Weaver and one by McMullin. Only 2 safeties were made by players with no involvement in the conspiracy.

The aftermath of the game sparked with a high drama which made the action on the field pale by comparison. Some of the comments were rather innocent. Christy Mathewson informed his readers that Tris Speaker had said, "Cicotte's last three games in the regular season had been bad, and this is his fourth." Most condemning was Ray Schalk's bitter accusation made to Chicago sportswriters immediately after the game. He said Cicotte repeatedly crossed him up, paying no attention to his signs. It was never reported. That evening Chicago *Herald and Examiner* sportswriter Hugh Fullerton confided to Fred Lieb, a reporter with the New York *Sun*, "I don't like what I saw out there today. There is something smelly. Cicotte doesn't usually pitch like that."

That evening at the Sinton, reporters bombarded Gleason with questions: "What happened? What was the matter with Cicotte?" Gleason smiled and answered patiently, "The boys never got started today, and, anyway, we should have never scored a run. So there's no use worrying over the game. A beating like that was just what my gang needed. You'll see them fighting out there tomorrow. Just wait and see.

"There were a lot of mistakes made in that game of ball. Maybe I made one myself in starting Eddie Cicotte instead of a left-hander. I think left-handers will bother the Reds more than right-handers." Efficient scouting reports would have given him the answer. The Reds did have four left-handed regular everyday players in the opening lineup. Kopf, a switch hitter, would bat left. Wingo, the catcher and a lefty, alternated with Bill Raridan, and Ruether also hit from the portside. That made seven lefties facing Cicotte. And Ruether, who smashed 2 triples and a single in the first game, was not an automatic out by any means. He was one of the best hitting pitchers in the majors, batting .261 for the season on 24 hits in 92 tries.

Gleason went on: "But Cicotte was a good pitcher today. He was going all right, but he was outguessed. We know several places where he should have used a spitter instead of a fast one. We know a lot more about the Reds than we did. We know a lot more about Dutch Ruether's pitching than we did. I don't think he can beat us in another game."

But there was at least another sportswriter who didn't think Cicotte was a good pitcher earlier that day, Ring Lardner of the *Tribune*. Ring had worked as the sports editor of the Boston *American* when Cicotte was still with the Red Sox. It was Lardner who clued Comiskey in on plucking the unhappy right-hander from the Red Sox on waivers. Lardner called Cicotte "the best all-round ball player among major league pitchers."

The night of the first game, Lardner, suspicious of Cicotte's fielding, invited the pitcher to his room for drinks. Lardner asked Cicotte point blank if he deliberately blew the game. What was Cicotte going to say? Of course he promptly denied it.

"What was wrong?" Lardner asked. "I was betting on you today." Cicotte said he was just off form and everything would turn out okay.

In the meantime, Gleason, who had put on a mask of lightheartedness for the benefit of the sportswriters, was in inner turmoil. He suspected the worst. So did Comiskey. Shortly after 11 P.M. Comiskey summoned Gleason to his room.

"Do you think they're throwing the series?" Gleason said he didn't know. "Answer me," Comiskey demanded. Gleason admitted something was wrong but couldn't put his finger on it. But he must have known what Schalk told reporters about Cicotte ignoring his signals.

Comiskey couldn't sleep. About 2:30 in the morning he decided that he had to make a move. The entire National Commission was billeted at the Sinton. But he hardly could approach the chairman of the commission, Garry Herrmann. He also was owner of the Cincinnati Reds. How could he dampen Herrmann's spirits by telling him the White Sox might be giving the Reds the Series? It would sound like a lame alibi for the Sox defeat. Nor could Comiskey approach Johnson. They were now implacable enemies. Johnson probably took extra pleasure in seeing Comiskey's club absorb a whipping even though he was president of the American League. Comiskey was left with only one alternative. That was to take his case to John Heydler, the president of the National League. He woke Heydler and told him his story.

"Impossible. You can't fix a world series, Commy," was Heydler's quick response.

Nevertheless, Heydler felt it was his responsibility to inform his counterpart in the American League. He roused Johnson out of bed. Johnson's only disdainful retort was, "This is the whelp of a beaten cur!" Johnson was totally disinterested.

Earlier that evening at the Sinton another White Sox official, secretary Harry Grabiner, had taken a phone call in his room from a nationally known gambler named Monte Tennes. Tennes wanted to talk to him about the World Series. Not wanting to be seen with a well-known gambler, Grabiner arranged to get the information through another White Sox intermediary the next morning. Tennes told Grabiner that something was wrong. The odds shifting from 7 to 5 in favor of the White Sox the night before the game to 7 to 5 favoring Cincinnati just before game time indicated trouble. Tennes said he didn't have any proof, but "being a gambler by profession it was apparent to him the White Sox had been reached." Grabiner would sit on his information until the teams returned to Chicago.

Cynics, doubters, the suspicious and the innocent saw the fourth inning of the second game as the decisive frame that led to the second White Sox defeat before another standing room crowd of 29,690.

Two lefties, Williams and Sallee, were hooked up in a scoreless duel when Williams walked 3 batters and allowed 2 hits that were converted into 3 runs. Sanborn called it "almost criminal wild pitching . . ." in his lead.

Immediately there was concern that Williams, reported to be a pinpoint control pitcher, would walk three batters in one inning. But as Victor Luhrs points out in his amusing, keenly analytical treatment of the 1919 world series in *The Great Baseball Mystery*, all the batters walked on 3 and 2 counts and Schalk argued with umpire Billy Evans on several of the calls. As for Williams' pinpoint control—he averaged only 1 walk per game in 1919—there were documented incidents during the latter part of the season when he'd let his control get away from him.

In 1919 Williams walked 58 and struck out 125, a little better than 2 to 1 in favor of strikeouts, which is a good ratio for any effective pitcher. In 1918, however, when Williams played only part of the year, he walked 17 more than the 30 he struck out. In the championship season of 1917, he struck out 85 and surrendered 81 passes. In his first year with the White Sox in 1916, Williams turned in 138 strikeouts compared to 65 bases on balls. In his career he had walked 347 batters and struck out 515.

Williams opened the fatal fourth by walking Rath. Daubert sacrificed. Groh walked. Roush lined a single to center, scoring Rath. On Felsch's throw to the plate, Groh raced to third, but Roush held at first. Roush then went down stealing on a spectacular play. Collins raced in as if to take Schalk's short throw. The ball went through to Risberg backing Collins who tagged Roush coming in. Groh held third on what looked like a busted double steal attempt. Duncan walked. Kopf then slammed the first pitch into left-center for a triple, scoring Groh and Duncan.

Cincinnati scored its fourth and final run in the sixth when Roush led off with a walk. Sacrificed to second, he scored when Neale lined a single to left. All Reds runners who had scored reached base on a walk.

The White Sox rallied to pull within two in the seventh. With 1 out, Risberg lined a single to left. Schalk smashed one down the right field foul line and sprinted to second. Neale's throw bounced away from Rath and Kopf and rolled all the way to the fence back of third, allowing Risberg and Schalk to score.

The Sox, who outhit Cincinnati 10 to 4, were thwarted all afternoon by "highway robbery that was ultra sensational by the Reds . . ." In the first inning Eddie Collins walked. Weaver smashed a liner towards left but Kopf "stabbed" it and threw to first to double up Collins. The Sox tried to nibble at the Red 4 to 0 lead in the sixth. Kopf again proved the culprit when he "hurled himself in front of Eddie Collins' liner" to start off the inning. Weaver then lined the ball over Duncan's head in left. The ball hit the railing and bounced back to Roush whose relay stopped Buck at second. Jackson struck out and Buck moved to third on a balk. Then Felsch really must have kissed one according to Sanborn's rhapsodic description: "Hap hit a ball several miles over center field and it would have been good for a home run if he had hit it in any other direction on account of the geography of Redland Park. Here it was possible for Roush to tear back to within a few feet of Western Avenue and pick the pill out of the sun over his shoulders while running at top speed. It was the catch of a lifetime and it squelched one of the most likely looking rallies the White Sox made."

In the eighth with the Sox trailing, 4 to 2, Felsch and the Sox were victimized again. With one down Daubert grabbed Jackson's hot smash back on the grass far behind first base. He threw to Sallee but the pitcher was slow covering the bag and the ball got away enabling Jackson to scamper to second. Felsch then lined a screamer toward left field but Groh reached up and knocked it down. He retrieved the ball at his feet and threw to Daubert who picked the ball out of the dirt. The amazing Red defense choked off another budding Sox rally in the ninth. Gandil opened with a single to center. Risberg than slashed one up the middle for what looked like another base hit but Rath raced behind second, grabbed the ball, flipped to Kopf for the force out and the shortstop relayed it to first to complete a lightning-like twin killing.

Buck distinguished himself in one of two other appearances at the plate. He tried to spark an attack when he lashed a single to center to start the fourth inning on the first pitch. Jackson followed with a single to left on another first pitch. Weaver stopped at second. Both runners advanced as Felsch sacrificed again on the first pitch. Gandil followed suit by swinging at Sallee's initial offering but could only bounce to Daubert, who threw Weaver out at the plate by 12 feet. Gandil stole second but Risberg popped to Daubert to end the threat. In Buck's only other at bat, he grounded to Kopf in the eighth.

On defense Buck handled only 3 putouts. Sallee popped to him in the third, Kopf fouled out in the sixth and Rath lined out in the seventh.

The 10 White Sox hits were distributed among Jackson, who charted 3 including a double; Weaver, who collected 2 including a double; Schalk, who hammered out 2 with a double; and Gandil, Risberg and Williams with one each.

Though Williams had allowed only 4 hits and the White Sox seemed to have been stymied by a tremendous Cincinnati defense, there was restiveness in the press box. The 3 walks by Williams in what was becoming known as Cincinnati's lucky fourth weighed heavily on the minds of the scribes reporting the Series.

Grantland Rice recalled: "I was sitting next to Lardner

when Ring started pounding his typewriter furiously. He kept humming, 'I'm Forever Blowing Bubbles.' His bitter parody of that song, dedicated to Williams, opened with, 'I'm forever blowing ball games . . .' "

After the game an interested spectator named Kenesaw Mountain Landis said, "The Reds are the most formidable team I've ever seen."

At the same time, after filing their stories with no revelation of their suspicions, a group of sportswriters led by Lardner and James Crusinberry headed for a saloon in Bellevue, Kentucky, on the far side of the Ohio River. Imbibing a few drinks as was his custom, Lardner led his cronies in the singing of his mocking parody.

> "I'm forever throwing ball games
> Pretty ball games in the air,
> I come from Chi
> I hardly try
> Just go to bat and fade and die.
> Fortune's coming my way,
> That's why I don't care.
> I'm forever throwing ball games
> And the gamblers treat us fair."

That night on the Pullmans back to Chicago, Lardner is supposed to have sung his special rendition for the benefit of the White Sox players and assorted friends. If it is true that Lardner crooned his bitter lyrics within earshot of the ballplayers, then the whole team, whether involved in the conspiracy or not, knew of the suspected fix. Certainly they were aware of the rumors, along with everyone else in Cincinnati. Quartered in the same hotel, is it possible that those White Sox players not touched by the gamblers didn't have even an inkling of what was going on?

Obviously Cincinnati ballplayers weren't immune to the wildfire of the fix rumor sweeping the city. Edd Roush recalled later in *The Glory of Their Times* by Lawrence S. Ritter: "Yes I knew at the time that some finagling was going on. At least that's what I heard. Rumors were flying all over the place that gamblers had got to the Chicago White Sox, that they'd agreed to throw the World Series. But nobody knew anything for sure . . .

"We beat them in the first two games, 9 to 1 and 4 to 2, and it was after the second game that I first got word of it. . . . So the evening after the second game we were all gathered at the hotel in Cincinnati, standing around waiting for cabs to take us to the train station, when this fellow came over to me. I didn't know who he was, but I'd seen him around before.

" 'Roush,' he says, 'I want to tell you something. Did you hear about the squabble the White Sox got into at the game this afternoon?' And he told me some story about Ray Schalk accusing Lefty Williams of throwing the game, and something about some of the White Sox beating up a gambler for not giving them the money he'd promised them.

" 'They didn't get the payoff,' he said, 'so from here on they're going to try to win.'

"I didn't know whether the guy made it up or not. . . ."

On the morning of October 3, the *Tribune* bannered: "PRESIDENT IS 'VERY SICK' " Wilson had spent the previous day in bed and his condition was described as "grave." Chicagoans riveted their attention on another crisis in their backyard other than the World Series. A mammoth strike gripped the nation and Chicago's southern neighbor, Gary, Indiana, and its environs, were in the vortex of the conflict.

Back in Chicago, Grabiner phoned Heydler about his earlier report from gambler Monte Tennes. Heydler answered that "rumors regarding World Series had always cropped up . . . the games looked to him as though they were played honestly that nothing . . . stood out in either game one or two that might look suspicious."

Buck sought to rouse his teammates and the fans by acting as an optimistic cheerleader. The Chicago *Daily News* before the third game headlined: "WEAVER PREDICTS A VICTORY. Sox Third Baseman Refuses to Be Disheartened by Defeats." Buck, "whose smile hasn't been erased by two stinging defeats," said, "It takes five games on the winning end for a club to win in this league.

"We'll get 'em sure on our home lot," Buck continued. "The Sox have been just a fair road team all the year, but they have been almost unbeatable on their own grounds. We have the best little pitcher among the recruits in either league under cover. We'll show 'em something today."

The *Daily News* commented, "Many Sox fans will be glad to hear this. Buck's optimism is contagious and it has spread to other members of the club."

Did Buck really believe the Sox were going to make a fight of it or was he bluffing with a false bravado, misleading his loyal fans who made him by this time the most popular player on the team? He probably meant it. When he walked out of that meeting at the Sinton Hotel, there had been no expressed common agreement, except for his own vehement withdrawal, as to who had cast his lot with the conspiracy and how they would proceed to throw the games.

True, there was turmoil in the Sox clubhouse after the second game. Buck couldn't erase the fact that Schalk went after Williams, accusing him of throwing the game, and manager Gleason had sprung for Gandil's neck. Other players pried the antagonists apart before any damage was done. Perhaps Buck sought by a public rallying cry to unite the divided forces. On the surface of things the White Sox as a team made a valiant bid to try to win the second game. One had to give credit to the Reds for playing great defensive ball.

When the gates were thrown open at Comiskey Park at 9:25 in the morning the first of the crowd to enter was probably a Cincinnati fan named Roland Ryan of Elyria, Ohio, a soldier stationed at Ft. Sheridan, recuperating from wounds suffered in the Argonne Forest during the war. He had arrived at the ticket window early Thursday evening and stayed in line all night equipped with a soap box for a seat, a small basket of food for lunch and cigarettes filling his pocket. Behind the soldier was Carl Schaeffer, a striking steel worker from the South Chicago mills and the third man in line was an amateur swimmer named W. J. Henry.

There may have been a line all night but those fans who went through the long vigil did so for naught. The count of the crowd for the first game in Chicago was a surprising low figure of 29,126. It seemed, as so often is the case of a giant sports event, the word got around that tickets were not to be had, so great was the crunch of people at the ballpark. In reality 5,000 seats went begging in the pavilion and bleacher sections. All the reserved seats were filled.

By 2 o'clock game time, the temperature was a pleasant 75 degrees. Throughout the afternoon it would steadily rise to a summery 84 degrees by 4 o'clock. But the game didn't last that long. Little Dickie Kerr, affectionately called a midget in the headlines, put on a David versus Goliath act and disposed of the Reds in exactly 1 hour and 30 minutes, pitching a brilliant 3-hit shutout to win, 3 to 0, against right-hander Ray Fisher. Nemo Leibold replaced Shano Collins for the only change in the White Sox lineup.

Even in defeat the Reds continued to play fantastic defensive baseball. On the first play of the game, Leibold, who at 5 feet 5 inches was even smaller than Kerr, smashed a line drive to right that looked like a sure bingo but Neale raced in to make a shoestring catch, landing on his neck.

In the second inning the White Sox would finally take the lead for the first time in the series. The crowd roared as Jackson started it off with a single to right. Felsch's attempt to sacrifice shot straight back to Fisher who heaved the ball into center field trying to cut down Jackson at second. Jackson fell as he rounded second but got up in time to reach third ahead of Roush's peg to Groh. Felsch, in the meantime, raced all the way to second. With the infield pulled in, Gandil slapped a single between Rath and Daubert, scoring Jackson and Felsch. Risberg walked. It looked as if the rally was gaining more steam when Schalk laid down a beautiful bunt towards third, but Gandil "loafed" on his way to third and was forced out on a throw from Fisher to Groh. Kerr also grounded to Fisher who threw to Groh forcing Risberg. Groh ended the inning by making a one-handed stop of Leibold's hard drive and throwing him out.

In the third inning Weaver and Eddie Collins combined to launch a scoring threat but it ended ingloriously. Collins opened the inning by lining a single over short. Kopf almost flagged the ball as he leaped into the air and just tipped it with his glove. Buck shot the ball through short on a hit and run as Kopf moved out of position to cover second. But the big guns failed to explode. Jackson popped up and Felsch again stung the ball, but Groh came up with another one handed stop that he converted into a double play.

However, the White Sox added an insurance run in the fourth. But first Groh performed another pretty play for Cincinnati as he ran in on Gandil's hit, scooped up the ball and threw him out. Risberg then powdered a liner to right which hopped past Neale for a triple. Schalk then squeeze bunted a twisting ball that got past Fisher, scoring Risberg.

In Buck's other appearances at the plate he popped to Daubert in the first, bounced to Fisher in the fifth and grounded to Rath in the eighth. On the infield Weaver handled 4 assists. He easily threw out Raridan in the third, took charge of Fisher's soft roller in the fifth, snapped up Groh's grounder in the sixth and tossed out Groh again to end the game.

On the morning of Saturday, October 4, the *Tribune* bannered: "WILSON A LITTLE BETTER." It could have said the same thing about the White Sox. Chicago fandom, with the Sox down 2 games to 1, took heart and packed Comiskey Park with a throng of 34,363. Gleason called upon Cicotte to go back on the hill against Jimmy Ring.

But once again Cicotte strangely fell into fielding lapses so unlike him, and once again they were limited to one critical inning. Because of that peculiar inning, the fifth, Cicotte surrendered a tight pitching duel by a narrow 2 to 0 score. Of course, the White Sox attack sank into a coma with only 3 hits—a double by Jackson and singles by Felsch and Gandil. That didn't exactly help matters.

The fatal inning started with Schalk pouncing upon Roush's tap in front of the plate and throwing him out. Then things began to unravel. Sanborn supplies an eyewitness account: "Duncan hit a sharp bounder which squirted off Eddie's mitt a little ways toward third. He recovered the ball in plenty of time to get his man, but nervously hurried the peg and shot it wide of first base. When Schalk recovered the stray pill Duncan was on second. Kopf followed with a hard single to left. It was hit so sharply that Duncan had no chance to score, but stopped on third when Jackson fielded the ball cleanly and winged it toward the plate.

"For some reason Cicotte tried to cut in on the play with one hand, and deflected the ball just enough to keep Schalk from stopping it. Duncan scored and Kopf reached second. Neale then hit a medium boiled fly to left which was good for two bases, because Jackson was playing close in for him. Kopf raced home with the second run and the game was on ice." Outside the fifth inning only three Red runners reached first base.

As for Buck's individual efforts, on offense he flied to Neale in the first, grounded to Daubert in the third and fifth. In the eighth Rath made a great running catch of his pop-up on the right field foul line. At third base, Buck threw out Neale in the third and Groh in the sixth. In the seventh, "Weaver made a great stop of Duncan's hot one and threw to Gandil in time to get him by fifteen feet."

Strangely enough, after four games, the White Sox, who had the most explosive hitting attack in the American League, could claim the responsibility of scoring only one run by their own prowess. The rest were gifts of the Cincinnati defense which had generally performed superbly. Buck had nothing to say in public.

Only an hour and a half after the game ended at 3:37 P.M., violence broke out in Gary, Indiana, in the two week old steel strike. Striking white men, coming out of a mass meeting, attacked black workers on a street car who were being employed by the steel mills as scabs during the strike. Racial prejudice and hatred spilled over into the labor conflict, making the antagonism even more bitter. Indiana Governor James Goodrich rushed the state militia to Gary to restore peace.

Back on the baseball front, the *Tribune* of Sunday morning, October 5, carried an ominous story without a byline. The headline read: "RECORD BETTING CAUSE OF ALARM; STARTS SCANDAL, Heavy Wagering Brings About Unpleasant Comment." The story followed: "Betting on the present world's series between White Sox and Reds has been heavier than in any previous post-season clash. It has been so heavy as to give concern to those interested in the sport, not for anything that has happened as yet, but because of the gossip or scandal which might sometime develop. . . .

"Even wagers running into four figures carry no danger where they are placed between individuals. It is when one man or a syndicate makes up a big pool to be wagered wherever it can be placed that a condition arises where unpleasant comment may be aroused.

"In the present series seemingly unlimited amounts of money to be placed upon the Reds appeared from the same source in Cincinnati after the first game. Much of it was covered by the Woodland Bards to their sorrow. Commissioners (pre-Las Vegas odds-makers) were in the leading hotels asking all comers for a wager. After the first game they began to offer liberal odds. It did not seem to be Cincinnati money, for the followers of the Reds appeared chary of backing their choices at anything like natural odds.

"This sudden influx of coin started several unfounded rumors which fortunately did not gain general circulation. But it is suggested the danger of such possibilities and what could follow from the idle talk [is] common after nearly every big sporting event.

"The difficulty of fixing a baseball game, aside from the honesty of the players and the almost sure detection even [if] it were possible to find one black sheep, is so great, as to be almost negligible.

"This heavy betting, however, is a danger sign. . . ."

Rain on Sunday forced the postponement of the fifth game. But most of the White Sox showed up anyway at the ballpark in the morning. Gleason held a team meeting. All he told the press was, "We just talked things over among ourselves." It may have been at this meeting that Gleason asked the players if what he heard about the rumors were true. If he did, none of the players offered any concrete response. Chick Gandil, in his 1956 interview in *Sports Illustrated,* said there was a meeting before the fifth game. He said those players involved in the fix "got huffy" and the others "kept quiet." He said Gleason "let the matter drop."

By 2 o'clock the only White Sox hanging around the clubhouse were Gleason, Lowdermilk and Sullivan. Lowdermilk and Sullivan were playing a modified game of Canfield, a form of solitaire. An out-of-town reporter asked Gleason, "Will it be Williams tomorrow?"

"No, I think I'll go in myself." Gleason had started in baseball as a pitcher.

Gleason talked to Crusinberry: "It's the best team that ever went into a world's series. But it isn't playing the baseball that won the pennant for me. I don't know what's the matter, the players don't know what's the matter but the team has not shown itself thus far."

Crusinberry searched for an answer: "But one must find some sort of excuse for the things the Reds have done to the Sox in the four games played. Anyway, right in the first game they were pitching in the proper manner to the various batters and they were playing in the proper places to handle anything hit by the Sox. They acted like a bunch that had been playing in the American league all summer and seemed well instructed on the dope that they made few mistakes. But Gleason hasn't any strategy board. He had a spy watching the Reds about batting peculiarities and defense." That spy, of course, was Fred McMullin, a member of the secret cabal planning to surrender the fort.

Late Sunday night, Gary mayor William F. Hodges called for more militia as new fighting broke out in four sections of the city. Not far from this bitter, violent industrial strife, the World Series continued. Many of the players on both teams may well have pondered about the strike since they came from families that worked in the mills.

Hope sprang eternal in the hearts of White Sox fans as 34,379 filled Comiskey Park to capacity on Monday, October 6. But that's about all that did spring. The White Sox submitted meekly as Hod Eller shut them out for the second game in a row, 5 to 0, on only 3 hits. Buck had 2 of the 3, an infield single in the first and a triple in the ninth.

Hod struck out 6 batters in a row in the second and third innings. In the second Gandil went down swinging. Risberg was called out on strikes and Schalk fanned. In the third Williams took a third strike. Leibold, who was the only strike out victim to touch the ball with a foul into the stands, looked at a third strike, and Eddie Collins went down swinging. In all, Eller struck out 9.

Williams matched Eller inning for inning through the fifth, allowing his first hit in the fifth when Kopf led off, singling to center. Williams held the Reds to 4 hits over the eight innings he pitched but 3 were bunched in the sixth when the roof caved in for 4 runs.

Eller led off by hitting a fastball to left-center over the heads of Jackson and Felsch. Felsch's throw got away from Risberg, allowing Eller to reach third. Rath singled to right, scoring Eller, and Daubert sacrificed, Weaver to Gandil. Groh walked. Roush smacked a long drive to center. Felsch tore back, got his hands on the ball but dropped it. It was judged a triple, sending Rath and Groh home. Eddie Collins took Felsch's throw, relayed it to Schalk, who appeared to have tagged Groh as he charged in on a head-first slide. When umpire Rigler called Groh safe, Schalk jumped over Groh and "dug his hands into Rigler's chest protector as he protested." Rigler waved Schalk out of the game. Byrd Lynn came in to catch for the White Sox. Duncan flied to Jackson. Roush tagged up and headed for the plate. Jackson's throw beat him but Lynn dropped the ball, allowing the fourth run to score.

In the ninth Erskine Mayer replaced Williams on the

hill and the Reds proceeded to score a run without a hit. Roush opened the inning by driving a hard smash to Eddie Collins, who fumbled the ball for an error. Duncan walked. Kopf sacrified, Weaver to Gandil. Roush scored as Risberg threw out Neale.

The White Sox threatened twice and Weaver's role was paramount each time. In the first Leibold walked and scooted to second on Eddie Collins' infield out. Weaver caromed a single off Eller's glove, Leibold advancing to third. But the rally collapsed when Jackson popped out to Groh along the third base line and Felsch flied to Duncan in short left. With 2 outs in the ninth the crowd roared as Buck powered a triple to right-center but Jackson ended the game grounding out to Kopf.

Besides his two hits, Weaver rolled out to Eller in the fourth and bounced out to Kopf in the sixth. Other than handling the 2 sacrifice bunts, the only other play that came Buck's way was in the third when he gathered in Eller's pop-up on the pitcher's mound.

After 5 games the White Sox had still scored only one run by their own effort.

Of far more concern to the nation than White Sox defeats was the volatile steel strike situation. Shortly after 6 P.M. Monday night following the White Sox's 5 to 0 defeat, about 1,000 veterans of the Fourth Division "created a sensation" as they marched from Ft. Sheridan, just north of Chicago, down Michigan Avenue on their way to the outskirts of Gary. General Leonard Wood had just declared martial law in Gary and its neighboring towns of East Chicago and Indiana Harbor. Ready for instant action were sixteen machine guns, sixty automatic rifles, trench mortars and one pounders. The reason for all this ready force was that thousands of Gary steel workers had participated in a parade and mass meeting against the orders of the mayor, police and militia. The unions announced that 367,000 steel workers were out on strike around the country. More troops were on their way from Omaha, Nebraska, to Gary.

As the *Tribune* bannered on Tuesday morning: "U.S.

REGULARS RULE GARY" and another head reported: "Wilson Grows Better Under Enforced Rest," a sports page headline focused on the troubled White Sox: "What is Wrong with White Sox? Gleason Asks." In an interview with Crusinberry after the 5 to 0 loss the manager said: "I don't know what's the matter but I do know something is wrong with my gang. The bunch I had fighting in August for the pennant would have trimmed this Cincinnati bunch without a struggle. The bunch I have now couldn't beat a high school team.

"I'm convinced that I have the best ball club that ever was put together. I certainly have been disappointed in it in this Series. It hasn't played baseball in a single game."

Crusinberry talked to Gleason later that night at the hotel and said Gleason clearly indicated that there was something wrong and that he intended to find out what it was.

"You know it doesn't seem possible that this gang that worked so great for me all summer could fall down like this. I tell you I am absolutely sick at heart. They haven't played any baseball for me. I thought all of them were my boys. I felt like a school teacher might feel toward his pupils. I loved those boys for the way they fought for me all summer. . . .

"But they aren't playing baseball. Not the kind we played all summer. If they had, the Sox would just about have the world's championship clinched by this time. Something has happened to my gang. If they would just play baseball for me the rest of the series, they might even pull it out yet. The team I had most of the time all summer would do it. I haven't had the same team on the ball field in a single game."

For the record Gleason held back from saying he suspected that some of his boys were laying down. Perhaps he hoped his public declaration might turn the team around when they took the field in Cincinnati for the sixth game.

Not much hope remained for any more Sox heroics at the end of 4 innings of the sixth game at Redland Field. They trailed 4 to 0 and Dutch Ruether was hurling for the Rhinelanders. Dutch limited the Sox to 1 unearned run in the opener. Now it appeared they were on the brink of fold-ing their hand in what looked like the final game of the World Series. But they picked themselves off the canvas and scratched and clawed back for a 5 to 4 ten inning victory. The crowd of 32,006 and the rest of the inhabitants of Cincinnati would have to take a rain check on their celebration.

Sanborn, in his exuberance, didn't hesitate to put in public print what a lot of people were suspecting: "Their work in this battle silenced all the dangerous gossip that had been circulated by disgruntled gamblers, and convinced even their enemies that as a team the White Sox take off their lids to no one when it comes to gameness. . . .

"From a baseball standpoint it was a poorly played game, and the White Sox gave a sorry exhibition at times defensively besides making a couple of breaks on the bases that were punk. . . .

"But as an exhibition of sheer bulldog grit and fight, with apparently everything conceivable conspiring against them, it was the most wonderful uphill battle I ever saw on the diamond, and at its conclusion 99 percent of the Red rooters stood up and said so unmistakably, even though it cost a lot of them a lot of dough."

Both third basemen—Weaver and Groh—tattooed base hits in the first inning after two outs. Buck smashed a grounder just out of Kopf's reach into center field. But Jackson could only pop up to Groh. Groh doubled to right-center and Roush slapped one up the middle but Risberg was able to skirt over and knock it down for a base hit. When Groh overran third Risberg whipped the ball to Weaver to erase the Reds third baseman.

Despite some wobbly defense in the second inning, the White Sox escaped without any damage. Risberg fumbled Duncan's easy roller. Kerr, seeking his second win, seemed upset and walked Kopf on 4 straight pitches. Then he made a "nifty" play on Neale's bunt, threw wildly to Weaver at third who saved the day by making a one-handed stab of the ball and touching the bag in time to force Duncan. Kerr held the next two batters in check.

The Sox tried to launch an attack in the third but the

Cincinnati defense, extraordinary during the entire Series, kept the lid on. Schalk opened with a walk and was sacrificed to second by Kerr. Shano Collins skied to Roush in short center. Then Eddie Collins powered a lusty liner into left-center, but Duncan intercepted the ball on a great running catch.

Cincinnati broke out in front with 2 runs in the third. With 1 out, Daubert singled to right. He then raced for second as Groh took a called third strike and overslid the bag, but Collins had to reach for Schalk's low throw, giving Daubert a chance to scurry back safely. Roush gained passage to first base when Kerr hit him with a pitched ball. Duncan doubled to right-center, scoring Daubert and Roush with the first runs scored against Kerr in 12 innings. Felsch squelched any further damage when he sprinted into deep center to haul in Kopf's long drive.

It looked as if the White Sox would start the fourth on a positive note when Buck teed off on a long drive, but Duncan continued his scintillating fielding performance by catching up with the ball before it hit the turf.

Shaky White Sox fielding mixed with timely Reds hitting propelled the National Leaguers to a 4 to 0 lead at the end of four. Neale opened the frame by drilling the ball to right-center. When Shano Collins overran the ball, Neale scooted around to third for a triple. Eddie Collins threw out Raridan, Neale holding third. Ruether then collected his fourth hit in 5 tries when he slapped a bounder just a foot inside the left field foul line. The ball veered into the stands for a ground rule double and Neale easily jogged home with a score. Ruether dashed for third as Risberg gobbled up a grounder off the bat of Rath. Swede tried to cut off the Cincy hurler but his throw hit Ruether in the back and rolled into foul territory, Weaver giving chase. Ruether scored and Rath pulled up at second. He then stole third on a poor throw by Schalk that Buck couldn't handle. But the Reds attack came to a halt when Rath tried to score on Daubert's fly to Jackson. Jackson's throw to the plate doubled him up to end the inning.

Now trailing 4 to 0, the White Sox managed to squeeze out their first run in 27 innings in the fifth on only 1 hit. Lax base running by Kerr, reminiscent of Faber's errant journey on the base paths in the 1917 World Series, aborted any possibility of further scoring. The inning started in a most promising fashion. Ruether walked Risberg and Schalk to start the inning. Kerr smacked a grounder to deep short which Kopf could only knock down. The bases were loaded with three outs to go. Shano Collins could only lift a fly ball not far behind second base. Roush sauntered in to catch the ball. Eddie Collins then sent Roush back peddling into deep center to get his drive, allowing Risberg time to score. Roush fired to third, holding Schalk at second. But Kerr, thinking his battery mate had progressed to third, lit out for second. But when he realized his blunder, he froze in the base path allowing Groh, who ran across the infield, to tag him out.

There were some scary moments for the White Sox in the bottom of the fifth but they escaped unscathed. After one out, Roush pumped a low liner to right which looked like it would fall in for a hit, but Shano Collins raced in to capture the ball at his knees. Duncan came to the plate with the roar of the crowd ringing in his ears for his defensive gems of the afternoon. He responded by powering the ball to deep-center. Felsch apparently had difficulty getting a bead on the ball. He ran in circles under it, grabbed for it, touched it and then dropped it for a three base error. Fortunately, Risberg tossed out Kopf to end the threat.

Finally, in the sixth inning of the sixth game, the White Sox let loose with their best scoring effort in the series. It started with the cooperation of the Reds when Weaver, leading off, popped the ball into short left field. Both Duncan running in and Kopf retreating hesitated making the catch, thinking the other had command, and the ball fell greenward, allowing Buck to motor to second for a double. Jackson, wasting no time, immediately singled to center, scoring Weaver. Felsch connected for a long drive to left, allowing Jackson to circle the bases to score. Alert fielding by Duncan stopped Felsch at second with the potential tying run. On the mound Ring replaced Ruether for the reeling Reds. Gandil

popped to Daubert for the first out after his attempts to sacrifice failed. Felsch traveled to third while Kopf threw out
Risberg for the second out. Schalk then stroked a ball towards left which Groh could only manage to tip. It skidded
over to Kopf but evaded his grasp for a single. In the meantime Felsch scooted home with the tying run.

The White Sox might have won the game in regulation
time in the eighth but more dramatic fielding by the Reds
delayed the ultimate outcome. Jackson opened the inning
with a walk. Felsch flied to Neale. Then Ring issued a pass
to Gandil on 4 pitches. He followed with a 3 and 2 count on
Risberg when the Sox shortstop kissed the ball for a "terrific liner" to short center field. It looked like a guaranteed
hit but Roush executed another of his patented robberies,
this time making a sparkling "shoestring catch" and then
leisurely tossing to Rath to double Jackson who already had
rounded third base.

The Reds also threatened in the eighth. Gandil made a
nice catch of Duncan's foul fly far behind first, near the outfield box seats, to start the inning. Kerr nabbed Kopf's line
drive and called time to recover from the blow on his pitching hand. With two out Neale drove a single to left and
Gleason ordered James to warm up. Raridan slapped the ball
off Kerr's glove for a single. Fortunately the inning came to a
close when Ring forced Raridan at second.

The fruitful tenth got underway when Buck registered
his third hit of the game. His short fly took a bad hop past
Duncan who tried to make another daring catch but this
time his effort misfired and Weaver sprinted to second for a
double. Jackson, attempting to sacrifice, bunted safely in
front of the plate, pushing Weaver to third. Felsch struck
out. With the Cincinnati infield drawn in for a play at the
plate, Gandil poked a slow, high bouncing ball into center
field, scoring Weaver with what proved to be the winning
run. Jackson halted at second where he was doubled off
when Risberg lined to Kopf.

The Reds went down one-two-three in their half of the
tenth.

In Buck's other action, he grounded out to Rath to end

the seventh and then reciprocated by taking Rath's grounder and throwing him out to lead off the ninth.

Now the White Sox trailed 4 games to 2. They were still on the ropes but Buck, always the sparkplug and eternal optimist, told the press: "That was the first of the four games we needed. Tomorrow we will win by an easier score."

Gleason, too, issued a signal of hope after the Sox 5 to 4 triumph. "If we win the next game we will win the world's championship."

The former owner of the Chicago Cubs, Charles Murphy, who could recall more than one city series when the southsiders got off the floor to knock his team out, said: "I learned a lesson a long time ago. Those White Sox can come from behind better than any team I ever saw. I am not predicting the World's Championship for the Reds until they have that fifth game over with the last man out, and the bats in the bat bag."

At first glance it was strange, inexplicable. Only 13,923 fans bothered to attend the seventh game at Redland Field for what could have been the coup de grace against the White Sox. But Garry Herrmann had a ready explanation for the sparse gathering. He had himself to blame. He didn't put the tickets on sale until the sixth game was over.

Cicotte took the mound against Slim Sallee. He had convinced Gleason to send him out again to make amends for his two previous failures. One change was made in the outfield for Chicago. Shano Collins and Hap Felsch traded positions. Gleason decided Collins would follow the ball better than Felsch because of his long experience in the sun field. No one seemed to have asked how Hap would be able to manage the sun in right field.

The *Tribune* head carried the joyful news: "SOX BATTLE TO THIRD VICTORY, 4-1." Sanborn caught the essence of the moment: "Fighting again like bulldogs at bay, Chicago's White Sox licked the Reds today in the seventh game of the world's greatest world's series and gave Eddie Cicotte a chance to regain his laurels brilliantly."

The White Sox jumped off to a one run lead in the first.

Shano Collins opened the game with a single to center. Eddie Collins sacrificed. Then Buck "drove Roush back half a mile after a long fly." Jackson came through with a single to left, scoring Shano. Joe got hung up between first and second after Groh cut off Duncan's throw to the plate and fired to Rath. Jackson scrambled back to first and landed safely when Daubert muffed Rath's poor throw. The chief scorer was J. G. Taylor Spink, publisher and editor of the *Sporting News*, and he awarded the error to Daubert. Felsch beat out a slow roller to third but Gandil ended the inning by grounding to Kopf for a force out at second.

The White Sox picked up a second run in the third. Shano Collins again started the inning with a single, a smash off Sallee's glove that shot over second base. Kopf couldn't make a play on a bounder by Eddie Collins to deep short. Then Weaver followed with a tap to the busy Cincinnati shortstop who stepped on second forcing Eddie Collins. Kopf then fired to first but the ball hit Collins in the shoulder and caromed away. Kopf claimed interference on the throw which umpire Rigler allowed and called Weaver out for a double play. In the meantime Shano Collins reached third and came home on Jackson's single to left. Felsch forced Jackson to end the inning.

Cincinnati's inner defense collapsed in the fifth, allowing the Sox two more runs which proved more than enough to insure victory for the Pale Hose. For the third time in the ball game, Shano Collins led off an inning but for the first time he couldn't produce; he flied to Neale. Eddie Collins singled to center for his second hit. Buck drilled a hard grounder towards third. Groh stabbed the ball, fell down and fumbled but recovered only to throw wildly to first. Rath followed with an encore miscue as he missed Jackson's roller which hit him in the ankle and bounded away. With the bases loaded, Felsch singled to center, scoring Eddie Collins and Weaver. Jackson stopped at second. That was the end of the line for Sallee who was replaced by Ray Fisher. Fisher extinguished the Chicago fire by handling Gandil's tap to the mound and striking out Risberg.

The Reds lost a chance to score in the bottom of the fifth. With 1 out, Neale, who wielded the hottest Red bat in the series, singled to left. Wingo walked. Moran sent his slugging pitcher, Dutch Ruether, to swing for Fisher, but this time Ruether, who clouted 2 triples in the first game, fouled weakly to Weaver. Buck handled Rath's easy tap to end the inning.

The Reds got on the board in the sixth when Groh's hit sailed over the temporary fence along the left field foul line for a ground rule double. Cicotte took Roush's tap, appeared to have a play at third, but chose to throw to first for the sure out. Duncan followed with a single to center scoring Groh with the lone Cincinnati tally of the afternoon.

To conclude the National Leaguers' trying day in the field, Roush, who had a spectacular series defensively, ran into short center to handle Risberg's fly but dropped the ball for the fourth Reds error of the game. Risberg tried to leg it to second, but Roush redeemed himself by recovering the ball in time to throw to Rath who put the ball on Swede. On a great play to end the inning, Kopf raced into deep short for Schalk's smash and threw him out.

In Buck's other efforts, he was called out on strikes to lead off the seventh. Neale fouled out to him in the second and he threw out Duncan to end the fourth.

After the game Buck beamed, "We faced even bigger odds in one of our city series against the Cubs. But we won out just the same."

Back at the Sinton Hotel, Gleason exuded freshly found confidence: "They are licked sure. I don't see a chance for the Reds to win another game. I feel absolutely certain we can take the next two and then it will be over.

"You see, this isn't the same ball team that was playing for me in the first three or four games. My gang that went through the summer and knocked everybody down in the American league race is back with me. I was the sickest man that ever walked when we left Chicago Monday night to come down here. I hadn't had a wink of sleep in two nights and felt as if I never would be able to sleep again.

"It wasn't because my fellows were beaten. It was because they weren't playing any baseball. Well, tonight, I expect to sleep like a schoolboy on that train ride to Chicago. I haven't felt so good in years. My gang is back playing ball again. When it is playing ball I can see no chance for the Reds to beat us, except through some remarkable break in luck, and that isn't likely to happen.

"Honestly, I could have hugged every one of them after that game today. And we haven't won the championship at all. We have to win two before they win one. But I could hug the fellows because for the last two days they have hustled and fought and come through for me, as I knew they can [sic] come through."

Gleason was aware of some smelly Sox befouling the ball club. So what was his motive for his exaggerated, almost maudlin praise of his players? Was he simply putting on a brave front? Or did he hope to retrieve all the strays back to the ranch for a final drive to the championship?

Ring Lardner, who sensed something was wrong from the start, continued to write humorously about the series in his nationally syndicated column which appeared in the *Tribune*. A *Tribune* headline on October 9, destined to be the last day of the World Series, reflected the facetious treatment Lardner dished out for public consumption: "WELL GENTS, RING DIGS UP A HEAP OF BALL SCANDAL; Lardner Discovers That Series Is Being Played with Round Ball."

Gleason stubbornly nominated Williams to pitch the eighth game in Chicago on Thursday, October 9. Williams had not only lost 2 games but was accused by Schalk of purposely ignoring his signals. Williams was deeply entangled in the fix. According to Eliot Asinof in *Eight Men Out*, Rothstein sent word to Sport Sullivan not to waste any more time and get the World Series over with pronto. On the night before the game, as Williams and his wife were returning to the hotel after dinner, they were accosted by a strange man who threatened both with bodily harm if Williams didn't blow the game quickly.

Williams, probably scared to death not only for himself but for his wife, promptly delivered the goods to the gamblers. The suspense of a White Sox comeback faded almost as soon as the eighth game began. Before the entire crowd of 32,930 had settled into its seats, the Cincinnati Reds had splattered Lefty Williams with 4 straight hits and 3 runs in ⅓ of an inning.

The horrendous first inning started innocently enough when Rath popped to Risberg. Then came the deluge. Daubert slashed a low, hard liner to center that Leibold tried valiantly but vainly to snare with a daring shoestring catch. Groh singled to short right, advancing Daubert to second. Roush bounced a double over first, scoring Daubert and dispatching Groh to third. Duncan doubled down the left field foul line, sending Groh and Roush to the plate. After Williams had pitched one ball to Kopf, Gleason finally had seen enough and yanked his starter off the mound in favor of Bill James. James lost Kopf on a base on balls but followed up by striking out Neale. Roush drove in the fourth run of the inning when he singled over Gandil's head to score Duncan. Eller, the ninth man to bat, ended the assault by flying to Felsch.

The White Sox tried to bounce back immediately. Leibold drove a single to left and Eddie Collins ignited the crowd with a double to left-center. But the rally fizzled quickly. Buck disappointed the roaring fans by taking a third strike. Jackson lofted a long foul down the left field foul line that Kopf pursued and caught for a great play. Felsch struck out.

The Reds added a fifth run in the second. After 2 outs, Groh singled to right and scored on Roush's double to left-center. On the throw to the plate Roush decided to make a run for third, but realized he couldn't make it and tried to dash back to second. He was tagged out. The play went from Leibold to Risberg to Schalk to Weaver to Eddie Collins.

Buck sparkled defensively in the Reds' third. He threw out Duncan to start the inning and then raced behind the pitcher's mound to snare Kopf's bounder and whipped the ball to first for the out.

The Sox made a slight dent in the Cincinnati lead in the bottom of the third. First Eddie Collins lined to Duncan. Then Buck looped one into short right-center that looked like it would fall in for a double, but Rath, running out with his back to the ball, made a great catch. Jackson made sure no one would catch up with his blast as he smashed the ball into the right field bleachers. It was to be the only home run of the World Series. Felsch grounded to Kopf to end the inning.

In the Cincinnati fourth, the White Sox cut down a potential run. Eller, who had reached base by getting hit by a pitched ball, later tried to score from second on Daubert's single to center. A great throw by Leibold caught him at the plate.

The Reds hiked the score to 6 to 1 in the fifth. With 2 out Kopf spanked the ball into the right field corner for a triple and then scored on Neale's slashing drive past Risberg.

In the fifth inning the White Sox attack tried to revive but again Cincinnati's defense stifled an attempted uprising. There was also a questionable tactic pulled by Gleason. Today, with a team trailing 6 to 1, and with a relief pitcher leading off, most likely a pinch hitter would go to the plate. It wasn't unlikely then either. But Gleason, who had a specialist pinch batter in Eddie Murphy on the bench and Dick Kerr waiting in the wings to take the mound, chose to let James bat for himself. He struck out. Leibold smashed a drive towards left field but Kopf "made a sensational running stop and got him with a lightning throw." Eddie Collins tested Kopf again but the Cincy shortstop "made a beautiful stop" and threw him out easily.

By the end of the Reds' sixth inning the debacle of the White Sox seemed complete. The once proud Chicagoans were now being battered by a 9 to 1 score. Eller opened the inning by reaching first on a hit that eluded James and Collins. James then walked Rath to gain his own pass to the showers in favor of Roy Wilkinson. Daubert bunted for an intended sacrifice but all hands were safe when Schalk threw wildly to Weaver, trying to gain a force out. Groh struck out. Roush slapped a bouncer over Eddie Collins' head, scoring Eller and Rath. Daubert circled to third and Roush pulled up at second. Duncan singled to center registering Daubert with the third run of the inning and Roush moved over to third. On Leibold's throw to Weaver, Duncan pedaled to second. Kopf walked. Weaver scooped up Neale's grounder and threw to Schalk for a force on Ruether. Mercifully Kopf strayed too far off second base and Schalk picked him off on a throw to Risberg to end another embarrassing inning.

Buck tried to start something in the home half of the sixth with a hot smash that Daubert couldn't handle. The ball rolled beyond first base for a hit. Both Jackson and Felsch connected for long drives to center but Roush smothered each one for outs. Gandil flied to Neale to end the inning.

Cincinnati scored its last run after Wilkinson hit Roush to open the eighth. Duncan sacrificed. Weaver handled Kopf's foul pop-up. Neale walked. Raridan singled to left scoring Roush with the Reds' tenth run of the game.

The last of the eighth was Chicago's biggest scoring inning of the World Series but it fell far short of any meaningful consequence. It was the last desperate gasp of a mortally wounded creature. The inning started uneventfully as Leibold flied to Neale. Then the vaunted Chicago scoring machine, which had been held in check for the entire Series, finally let loose. Eddie Collins singled to center, and Weaver lined a two-base drive over Daubert's head, sending Collins to third. Jackson pounded a double to right, scoring Collins and Weaver. The attack stalled as Felsch popped to Daubert. Gandil delivered a fly ball to Neale in right, but when Greasy lost the ball in the sun, Gandil loped around to third, getting credit for a triple and a run driven in as Jackson scored.

Roush then messed up Risberg's fly ball in short center, allowing Gandil to score. Ironically, Edd's only other error was in the eighth inning of the previous game and it also came off the bat of Risberg on a short fly to center. Rath, though, threw out Schalk to end the nuisance uprising.

For just a brief moment, the White Sox faithful may have felt another gargantuan rally might be in the offing in the ninth. Murphy, batting for Wilkinson, reached first base by getting hit by a pitch to start the inning. Leibold then tore into one that looked like a sure double but Roush "made a wonderful diving catch of the drive" that just about put the seal of doom on the White Sox disaster. Eddie Collins kept the rally alive with a single to center, Murphy holding at second. But all Buck could do in his last appearance in the World Series was fly to Neale with Murphy taking third after the catch. Collins stole second without drawing a throw. The most memorable World Series in history ended when Rath tossed out Jackson for the final out.

Buck came out of the World Series with a stellar performance behind him. His classy .324 batting average was second on the White Sox only to Jackson's robust .375 mark which led all hitters on both teams. Greasy Neale surprised everyone by topping all Cincinnati swingers with a .357 average while Edd Roush, the National League's batting champion, slumped to a mediocre .214. Ray Schalk, not known for a charged bat, tied Buck in hitting, giving them the third highest batting averages in the Series. The Reds did stop Eddie Collins, one of the American League's premier batsmen, who could only muster a tepid .226.

In head to head competition with his counterpart, Buck far outshone Heinie Groh in fielding and hitting. A short series such as the fall classic, even with its aberration of 8 games, doesn't really make comparisons reasonable, but going into the World Series Heinie seemed to have a bit of an edge over Buck in reputation, at least among a number of sportswriters. Comparisons were unavoidable. In the final statistics, Buck overwhelmed Groh at the plate with his .324 batting average, getting 11 hits in 34 at bats while Heinie struggled for only 5 safeties in 29 tries for a skimpy .172 mark. In the field both third basemen handled 27 chances. Weaver played flawlessly while Groh committed 2 errors. Putouts and assists were almost identical. Buck had 9 putouts and 18 assists while Groh figured in 8 putouts and 19 assists. In fairness to Groh, he did enter the Series playing with a taped finger on his throwing hand.

The World Series of 1919 rewarded the players with

their richest purse in history since they began sharing a piece of the gate receipts for the first 5 games. Most of the Cincinnati players picked up checks for $5,207.01. They had voted three half shares. The White Sox voted twenty-four full shares which netted each player $3,254.36.

In one of the early advertising testimonials, Buck, Cicotte, Jackson and Felsch earned a little extra money by endorsing an ointment called TURPO. The ad appeared in the *Tribune* on October 2 and ran two columns, the full length of a sports page. There were sketches of each of the players in action with their few words of praise for the product in letters they supposedly wrote to the company. Buck allegedly said: "Give me Turpo all the time. I prefer it to any liniment or ointment as far as cuts, sprains, or bruises are concerned. I have used it and I know."

On the morning of October 10, the *Tribune's* first sports page trumpeted: "REDS ARE NEW WORLD'S CHAMPIONS." Sanborn wrote: "It was significant that they [Cincinnati] burned up the White Sox by a score of 10 to 5 on the anniversary of the day Mrs. O'Leary's cow burned up nine-tenths of Chicago forty-eight years ago. . . .

"The world's series was over five minutes after yesterday's game started and uncovered the guy at whom Dame Rumor has been shooting for a week." If Sanborn meant Williams he didn't go to any pains to elaborate on his unvarnished accusation.

Sanborn did praise the White Sox' courageous effort to get back in the game: "Yesterday under a handicap that would have made the average team quit, the White Sox hammered Eller's shiner for ten hits, and if Edd Roush had not come to the rescue with a miraculous catch in the ninth inning we might now be in Cincinnati for the ninth game of the series."

But the recoil of the Series in the form of recrimination and suspicion virtually buried any kind words that may have been offered on behalf of the White Sox. Sanborn: "The final result has left breaches in the White Sox harmony, feelings of resentment toward some of the players who did not perform up to expectations so deep as practically to impel changes in the personnel of the squad before the season of 1920 impends."

In the same edition of the *Tribune*, Crusinberry closed in on the reality of the situation but backed off in the end: "There was more discussion about the playing of the White Sox than about the peace treaty after the last game. Stories were out that the big gamblers had got to them. But all of them sounded like alibi stuff even if true and Manager Gleason had no excuse to offer for the defeat except that the Reds had played better baseball."

Gleason told Crusinberry, "I was terribly disappointed. I tell you these Reds haven't any business beating a team like the White Sox. We played the worst baseball, in all but a couple of games, that we have played all year. I don't know yet what was the matter. Something was wrong. I didn't like the betting odds. I wish no one bet a dollar on the team." Gleason of course did not reveal his deepest suspicions. Or what he really knew.

But on the same day (the day following the World Series), Chicago *Herald-Examiner* sportswriter Hugh Fullerton, who suspected foul play before the Series opened, sent shock waves through the baseball world: "Yesterday's game in all probability is the last that ever will be played in any world series. If the club owners and those who have the interests of the game at heart have listened during this series, they will call off the annual interleague contest. . . . Yesterday's game also means the disruption of the Chicago White Sox as a ball club. There are seven men on the team who will not be there when the gong sounds next spring, and some of them will not be in either major league."

Fullerton, however, couldn't come up with any hard evidence to support his suspicions when Comiskey called him in to his office to explain what information he had.

One day after the Fullerton bombshell, Comiskey promised a reward of $10,000 "to any one who could furnish him with a clew that would lead to any proof of the truth of the reports" that the White Sox were not trying in the World

Series. Comiskey shortly afterwards told the public: "There is always a scandal of some kind following a big sporting event like the world series. These yarns are manufactured out of whole cloth and grow out of bitterness due to losing wagers. I believe my boys fought the battles of the recent world series on the level, as they have always done. And I would be the first to want information to the contrary—if there be any." He raised the reward another $10,000. "I would give $20,000 to anyone unearthing any information to that effect." On second thought, Comiskey realized he was acting like a spendthrift and quickly reduced the reward back to $10,000.

Several Chicago gamblers who had lost heavily betting on the White Sox, informed Grabiner that a St. Louis movie theatre operator and gambler named Harry Redmon possessed information about the allegedly fixed series. Grabiner and another White Sox official, Norris "Tip" O'Neil, traveled to East St. Louis and interviewed Redmon on Sunday, October 12. Redmon had dropped about $5,000 on the Sox and was eager to recoup his losses. Redmon related details of the World Series fix that were essentially what later became public knowledge. Yet Comiskey, Grabiner and other members of the Sox official family maintained their silence, and Redmon came away empty handed.

Whatever his motives, Comiskey did hire detectives to shadow his suspected ballplayers, but no solid evidence was uncovered. He said on December 15, "I am now very happy to state that we have discovered nothing to indicate any member of my team double crossed me or the public last fall. We have been investigating all these rumors and I have men working sometimes twenty-four hours a day running down clews that promised to produce facts. Nothing has come of them.

"Do not get the impression that we quit investigating. I am still working on the case and will go the limit to get any evidence to bear out the truth of these accusations. And if I land the goods on any of my ballplayers I will see to it there is no place in organized baseball for them.

As Comiskey vowed to continue to run down all the

rumors, the *Tribune's* Sanborn revealed how much of the World Series fix was already common knowledge. Notice his use of the word "scandal" more than nine months before the affair found daylight in the criminal court. Sanborn wasn't the first to use the word, but from that point on it would be a popular tag to the World Series. He wrote, "Although the details of the 'scandal' are probably known to practically everyone who speaks baseball, it may be necessary to inform a few. In brief, it was the effect that six, seven or eight White Sox (the number varies according to the source of the rumor) met in a hotel room in New York, Boston, or Chicago (the place also is elusively variable) before the world's series and split anywhere from $20,000 to $100,-000—depending on the narrator—of a gambling clique's bankroll under an agreement to let Cincinnati win the world's series.

"The report was circulated directly after the Reds won the first two games of the series in Cincinnati. THE TRIBUNE was in possession of the alleged 'facts' immediately. So were Comiskey and Gleason. The White Sox themselves were informed at once of what was being said about them at a meeting called by Mr. Gleason in their own club house."

The *Sporting News* featured a two column head on December 25: "REVIVAL OF SERIES SCANDAL EMPHASIZES NEED OF INQUIRY." Four days later Comiskey and Grabiner met with two St. Louis gamblers, thought to be Harry Redmon and Joe Pesch, in the office of attorney Alfred S. Austrian, legal counsel for both the White Sox and the Cubs. Austrian knew how to cover all bases.

Speaking for Comiskey, Grabiner told the press: "The St. Louis parties came here at the request of Mr. Comiskey. There had been many rumors that they could give information of value. It developed, however, that they could tell only what some one else had told them and that they knew nothing we hadn't heard before."

On the last day of 1919, the *Tribune* headlined: "INVESTIGATION OF ALLEGED SERIES SCANDAL TO BE CONTINUED; COMISKEY SILENT ON FUTURE PLANS TO GET AT TRUTH."

14

The Babe and the Rabbit Ball

As was their custom in recent years, Helen and Buck enjoyed the pleasures of sunny southern California during the winter break. They lived in Los Angeles or in one of its innumerable satellites. In all probability they visited with Hattie and Jim Scott. Buck played golf with Babe Ruth and convinced the home run king to join the baseball team he organized to play exhibition games in California. Ruth had been enticed to the West Coast with the possible offer of a movie contract. Buck also was seen with screen stars such as the matinee idol Douglas Fairbanks and popular cowboy actor Buck Jones. Jones would die tragically in the Cocoanut Grove night club fire in Boston in 1942.

While Buck, the ballplayer, buddied around with Ruth, the Boston Red Sox versatile slugging outfielder and pitcher who had become a superstar was fighting for a renegotiated contract. He was entering the second year of a three year deal calling for $10,000 a year but now was demanding new terms that doubled that figure. And Buck was at his side telling him he was worth the money. Ruth was seeking a reward for creating a sensation by smashing a record shattering 29 home runs in 1919. The previous record in the modern era was held by Gavvy Cravath of the Philadelphia Phillies who clouted 24 round trippers in 1915. Ruth's towering feat dwarfed previous home run totals including his

American League leading 11 homers in 1918. Frank "Home Run" Baker of the Philadelphia A's earned his nickname by leading the American League in homers with 9 in 1911, 10 in 1912, and 12 in 1913. Baker tied Sam Crawford of the Tigers for the lead with 8 in 1914. Bobby Roth of the White Sox and Indians managed to be the AL front runner with seven homers in 1915.

Said the Babe: "I have several propositions on hand, any one of which would pay me more than $10,000 a year." He denied plans to enter the boxing ring but he said he might go into motion pictures.

Ruth's salary squabble with the Boston Red Sox ended in January 5 when Harry Frazee, the embattled owner of the team, sold his phenomenal slugger to the New York Yankees for $100,000. Included in the deal was a loan of $350,000 from the Yankee ownership to Frazee, who was deeply in debt because of notes due to the previous owner of the Red Sox and his string of theatrical flops. (Frazee, a highly regarded theatrical producer despite his alcoholic benders, would strike it rich in 1925 by producing the highly successful Broadway musical, "No, No, Nanette.") Miller Huggins, the little Yankee manager, rushed out to California to sign Ruth at Ruth's price.

Babe Ruth's success in managing to renegotiate his contract and change ball clubs rubbed off on Buck Weaver. Buck was in no rush to get to spring training. Sanborn saw him watching the Chicago Cubs practice at Pasadena on March 6: "The Sox infielder has been playing golf all winter at one of the nearby beaches. He was quite enigmatical as to the date of his joining the Gleason tribe in training. Weaver's contract still has two years to run, but he does not expect to leave California before the end of next week, so it is uncertain whether he is planning to pull a Babe Ruth stunt by demanding a new contract or a trade to the Yankees or merely has a distaste for Waco as a training camp."

Sanborn asked Weaver why he lingered in California but Buck only smiled and told Cubs manager Fred Mitchell that he hoped the Cubs would win the pennant so the Sox and Cubs could get together in the World Series. Buck at the same time probably got the news that his counterpart at Cincinnati, third baseman Heinie Groh, refused to sign a $10,000 a year contract, demanding $11,000. Buck was getting $7,250. The Cincinnati ballplayers were demanding raises amounting to $72,000. Crusinberry commented: "Only a few years ago a magnate could have signed up a whole team of stars for the $72,000 raise asked by the Reds this year." Hod Eller, who had won 2 World Series games and struck out 6 White Sox in a row, demanded his salary be boosted from $4,000 to $20,000 a year.

But Buck couldn't stay away. He arrived in the spring training camp at Waco, Texas, only three days late. The cat was out of the bag, however. Reported the *Tribune:* "Buck Weaver, third baseman extraordinary . . . . had nothing to say regarding his previous ultimatum about more pay or a trade."

Buck got into his first exhibition game against Dallas on March 20, sustained a stone bruise on his right heel, and booted 2 grounders. The next day, opposing Fort Worth, Buck showed his "lack of practice" by muffing one ball and kicking away two more. Weaver watched part of the next game and then went back to the hotel. He said he was going home.

Weaver left for Chicago on Thursday, March 25, hoping to convince Comiskey to come through with a raise in pay. Gleason tried to persuade Buck that he was taking the wrong course, but Buck wouldn't listen. If he couldn't get an increase in pay, Buck said he would demand a transfer to the Yankees. Buck seemed to ignore that he had signed a three year contract the year before. Shades of Babe Ruth.

While Buck rode back to Chicago, Comiskey and Grabiner made it plain they weren't going to put up with what they considered irresponsible demands of their ballplayers. Grabiner said the White Sox were honoring their contract with Weaver and expected him to do the same. "Weaver himself asked for a long term contract last spring, and he got just what he wanted. If we had a bad season financially he would not expect us to ask him to take a cut in salary. We are willing to do our part, and he must do his if he wishes to play ball."

If Buck had any reasonable hopes of changing Comiskey's stance in altering his contract, they would be dashed by reading Comiskey's hard line statement a day after he left for Chicago: "Weaver signed a three year contract at his own demand and without my consent last spring, and he will live up to it or stay out of organized baseball for the rest of his life.

"He told me last spring all about his opportunities to make good up in Wisconsin, where he went during the war, and I advised him to stay there if he thought it was best for him. While I was out of town he came back and signed for three years with Kid Gleason and Harry Grabiner. If I had been there he would have had only a one year contract. Now he will have to live up to the terms he dictated if he wants to play in organized baseball."

Buck didn't tarry long in Chicago. Whether he managed to talk with Comiskey or not, he was back in Texas on April 1 resuming spring training. A *Tribune* story said he "seemed satisfied that he did not get more money out of Comiskey." Satisfied would hardly be the appropriate word. Resigned may have been more accurate. In his first full game back on April 2 Buck got the headline treatment in the *Tribune*: "WEAVER CLOUTS TWO DOUBLES IN 1 INNING AS SOX WIN, 12 TO 6."

Higher ticket prices greeted the fans as the new season started. Comiskey had fought his fellow magnates against raising admissions but the soaring contracts of ballplayers forced the move. The 25 cent ticket was now a relic of the past. And, wrote Crusinberry, "the $10,000 player has replaced the $2,500 performer . . . but regardless of diamond prima donnas and high prices the old game will be the same as twenty years ago."

Crusinberry wasn't entirely accurate in his assessment that "the old game will be the same as twenty years ago." Although the manufacturers and baseball executives denied altering the baseball, it underwent a metamorphosis with the use of an improved yarn and tighter winding in 1920. This ushered in the era of the lively ball and more robust batting averages. Astronomical totals in the home run derby, though, would still remain the exclusive province of George Herman "Babe" Ruth. Before the 1920 season opened, the major league owners voted to prohibit all freak pitches such as the shine ball, the emery ball and the spitball. Only veteran major league pitchers, who had relied on the spitter for their livelihood, would be allowed to continue with the pitch. The pendulum had definitely swung in favor of the hitters.

As the 1920 race got underway, White Sox players had broken up into factions, and internal troubles wracked the team. Crusinberry gave the Sox manager a vote of confidence: "Gleason is just the man to handle anything like that, and he'll handle it if he has to floor a few athletes to make his point clear." The antagonisms on the ball club did not disturb the well-oiled machine on the field. The players put up a united front and roared quickly into first place with 6 straight wins. Buck resumed his galvanizing action on the field as the campaign opened before 25,000 roaring fans in Chicago. He gained most of the attention right from the start as the Sox nipped Detroit 3 to 2 in 11 innings on a four-hitter by Lefty Williams. In the last of the eleventh, Crusinberry reported: "Buck Weaver, who had been ripping things up during the entire battle, scratched a single on a dizzy grounder down to the first baseman. He stole second and galloped home when Eddie Collins drove the ball to the fence in left-center.

"It was one of the most brilliant inaugurals Chicago ever witnessed. It didn't seem to matter that the prices had been raised. The bleachers that in former years were filled with blue shirted working men at 25 a throw were packed with white collar fellows at four bits each, presumably unfortunates who have to work for a salary. The pavilions accommodated a lot of people who didn't get there in time to get good places in the grand stand. The grand stand and boxes were packed with bankers, presidents of big corporations, plasterers, carpenters and bricklayers.

"Among those thousands were the countless bugs who, after the deplorable world's series of last fall, had raised a right hand and sworn, 'Never again.' They simply forgot all about the nasty rumors, the unexpected series defeats, the bum playing, and the other things, and went back for more.

"Buck Weaver, Eddie Collins and Claude Williams did a major portion of the stirring things accomplished by the Sox. Weaver poled 3 singles and a double in 5 trips to the plate, besides stealing second twice and scoring 2 of the 3 runs. He was holding out for more dough this spring. If he goes along like he did yesterday, he can get any amount he asks." Crusinberry was getting carried away, forgetting with whom Buck had to deal with for salary hikes.

Buck was enjoying his greatest start at the plate and was playing a spectacular brand of ball at third base as well. But he lost the security of playing third when Risberg was spiked in a game at New York on May 11. Swede's injury forced Buck to resume his original position at shortstop. Buck's spectacular performance continued there, however, and earned him special attention of the *Sporting News* on May 20. Over a close up shot of Buck on the front page rested the caption: "WORTH MOST ANY PRICE." Said the *Sporting News*: "George Weaver is having a wonderful year. . . . He started out in his old brilliant style at third, then shifted to short when Risberg was hurt, where he has been even more a star if possible. Not only is his fielding spectacular, but he is hitting at a tremendous clip, giving Joe Jackson a run for the honor of being the leading swatsmith on Kid Gleason's fast going bunch of wrecks." Whether at shortstop or third base, Buck continued on a hitting rampage that raged all season.

But it was Babe Ruth's mighty explosions that were causing a sensation in the American League and drawing huge crowds to all the ballparks. The Babe led the New York Yankees to town on June 16. The gold mine drawing card attracted 15,000 fans to Comiskey Park on a Wednesday afternoon, an unheard of crowd for a mid-week game. The big slugger didn't disappoint the bugs. He blasted his eighteenth homer of the season.

To hold the Babe to only one home run a game began to be considered a moral victory. The *Tribune* headline gleefully chortled: "SOX AND BIG WIND HOLD RUTH TO ONE HOMER . . ."

A new sportswriter for the *Tribune*, Irving Vaughn, witnessed the blast. He would remain one of the newspaper's leading baseball writers until after World War II. "Home run No. 19 was awe inspiring to say the least," wrote the overwhelmed Vaughn. "When Ruth came up to perpetrate it, his ears tingled from the taunts of the attending fans who had witnessed two strikeouts in previous appearances of the mighty one. Williams worked on him and got the count to two and two. Then came a beauty waist high. Away went the pill, eastward bound, and the bugs in the right field bleacher craned their necks to watch it pass overhead. When it came down it was far outside the wall. Just how far Homer No. 19 went in its travels is not known. It must have taken in at least 425 feet before it came down to earth. Then it rolled and bounced on its way across the soccer field."

The Babe mesmerized the baseball world with his gargantuan wallops. He drew thousands of fans from the opposing teams just to see him send one of his patented high flyers out of the park, even if it meant a loss to the home team. On Saturday, June 19, the White Sox beat the Yankees, 6 to 5, but Vaughn wrote: "Some 25,000 didn't get a satisfactory dividend on their investment. Most of them came not to see the Sox win or lose but in anticipation of witnessing 'Babe' Ruth in one or more of his home run acts. 'Babe' didn't put on his specialty stunt because a thrown ball jarred his scalp loose in the second inning and necessitated his retirement in the fourth."

It was Buck who knocked his old California golfing buddy out of the game. Ruth sauntered up to the plate to start the second inning accompanied by "a lot of whoops and yells." He responded by singling to center. Weaver snapped up the next hopper, stepped on second and fired to first for an attempted double play. But Ruth got in the way of the ball as he charged into the bag and got smacked over the right eye. He went down but regained his bearings in a few minutes and tried to stay in the game. When he got a dizzy spell, missing a fly ball, he decided to leave the field. Ruth suffered "a huge bump over his eye."

Despite the exhilarating fresh winds of excitement generated throughout baseball by Babe Ruth, the stench of gambling and fixed games would not go away. In early January, 1920, major league owners had been expected to take up the problem of gambling at their meetings but nothing came of it. "The gamblers," reported the *Tribune* on May 16, "are still doing business at Fenway park. Several hundred of them were gathered at their customary hangout in the right field pavilion." A little more than a week later the *Tribune* carried a front page banner: "CUBS PARK RAIDED; 47 BETTORS ARE JAILED." But the story confessed that most of the men were not professional gamblers. They were "just fans who wanted a little excitement on the side." Johnson announced he had hired a private detective agency to obtain evidence of gambling in every park in the league.

Reminders of the gambling problems were persistent. Lee Magee, who made the world tour as a member of the Giants, sued the Chicago Cubs for breach of contract in June. The Cubs released Magee after team president William Veeck learned directly from Magee on February 10 that he had made "intentional wild throws and otherwise" played to cause his team, then the Cincinnati Reds, to lose to Boston in a game at Boston on July 25, 1918. Magee implicated Hal Chase as the mastermind of the attempt to throw the game, which the Reds won anyway in the thirteenth inning. Magee lost the suit and in August signed to play with a semipro team in Kenosha, Wisconsin.

Chase by this time was out of major league baseball, having been given the heave-ho by manager McGraw in September, 1919. Chase left the Giants quietly and would never play organized ball again. Asked why this happened, McGraw, generally an expansive fellow with the press, would only say laconically, "I cannot talk of the matter."

But the president of the National League, John Heydler, provided the key to the matter later when he confided to Fred Lieb. Lieb, in his autobiographical work *Baseball As I Have Known It*, reported Heydler as saying, "I never was satisfied with my earlier acquital [sic] of Chase. I was unconvinced. Eventually I got a signed affidavit from the Boston gambler and a photographic copy of Chase's canceled check for five hundred dollars given him by a gambler as pay for throwing a game in 1918. I took this evidence to Charles Stoneham (owner-president of the Giants) saying, 'When I permitted Chase to play early last spring I said I had no real proof of Hal's throwing a game. Now I have that proof.' I handed him the affidavit and Chase's canceled check and then told Stoneham 'Please notify your manager that Chase will not play in any future game with the Giants.' Stoneham said, 'If that is the way it is, that's it.' The Giants owner took it quietly, saying, 'John, you had no other choice.' "

Giants third baseman Heinie Zimmerman fell under Chase's spell and was banished along with the slick fielding, scheming first baseman for throwing games in 1919. Heinie, who lived in New York, went back to work as a plumber. Chase returned to outlaw ball in 1920 and would be revealed later as a full fledged, full-time crooked gambler in the 1919 World Series.

Besides gambling and plugging leaks that continued to plague baseball, the National Commission had been drifting rudderless without a chairman since February 11. Herrmann had finally resigned and left office while the major league owners opened their annual meetings at the Congress Hotel in Chicago. One of the tasks of the owners was to consider candidates to replace him. But before this could be done, the two factions in the American League, split over supporting Johnson and his policies, had to be brought together, at least temporarily. Chicago, New York and Boston formed the anti-

Johnson forces while the other five clubs remained loyal to their league chief. Comiskey had been Johnson's enemy for several years. Owners Ruppert and Huston of the Yankees and Frazee of the Red Sox had become embroiled in a bitter fight with Johnson the previous summer. Frazee already had raised Johnson's ire for not controlling gambling at Fenway Park.

The conflict grew out of peculiar behavior by Carl Mays, the submarine pitching right-hander for the Red Sox. He finished his second inning in a game against the White Sox in Chicago on Sunday, July 13, before 22,000 fans, then stomped off the mound, walked through the dugout and continued to the clubhouse. Red Sox manager Ed Barrow heard Mays angrily predict, "I'll never pitch for this ball club again." Mays had been complaining about the poor support he was getting from his teammates. In the first inning the White Sox scored four times after a rookie second baseman failed to execute a force out at second base when he became befuddled by the base running of Eddie Collins. Barrow thought Mays was upset because catcher Wally Schang hit him in the back of the head when he tried to cut down Eddie Collins stealing second base. Barrow sent one of his pitchers to tell Mays the team was waiting for him to get back on the mound. The perturbed pitcher refused. He changed into civilian clothes, left the ballpark and departed for the East Coast.

Frazee phoned Barrow and instructed his manager: "Don't suspend this fellow. The Yankees want him and I can get a lot of money for him." New York purchased Mays for $40,000 and two pitchers two weeks later.

Johnson was enraged. He had ordered the ball clubs not to deal for Mays until the pitcher returned to good standings, so he canceled the deal, suspended Mays and ordered umpires not to allow Mays to play for New York. Ruppert and Huston immediately struck back by going to court and obtaining temporary injunctions to set aside Johnson's suspension of their new hurler. On October 25, the New York Supreme Court "granted a permanent injunction restraining Johnson from interfering with Mays' performing with the

Yankees." Although Johnson would remain president of the American League until the end of the 1927 season, the Mays decision signaled the end of his once czarist-like dominion over the league he created and nurtured for so many years. In essence it really meant the end of the National Commission.

Somehow the two factions were brought together by William Richardson, part-owner of the Washington Senators, who said he was neutral in the controversy. It must have been a masterful stroke of diplomacy to get Johnson to go along since his opponents made no secret of their desire to boot him out of baseball. Finally five candidates were selected by the major league owners as a possible chairman for the National Commission and subsequently approved by Heydler and Johnson.

The five finalists were U.S. federal district judge Kenesaw Mountain Landis, viewed as a friend of organized ball since the Federal League fight; Harvey T. Woodruff, sports editor of the Chicago *Tribune;* "Big Bill" Edwards, an ex-Princeton University athlete; James A. Walker, a New York state senator who later became the popular and flamboyant mayor of New York City; and John Conway Toole, a prominent New York lawyer.

The final choice would be made by the two league presidents. Heydler expressed a desire to make a decision quickly but Johnson said he needed more time to study their qualifications. By mid-summer Johnson still was not ready to name his choice. In fact he would never be ready to select from those five.

While the White Sox beat the Cleveland Indians at Comiskey Park on June 26 behind Buck's 3 hits, another ball game was in progress at Wrigley Field. A high school boy named Louis Gehrig hit a home run with the bases loaded to lead New York City's High School of Commerce to a 12 to 6 win over Lane Tech High, Chicago's prep champions, in what was called the high school world series. Young Gehrig already was known as the "Babe Ruth" of the high schools.

With the White Sox in the thick of the pennant race

with Cleveland and New York, Buck displayed more than
his daily high spirits, his always pleasant grin and his constant chatter in the infield. At the plate, Buck added dramatic histrionics to his repertoire in trying to push a run
across the plate. In the first inning of a game in the middle
of July, with 1 out and Nemo Leibold on third, Buck faced
pitcher Rollie Naylor of the Philadelphia A's. Crusinberry
describes the delicious chicanery attempted by the ebullient
Chicago third baseman. Naylor "cut loose with a wild pitch
that bent down into the dirt and cracked against the toes of
Weaver's right foot, then bounced up and hit catcher Cy Perkins in the neck and caromed off to the grand stand.

"Leibold ran in and crossed the plate. Perkins stood bent
over rubbing his Adam's apple. Buck Weaver lay on the
ground, smiling up at Umpire Tommy Connelly. It's doubtful if he knew whether the ball really hit Weaver or just hit
the ground and bounced up into Perkins' neck. If it didn't hit
Weaver, Leibold should be allowed to score. If it did hit Weaver, Leibold would have to return to third base, and Weaver
go to first.

"Weaver saw the situation. That's why he sat there smiling as if happy to see the Sox get a run. He wanted the decision made so that Leibold could score. Umpire Connelly
stood with his eyes on Weaver. He thought the ball hit him
on the foot, but knew if it did, it must have hurt like fury,
and there was Buck, smiling and happy as if tickled to see
the run scored.

"Nothing was said for a moment, and then the water
began to come into Weaver's eyes and his forced smile departed. There was a twinkle in Tommy Connelly's eye as he
said, 'Go back to third base Leibold and you get up and go
to first base Weaver.'

"Then Buck grabbed his injured foot and began rubbing
it. 'Say, it felt like the blood was running out of my toes and
filling my shoes,' said Weaver in telling about it afterward.
'But I thought maybe I could get away with it.' "

Going into August the White Sox trailed in third place
behind Cleveland and New York, only 4½ games off the

pace. But they had just been humiliated in New York, bowing 4 out of 6 times, including a 20 to 5 drubbing. In that disaster, the White Sox committed 7 errors, with Buck contributing 4. "They kicked and heaved the ball around in a manner that would have made a high school team ashamed of itself. . . . Only five were made in the first two innings."

Cicotte started on the hill and surrendered 9 hits in 4 innings. His relief, a lad named Spencer Heath, stayed around to get plastered for 6 hits in one inning. There may have been a legitimate excuse for this incredible collapse. White Sox traveling secretary, Walter Clark, had notified the hotel that the team would arrive in New York about 1 o'clock in the morning. "When they arrived no one behind the hotel counter had ever heard of them. Some of the boys got to bed by 3 o'clock A.M. and some later." The Sox may have been bothered by their lack of sleep on defense but they found enough energy to pound out 16 hits. Weaver kept up his attack at the plate, going 3 for 5 including a double.

It was obvious that the ball had been juiced up. Batting averages soared to new heights. As the pennant chase headed into August, Tris Speaker now topped the hitters with an amazing .412 average. In his wake followed George Sisler with .393, Joe Jackson at .392, Babe Ruth at .389, Sam Rice of Washington at .366, Eddie Collins at .357, Bob Meusel of New York at .350, Buck Weaver at .339, Happy Felsch at .328 and Shano Collins at .316. Buck was in heavyweight company and the Sox had five hitters in the elite ten.

Of all the heavy hitters none could come near attracting the huge crowds that swarmed to the ballparks to give witness to the towering blasts of the mighty Babe. Added to that, the Yankees, only 2½ games ahead of the White Sox, surged into Chicago for a critical four game series starting Sunday, August 1. Capacity for Comiskey Park in those years was 32,000 people, yet the headlines trumpeted that 40,000 enthusiasts propelled themselves like lemmings into the stadium. General admission stopped one hour before game time. The overflow crowd rimmed the outfield. Some of the crowd climbed a wall and "one mob rushed a bleacher gate and broke it down in spite of the resources of the police, who didn't take time to count those who eluded them. Whatever the actual count was, it was the biggest crowd that ever watched a ball game in Chicago."

Sanborn observed the mesmerized crowd: "And every pair of eyes were focused on Ruth from the time he sauntered into the arena all alone a couple of minutes behind the rest of the Yankees, until he had completed his fourth and last time at bat without getting his thirty-eighth four bagger." The *Tribune* headlined: "CICOTTE BLANKS RUTH AND YANKS." Cicotte threw a five-hitter as the Sox won, 3 to 0, to pull within 1½ games of second place. Ruth would never hit a homer against Cicotte.

It took an exceptional attraction to draw big crowds in daylight hours during the week in those years. Ruth was that singularly exceptional attraction. On Monday, August 2, 30,000 fans, many of whom ditched their jobs, swarmed out to Comiskey Park. They watched the Yankees win, 7 to 0, and saw the Babe pole his thirty-eighth homer of the season. The White Sox bounced back the next day, winning behind Red Faber, 3 to 1, before 27,000. Faber used his most effective weapon against Ruth. He walked him three times, and White Sox fans booed. They wanted to see the Babe swat one.

Dickie Kerr held Ruth to a single in the final game of the series as the Chicagoans mauled New York, 10 to 3, before another big crowd of 28,000. Ruth drew much of the 125,000 fans for the four game series. Of course the close pennant race with the White Sox in the thick of it had something to do with attracting the bugs, but those gargantuan throngs would not have been in the stands without Ruth as the special attraction. He packed them in wherever he essayed his Herculean swing.

Only a game out of second at the end of the Yankee series, the White Sox finally copped second place on August 9 when they swept a doubleheader from Washington. Buck played a key role as the Sox surged towards the league lead. The next day the Sox went into the last of the tenth, tied 3 to 3. "Weaver made a two base hit out of a single and then Jackson drove a long single on which Weaver rode home standing up." The next afternoon Weaver came through again, leading the Sox to a 2 to 1 victory. Buck "boosted a rainbow single over [third baseman Frank] Ellerbee's head with the bases full in the lucky seventh . . . and scored the two runs which enabled the White Sox to win their fourth straight from Washington and to climb a whole game closer to the lead."

That same day, August 11, former White Sox first baseman Babe Borton, who ironically was part of the trade to the Yankees for Hal Chase in 1913, was released by the Vernon club of the Pacific Coast League "for the good of baseball." And the following day the wife of a Salt Lake City outfielder went to bat in a special hearing requested by her to try clearing her husband from gambling charges that led to his suspension and release. The dike against corruption in baseball seemed to be leaking everywhere.

The White Sox had reeled off seven straight victories before losing the second game of a doubleheader against the Tigers at Detroit on August 14. But in defeat, Buck sparkled on defense. "Weaver made a great play to retire Cobb on a bunt towards third in the fifth. . . . Buck scooped the ball on the run and threw it without straightening up, nailing Ty by a step and causing a lot of trouble for Umpire Dineen because the local fans did not realize that Cobb had slowed up."

Cobb apparently ignored his own warning about trying to bunt against Buck. Weaver played a shallow third base, about 15 feet closer to the plate than other third basemen. His idea was to cut down more runners than he otherwise could even at the expense of a few more errors. His body and hand movements were as agile and as quick as the sudden spring of a cat. Cobb reminisced years later: "I'd see that filthy uniform standing there, the funny face grinning at me and I wanted to lay one down that line more'n anything in the world. The s.o.b.'d throw me out every time!" In talking to James T. Farrell, author of *My Baseball Diary*,

Cobb recalled: "Weaver was one third baseman I didn't try to bunt against. I was supposed to be a fast man getting to first base but I knew better than to lay one down in Weaver's direction. There was no chance beating out a bunt to him." Farrell wrote: "Weaver was supposed to have [a] standing bet with Ty Cobb that anytime Ty bunted towards third base, he could throw him out."

On the morning of August 16, the White Sox and Indians were virtually entwined in a tie for the lead. Cleveland gripped first place by a slim four percentage points. But later that day the baseball world was diverted from the torrid pennant race by the greatest tragedy in major league history. Cleveland's brilliant shortstop, twenty-nine year old Ray Chapman, was struck in the head by a pitched ball and died early the next morning in a New York hospital.

Chapman was batting against New York's Carl Mays at the Polo Grounds. Leading off the fifth inning with the count 1 and 1, Chapman, as usual, hugged the plate in a crouch. He tried to dodge a fastball streaking towards his head but the ball hit him on the left side of the skull. Chapman collapsed. Umpire Tom Connelly immediately called for doctors. Several hurried out of the stands. They brought Chapman to his feet when he should have been carried off the field on a stretcher. As he headed for the clubhouse with the help of two teammates, he collapsed again. Before being rushed to the hospital, "Chappie" regained consciousness in the clubhouse for a moment and told a close friend, "I'm all right. Tell Mays not to worry."

X rays revealed fractures on both sides of the head. Shortly before midnight Chapman underwent surgery and died just after 2 A.M. Ironically, Chapman, a nine year veteran with the Indians, planned to retire before the 1920 season. A year earlier, he had married the daughter of the president of the East Ohio Gas Company and was ready to go to work for his father-in-law. But Indian officials and fans persuaded Ray to come back for another season. Everyone could smell a pennant under the managerial reins of Tris Speaker and Chapman was a needed warrior in the Tribe camp.

Chapman was an outstanding fielder and had a sharp eye at the plate. Years earlier Comiskey sought to make a trade for the Indian shortstop while Buck was floundering in that position. Chapman led American League batters with 84 walks in 1918. He was no slouch as a hitter, either, batting .302 in 1917, .300 in 1919 and .303 at the time of his death. He was an accomplished bunter as well as shown by his major league record breaking 67 sacrifice hits in 1917 and he continued to lead the majors in sacrifice hits for the next two years.

Mays broke down completely when he heard of Chapman's death and refused to talk to anyone before giving himself up to the district attorney's office. With his eyes filled with tears, Mays was able to tell his story: "It was a straight fast ball and not a curve. When Chapman came to bat, I got the sign for a straight fast ball which I delivered. It was a little too close and I saw Chapman duck his head in an effort to get out of the path of the ball. He was too late, however, and a second later he fell to the ground. It was the most regrettable incident in my career and I would give anything if I could undo what has happened."

Harold "Muddy" Ruel caught Mays that fatal afternoon. Ruel, one of baseball's most respected, urbane, intelligent and sophisticated individuals, would become a successful lawyer and an executive in the baseball commissioner's office. He said the pitch most likely would have been called a strike had Chapman not crowded the plate in his familiar crouch and been hit.

The district attorney's office released Mays immediately, ruling Chapman's death "purely accidental."

But many other ballplayers were enraged and not so lenient. Mays had a reputation as a "head hunter," firing bean balls at opposing batters. Players on the Boston and Detroit teams were considering a petition to bar Mays from organized baseball. White Sox players publicly condemned umpires and league officials for not being tougher on Mays for hitting so many batters. The White Sox sent a floral piece to Chapman's home.

In what turned out to be a bit of hyperbole, Ban Johnson said, "I could not conscientiously attempt to make trouble for Mr. Mays. But it is my honest belief that Mr. Mays never will pitch again."

Cooler heads prevailed. Cleveland manager Tris Speaker said, "I do not hold Mays responsible in any way. I have been active in discouraging my players from holding Mays responsible and in respect to Chapman's memory, as well as for the good of baseball, I hope all this talk of this kind will stop. I realize that Mays feels this thing as deeply as any man could and I do not want to add to his burden."

Mays went back to the mound exactly one week after the fatal pitch and shut out the Detroit Tigers, 10 to 0, in New York.

One day after Chapman died a news story out of New York reported: "Introduction of headgear for batsmen is being considered by baseball club owners. . . . Humanitarian impulse quite as much as anxiety to protect the heavy financial investment in their star performers has moved club interests to consider headgear as a desirable addition to player's protective apparatus . . ."

Batting helmets were introduced into the major leagues in 1956, thirty-six years after Ray Chapman lost his life in the batter's box.

On August 21, five days after Chapman was struck down, the White Sox grabbed sole possession of first place. By August 27 they forged to a 3½ game lead by blasting the Yankees 16 to 5 in New York. While Buck knocked out 2 doubles, Ruth clobbered his forty-forth home run. George Sisler of the Browns trailed Ruth in the home run derby with 16. In the National League, outfielder Cy Williams of the Phillies led the home run race with 13.

It looked as if the White Sox were ready to spring ahead in a final stretch drive. The offense had been explosive and the pitching had returned to full strength with Red Faber recovered from a lame arm. The big four—Cicotte, Williams, Faber and Kerr—were all destined to win at least 20 games, the first major league mound corps to have four starters attain such lofty records.

But the White Sox couldn't hold on. They nose-dived

into a 7 game swoon. Their fielding became sloppy and Sanborn accused the Sox of running the "bases like high school boys." Suddenly their hitting evaporated as the Red Sox swept a 3 game series in Boston, forcing Chicago to surrender first place on September 1 to Cleveland.

When the White Sox returned home, Eddie Collins went to see Comiskey. He told the Sox owner that some of his teammates threw the Boston series. Perhaps he mentioned a rain soaked game in which "a return throw by Jackson got away from Risberg, and cost two runs." Or in the same game with runners on first and third and 1 out, first baseman Shano Collins snared a hard grounder. It looked like an easy double play "but Risberg could not find second base after taking the throw, so his return was delayed until the batsman beat it and let the runner score off third." How could Eddie Collins explain errors by Shano Collins, Dickie Kerr and himself—all in one inning? How could Collins distinguish beyond a reasonable doubt deliberate mishaps from honest mistakes? Comiskey absorbed the information, thanked Collins and sat on what might have been a bombshell. McMullin earlier in the season had approached Buck about getting in on some easy money. Weaver angrily rebuffed the utility infielder and warned if he ever brought it up again, he'd beat the hell out of him. Buck again chose to maintain his silence just as Comiskey did with Collins' allegations. Collins also decided to take the matter no further. According to Harold Seymour, author of *Baseball: The Golden Age*, "two of the Square Sox [later] testified that some of the players purposely tossed away a three game series at Boston on Chicago's last eastern trip of the season."

Cleveland and New York folded into losing streaks of their own but recovered simultaneously with the White Sox. The Chicagoans were matching the Indians and Yankees stride for stride despite allegedly tainted players. Or were the Sox winning and losing because players, rumored to be in the grasp of gamblers, were watching the scoreboard, and purposely matching their opponents to keep the race close? Were the Sox that strong that they could turn up the power anytime they wanted to? In any case, the three contenders could not have been much closer if welded together. The standings on the morning after Labor Day, September 6, showed Cleveland in first place with a record of 81-49 at .623; Chicago second, 81-51 at .614 and New York, third, 82-52 at .612.

As Buck and the White Sox pulled out of their slumps— Weaver had connected for only 2 singles in 27 at bats—far more troublesome developments erupted. They would have shattering consequences both for Buck and the team. A new gambling and fixing scandal hit the newspapers. Ironically, though the new allegations also originated in Chicago, this time it was in the bailiwick of the National League Cubs. President William Veeck of the Chicago club told the press on September 4 that he had received phone calls and telegrams warning that the Cubs-Philadelphia Phillies game on August 31 might be fixed, since Detroit gamblers were betting heavily on Philadelphia. On orders from Veeck, Fred Mitchell, the Cubs manager, replaced scheduled starting pitcher Claude Hendrix with Grover Cleveland "Pete" Alexander. Veeck promised Alexander a bonus if he won the game. The Cubs lost anyway, 3 to 0. Hendrix swore his innocence but was not taken on the road trip to Pittsburgh.

On September 5 Veeck asked the local chapter of the Baseball Writers' Association to open an investigation into the charges of crookedness among Cubs ballplayers. He told them, "My sole idea is to have this investigation open and effective that the charge can never be brought that the Chicago National League club attempted to protect in any manner whatsoever any player against whom there is any evidence." On the south side of town, a leading baseball executive may have squirmed at that pronouncement.

Veeck needed no help from the baseball writers. Within two days on September 7, Chief Justice of the Criminal Courts, Charles A. McDonald, called the Cook County grand jury into session to investigate the Cubs-Phillies game. He also recommended that the grand jury look into the problem of the gambling connection in baseball. McDonald did not reach his decision independently. He had been playing golf with his close friend, Ban Johnson, president of the American League and the most powerful man on the baseball commission. Johnson urged the judge to call the grand jury into session.

Now that the grand jury was beginning to turn the spotlight on gambling and thrown games, bookies publicly admitted they had avoided action on major league baseball. Until the 1919 World Series, Chicago bookmakers were among the leading operators handling bets from all over the country. When stories started circulating about fixed games again, ". . . the bookies folded their bankrolls and turned to other fields. One reformed baseball bookie . . . said, 'We now refuse to bet on anything that talks.' "

In the helter-skelter pennant chase, the White Sox slipped to third place on September 11, dropping a wild 9 to 7 clash to Boston while committing a wholesale lot of 6 errors. Risberg, Weaver and Eddie Collins each contributed two apiece. Though 6 errors in one game might have looked suspicious, it was not uncommon in those years for teams to commit errors on a grand scale.

On the following day Sanborn pointed scornfully to the major league moguls who dallied so long over the problem of gamblers and charges of fixed ball games. This was a change of tack for the veteran sportswriter who had generally supported the interest of the owners in the past. "If the promotors of professional baseball had heeded the warnings dinned into their ears for years against the inroads of the betting fraternity on their business they would have headed off much of the trouble that has come to them and which is still coming to them.

"Granting, for the sake of a point, that Chase was wholly innocent of the charges made, it would have been better if one man suffer injustice for the good of the game than that scores of ball players should be made to suffer the injustice of suspicion, [as] has been the result of inaction in the Chase case . . .

"The Chicago National and American League clubs,

which unquestionably have done more in recent years than any other clubs to throttle the gambling evil, have been the worst sufferer (sic) up to date."

As if to underscore the gambling problem, detectives raided the bleachers at Comiskey Park the next day and arrested five fans. In the meantime, big-time gamblers in the box seats near the home team dugout were unmolested according to a *Tribune* "investigator." He heard them wagering $300 to $380 on a bet "probably much larger than the total amount involved in the bleacher affair."

Off the field drama continued to rival the action on the diamond. New York *Sun* sportswriter Joe Vila, who had vouchsafed the honesty of the 1919 World Series in an article he had written the previous December, now charged that the World Series was crooked. Louis Comiskey fired a telegram to Vila the same day as the gambling raid at the ballpark, inviting him to appear before the Cook County grand jury and present any evidence he had of "crookedness in baseball." Vila did not appear.

As the day dawned on Thursday, September 16, the White Sox were still lodged in third place, 2½ games behind the leading Yankees and the Indians were sandwiched in second place, 1½ games out. Fourteen games remained on the schedule as the Sox were poised for their final drive for the flag. Of the fourteen six were against Cleveland and New York. The situation didn't look particularly bright since the Sox had won only 8 of their last 19 encounters. But playing their close rivals head to head would offer them more of a chance to leapfrog into the lead.

That afternoon the Yankees strutted onto the field for the beginning of a crucial three game series at Comiskey Park. More than 30,000 rabid fans, attracted by Ruth and the heated pennant race, screamed their delight as the Sox downed New York, 8 to 3, behind the slants of Dickie Kerr. The little left-hander earned the headline: "KERR HOLDS RUTH HELPLESS AT BAT." It was a mixed day of excitement and disappointment for the boys' band from Ruth's school in Baltimore. The boys had made a special trip to

Chicago and paraded around the field before the game. The Sox knocked the Yankees out of the top perch but they were still ensconced in third place.

Another mob of more than 30,000, which included thousands of women admitted free in a Friday afternoon Ladies' Day special, swarmed into the baseball palace of the world and again were rewarded with a Sox victory. Faber held on for a 6 to 4 win. The awesome respect for Ruth was shown again in the headline: "RED FABER HOLDS RUTH HOMERLESS." The Sox still trailed in third place, a game and a half out of the lead.

For the third day in a row, Chicagoans flocked to the ballpark and the huge throng overflowed onto the field and had to be contained by ropes that circled the outfield. The White Sox didn't disappoint their wild followers who had caught pennant fever. The *Tribune* headlined Sunday morning, September 19: "SOX ON RAMPAGE CRUSH YANKEES IN 15 TO 9 BATFEST." The Pale Hose pounded out 21 hits with Weaver cannonading four of them. The Sox edged into second place by sweeping the series but they were still a game and a half behind Cleveland who refused to buckle and only four percentage points ahead of New York.

Batting averages released that Sunday showed Jackson hitting a hefty .378, but it was only third best in the league, topped by Sisler at .397 and Speaker at .390. Eddie Collins ranked fifth with .366 and Weaver, swatting at a .331 clip, was twelfth highest, even outhitting Cobb, who was in a batting slump at .327. Hap Felsch trailed Buck at .330.

But all was not coming up roses. Right next to the headline chortling about the Sox final victory over the Yankees was a two column head that must have caused some anxiety among those concerned: "IS ANYTHING WRONG WITH SOX? 1919 WORLD SERIES SCANDAL REVIVED; FAN SEEKS ANSWER TO RUMORS! The article was supposedly written by Fred M. Loomis, a Chicago businessman who was said to be a personal friend of several members of the White Sox. He also was closely associated with Charles Ringling of the Ringling Brothers Circus. Loomis signed the letter but it was actually ghostwritten by the *Tribune* sportswriter James Crusinberry: "Widespread circulation has been given to reports from various sources that the world series of last fall between the Chicago White Sox and the Cincinnati Reds was deliberately and intentionally lost through an alleged conspiracy between certain unnamed members of the Chicago White Sox team and certain gamblers. . . .

"At this time, therefore, it occurs to me, and I know it likewise appears to others in the same light, that the game must be cleaned up. . . .

"An investigation might disclose that there is absolutely nothing to these reports. Therefore, there is all the more reason why an investigation should be made. . . .

". . . it makes no difference who is hit in the investigation, from the president of either major league down to the clubhouse boy in the smallest league in the country. The game must be protected. . . .

"There is a perfectly good grand jury located in this county. The citizens and taxpayers of Illinois are maintaining such an institution for the purpose of investigating any infractions of the law.

"Those who have in their possession the evidence of gambling last fall in the world series should come forward with it and present it in a manner that may give assurance to the whole country that justice will be done in this where the confidence of the people seems to have been so flagrantly violated."

Growing and persistent demands such as the so-called Loomis letter to investigate the 1919 World Series turned the attention of the grand jury away from the suspicions of a fix in the Cub-Phils' game of August 31. Shortly after the hearing got underway on September 22, the grand jury would be diverted from its expressed purpose of probing the gambling connection with baseball in general to focus completely on the alleged conspiracy of the White Sox to throw the 1919 World Series.

15

The Last Race

The White Sox left Chicago for their desperate three game series with Cleveland on Tuesday night, September 21. The grand jury hearing would start churning the next day in the Criminal Courts Building at 54 W. Hubbard Street. Though there seemed to be some understanding that the hearings would be public, the sessions moved behind closed doors. Whatever information leaked out of the jury room to the press was offered voluntarily by the assistant state's attorney Harley Replogle. His boss, state's attorney Maclay Hoyne, was vacationing in New York. A Democrat, he had been defeated in the primary election on September 15 and would soon be replaced by Republican Robert E. Crowe. Other revelations came from the witnesses themselves as they talked freely to reporters.

The first day's testimony caused sensational headlines. In heavy black block letters streaming across the front page of the *Tribune*, the long festering suspicions were exposed to blinding daylight: "BARE 'FIXED' WORLD SERIES." The drop head was even more condemning: "FIVE WHITE SOX MEN INVOLVED HOYNE AID SAYS." A quotation above the lead, lifted from the body of the story, was explosive: "The last world series between the Chicago White Sox and the Cincinnati Reds was not on the square. From five to seven players on the White Sox are involved." Assistant state's attorney Replogle made the electrifying charge but he did not divulge the name of any of the White Sox players.

Much of the early fireworks came as a result of bitter feelings between two ballplayers, Buck Herzog and Rube Benton, who had been teammates on the New York Giants. Herzog, now an infielder with the Cubs, dropped a bombshell the first day when he testified that two of his friends, Art Wilson and Norman Boeckel of the Boston Braves, had sworn in an affidavit the previous May that they heard Benton say a month earlier that he was "tipped off" by Hal Chase before the World Series to bet on Cincinnati. The Boston players claimed Benton said he had won $3,800.

Ban Johnson, Charles Comiskey and William Veeck also testified the first day but their information did not evoke any sensational headlines. But before entering the jury room, Johnson admitted to reporters that he had evidence of crooked ball games the year before. Why that didn't merit a big splash in the press is a mystery.

That Wednesday night Herzog told the *Tribune* what he probably testified before the grand jury. He said he and Benton had appeared before National League president John Heydler on June 25 in his New York office. Both told their stories, supported by affidavits. Benton accused Herzog of offering him an $800 bribe the previous September to lose to the Cubs. Herzog said Heydler listened to both stories and then presented him with a letter stating he was "convinced Herzog had nothing to do with gambling." According to Herzog, Heydler gave Benton "a calling." Heydler then said the whole matter should be dropped and kept quiet.

Rube Benton took the witness stand on the second day of the grand jury hearing. He denied betting big money on the Series although he admitted being aware of the fix. He struck back at Herzog by telling how the previous September Herzog offered him an $800 bribe to lose to the Cubs. Benton said Chase and Zimmerman also were in on the deal with Herzog. The Giant pitcher said he immediately reported it to McGraw but the Giant manager did not pursue the matter.

Herzog said he thought Benton was seeking revenge for a fine he laid on him when he was Benton's manager at Cincinnati.

In this netherworld of baseball, hidden from the unsuspecting fans, could Benton be considered an accessory before the fact and Heydler, Herzog, Wilson and Boeckle be considered accessories after the fact? Certainly Heydler, as president of the National League, had the greater responsibility to bring the scandal to light voluntarily before being called before a criminal grand jury. And what of Johnson, who admitted publicly the first day of the hearings that he had evidence of crooked ball games the year before?

Johnson threw more oil on the fire that Thursday, September 23, when he told reporters: "I heard several weeks ago a vague statement that the White Sox would not dare win the pennant this season. That statement was repeated several times, and within the last few weeks it has been hinted, more or less openly, that the Sox would not dare win because the gambling syndicate would tell what it knew of certain players in the Cincinnati-Sox world's championship games in 1919."

Johnson also admitted he knew about the holding up of salary checks of eight White Sox players following the 1919 Series. He said three players—Gandil, Cicotte and McMullen —had asked for help in getting their money from Comiskey.

By the end of the second day of hearings, Henry H. Brigham, foreman of the grand jury, expressed his dismay: "Chicago, New York, Cincinnati and St. Louis gamblers are bleeding baseball and corrupting players. We are going the limit in this inquiry, but at present we cannot give out evidence we have uncovered. I am shocked at the rotteness [sic] so far revealed." Despite Brigham's emotional reaction, the *Tribune* concluded that, "No indictments are expected."

In Cleveland that Thursday afternoon the ballpark was a "maelstrom of enthusiasm" with all the reserved seats sold for the entire series. Reflecting the widespread interest in the big series were the out-of-town sportswriters covering the games from Boston, New York, Pittsburgh, Detroit and

Buffalo. They could report that the White Sox steamrollered over Cleveland, 10 to 3, to pull within a half game of the lead. It looked as if the Indians were finally beginning to wilt under the unrelenting pressure of the Sox, who won their seventh game in a row. Cleveland's 3 errors helped boost the Sox score which had been ballooned by a 15 hit attack. Buck, however, could account for only one of them.

Wrote Sanborn concerning Johnson's statement that he was told the Sox dare not win the pennant: "Certain Sox players who have heard the report are said to have been spurred on to make every effort to win as a vindication, regardless of athletic honors or monetary reward."

But on Friday, the White Sox slipped back to a 1½ game deficit when they lost a tough 2 to 0 game that could have gone their way. They were stopped cold on a 3-hitter by a pitcher named Walter "Duster" Mails who had been recently discarded by the Brooklyn Dodgers. Faber went to the hill for the Sox and surrendered 9 hits. But the Indians could only scratch him for 1 run in the first and 1 in the second with the help of "flukey" base hits.

In the first inning left fielder Charlie Jamieson bounced the ball over Faber's head. Eddie Collins snared it behind second base but his throw was too late to get the runner. Second baseman Bill Wambsganss sacrificed. Then Jamieson scampered to third as Speaker was retired and scored on right fielder Elmer Smith's single to right.

Rookie Joe Sewell, who recently had been brought up from the minors to fill Ray Chapman's shoes at shortstop, led off the second inning with a scratch hit between first and second. Both Collinses tried to make a play on the ball but failed. Indian catcher Steve O'Neil missed a pitch on a hit and run and it looked as if Sewell would be a dead warrior at second, but the usually dependable Ray Schalk made a bum throw to second and Sewell was in safely with a stolen base. He then scored on O'Neil's single to center.

The White Sox had their chances to get back in the game. In the fourth inning 2 of their 3 hits were wasted when the fledgling Sewell robbed Shano Collins of a base hit and

turned it into a double play. In the fifth Mails struck out
Risberg. Then he suddenly lost his control and walked three
men in a row to load the bases. Prospects looked bright for
the Chicagoans to turn the game to their advantage.

Sanborn: "Weaver was next up and Buck tried his darn-
dest to get a base on balls too, but Mails regained his control as suddenly as he had lost it. He gave Weaver one bad
ball, then pitched a . . . ball across the heart of the plate.
Buck resisted the temptation to hit it out of Cuyahoga county
and took the strike. Then Mails broke two curves across the
plate and Weaver missed both of them.

"Eddie Collins was next and with the count of three
balls and two strikes, after he had hit three fouls in succes-
sion, swung at a bad ball and struck out. That was the ball
game."

Although the grand jury recessed Thursday afternoon
for a long weekend until the following Tuesday, there was
no dearth of stories to keep the kettle boiling about the alleged Series scandal. Before the final game in Cleveland the
White Sox learned that the names of eight players whose
paychecks and bonuses had been held up by Comiskey after the World Series became public. They were reported to
be Buck Weaver, Happy Felsch, Claude Williams, Swede Risberg, Joe Jackson, Chick Gandil, Eddie Cicotte and Fred
McMullin.

There were also leaks out of the grand jury room that
gamblers had testified that Hal Chase and Abe Attel, former featherweight boxing champion, were the leaders of a
$100,000 ring to bribe Sox players.

Mindful of Ban Johnson's charges that some White Sox
players would not dare win the pennant because of the gamblers' grip on them and the fresh allegations coming out of
the grand jury investigation, the White Sox stormed ahead
and captured the last game of the Cleveland series on Saturday, September 25, by a score of 5 to 1, lifting themselves
back to within a half game of the lead. The Tribune headlined: "SOX GIVE LIE TO 'DON'T DARE WIN'." Sanborn:
"Chicago's White Sox did their best to give the lie to the re-

port they did not dare get into the world's series of 1920 by licking the Indians today. . . .

"Lefty Williams pitched a remarkable game against the Indians, considering the strength of the enemy and the latest development in the grand jury investigation. He held them to five hits and would have shut them out on a clear field, because the only run Cleveland made resulted from a fly into the crowd.

"Nearly 31,000 jammed their way into the local plant and by invading the short right field area made any healthy fly hit in that direction good for two bases. . . .

"The White Sox on the 'doubtful' list were the men who won the game. Joe Jackson slammed a home run high over the right field wall in the fifth inning. . . . In addition to his Babe Ruth blow, Mister Joe hammered out two doubles each of which landed against the right field wall . . .

"In addition to his remarkable pitching feat Williams delivered two safe hits in four times up. One of them was a double which scored a run in the fourth." Buck did nothing in three trips.

Worse news than not getting any hits awaited Weaver back in Chicago. A *Tribune* headline unequivocally announced Sunday, September 26: "FIRST EVIDENCE OF MONEY PAID TO SOX BARED." The story focused on Buck in particular. In reality there was no evidence but only hearsay testimony that cast suspicion on Buck because of a story of a mysterious package delivered to his home by Fred McMullin during the World Series. The package was supposed to be in the shape of currency. An unidentified witness had testified that Weaver's dentist told him that he, the dentist, "heard the details from Weaver's mother-in-law, Mrs. Cook, who was said to have been present at Weaver's home when the delivery was made.

"The report is that Weaver was out when McMullin called with the package, that after waiting a long time, McMullin left the package and departed. When Weaver came home and learned what happened he is said to have stormed and refused to touch the thing, but later accepted it.

"Just what the packet contained never was learned, nor was it learned whether McMullin delivered packages to other Sox. If the proper witness is procured the mystery may be cleared up." Assistant state's attorney Replogle was seeking to find the dentist. Wouldn't it have been more appropriate to question Buck's mother-in-law? On such flimsy hearsay testimony the *Tribune* felt justified in writing an unwarranted headline that caused Buck more grief. As the story already admitted, the package could have contained any number of things. If it were a payoff would McMullin foolishly abandon incriminating evidence with Buck's mother-in-law?

On Sunday the White Sox were back in Chicago to close out the home season against the Detroit Tigers, only a half game out of first place. Buck obviously heard the stories. He skipped breakfast. He gulped down a candy bar that unsettled his stomach. But he went out to play hard under a dark, sullen sky that probably reflected some of his feelings.

Buck must have felt better as a big crowd of 28,000 loyal bugs cheered loudly while the Sox took the field. It appeared to be a kind of affirmation of faith in support of the team regardless of the threatening storm hovering over it. By this time the loudest cheers were reserved for Buck who had become the most popular of all White Sox players. A sportswriter named Dean Snyder had written: ". . . there's naturally something about Buck that makes him sweeter than any of them—Collins, Schalk, Jackson."

As the Detroit series opened Buck was hitting around .330, the highest of his career so late in the season. But his special quality through the years was his boyish hustle and bubbling spirit, his constant grin and chatter as he sprang around the infield with ballet grace. His quick, lightning-like reflexes afforded him to make plays no other third baseman would even think of chancing.

Observed Snyder: "There is something of the born leader in the Pale Hose third sacker. Whether in the field or at the bat, he's bristling with the attack spirit. It's the dare stuff in all his ball playing that has entitled him to the seat of honor on the 'sweet' ball players row."

In the days when there were no numbered or named uniforms, Buck was easy to spot on the field. If you couldn't distinguish Weaver by his enthusiasm, all you had to do was locate the player with the dirtiest uniform.

The White Sox whipped the Tigers, 8 to 1, but Cleveland beat the Browns to maintain their one half game lead.

As Buck headed out of the ballpark, he was questioned by a reporter. Asinof, in his intensive study of the 1919 World Series scandal *Eight Men Out*, records the scene:

> "Hey, Buck, lemme buy you a beer!"
>
> "No, thanks."
>
> "You know the story about you in the grand jury?"
>
> "I don't care none."
>
> "They're saying McMullin brought you money—"
>
> "Look, I didn't get no money. Not from nobody!"
>
> "They're saying there was witnesses. This package—"
>
> "A package. So what! I got lots of packages. All the time. Especially in the series. People send me presents. All ball players get presents, more or less. See this shirt? A present. Neckties. I get silk neckties maybe twelve each year. You know that? Fans send me neckties. Does that make me a crook?"
>
> "Then you didn't get any package from McMullin?"
>
> "No! I suppose before this investigation is over they will have every ball player in both leagues branded as a crook."
>
> "Well, you gotta admit they've got some evidence of business being done—"
>
> "Look, I'm gonna go before that grand jury on my own and cut loose with a lot of stuff from the shoulder—"
>
> "They say you haven't spoken to Eddie Cicotte since the series last year. It's common talk. Do you mind saying for publication why you're sore at him?"
>
> "I won't answer that question in the papers. If the grand jury asks me that question I might or might not answer. I'm a long way from being a squealer."

Weaver finally realized, as the reporter was taking notes, he shouldn't have talked to him at all.

"Lemme alone," he grunted.

McMullin, also questioned by reporters about the mysterious package said he "had been at Weaver's home often but that he knew absolutely nothing about any packages that looked like money.

In addition to the tale of the mysterious package, the traffic in World Series scandal stories remained hot and heavy during the weekend even though the grand jury was in recess. On Saturday, September 25, Charles Weeghman, the Chicago restauranteer and former owner of the Cubs, told the press that well-known Chicago gambler, Monte Tennes, had told him the World Series games were fixed as early as August when he met Tennes at the Saratoga, New York, race track: "Tennes told me a New York gambler had advised him to bet on the Cincinnati Reds. He said the New Yorker told him the series had been fixed and seven White Sox players had agreed to lay down. He mentioned their names and said the tip was straight but he didn't want it. He liked baseball, but wouldn't go in on a crooked deal. I understood in spite of the tip he lost $30,000 on the Sox."

Weeghman said he didn't remember if he told Heydler about the story but "thinks" he did. Weeghman "thought it so preposterous that he could hardly credit it and the matter may have slipped his mind."

Tennes volleyed back Weeghman's shot on Sunday: "I'm willing to tell them (grand jury) all I know about baseball and betting on baseball—but I can tell them nothing about fixed games. I know nothing about fixed games.

"I never told Charles Weeghman about fixed games. Weeghman's intentions are good I'm sure, but I believe he was misunderstood. Whether Weeghman and I met at Saratoga I can't say. I remember meeting him at a race track last summer. Of course we talked baseball—one would have to talk baseball with Charley. I told him I had bet or intended betting on the White Sox. I don't remember which it was. I bet on the White Sox. I lost my bet, and I made no cry of fraud." Perhaps Tennes also forgot, according to Bill Veeck's *The Hustler's Handbook*, that he called Harry Grabiner after the first game and expressed his suspicions that the World Series might be fixed. In fact Grabiner in his diary wrote that Tennes said ". . . it was apparent to him that the White Sox had been reached."

That Saturday Ban Johnson was in New York having a long talk with Arnold Rothstein, described by the *Tribune* as a "millionaire turfman." Rothstein denied the charges making the rounds that he was the kingpin of the gambling syndicate responsible for the fixing of the World Series. Johnson came away from the interview "convinced Rothstein wasn't in on the frame up" even though the New York gambler admitted he knew about it. Weeghman in Chicago said he "doubts a man of his standing would be mixed up in a thing like this." But stories surfacing that same day mentioned the name of Nat Evans as the front man for Rothstein in the plot. In Rothstein's supporting cast were said to be "Nicky" Arnstein, indicted as a bond thief, but better known as the husband of Ziegfeld Follies' star Fannie Brice, and Abe Attel, the former featherweight boxing champion.

It was also reported that Sunday morning that Schalk wanted to tell all he knew about the scandal to the grand jury. Not only had he fought with Williams during the World Series but he was apparently suspicious about the efforts of two White Sox pitchers during the last two months of the current season. However, it was learned that Schalk and other White Sox players would not be called to the witness stand for some time since Replogle and the jury "did not wish to interfere with the Sox chances of winning the pennant."

Then Comiskey, after the Sox victory over Detroit Sunday, blurted out at the ballpark that he was convinced after the first game of the World Series that someone had "fixed" some of his players. That was contrary to all his public statements since the World Series which defended his team.

The *Tribune* headlined Monday morning: "SOX SUS-

PECTED BY COMISKEY DURING SERIES." Comiskey spewed his venom towards Ban Johnson: "There's one man working on this investigation whom I did think was sincere in it, but I believe now he's using it for his own personal gain. It was a terrible thing to see a story printed of crookedness of the White Sox recently just before they went into a tough series against New York, but it was still worse to follow with a statement of blackmail of my players by gamblers just before they went into a series against Cleveland, a club in which this man is interested. I refer to Ban Johnson, president of our league."

Johnson did have a stake in the Cleveland Indians. He had made a loan to James Dunn, the owner of the ball club, and held some notes as collateral. Comiskey seemed to have been caught on the horns of a dilemma. On one hand he admitted he harbored some crooked ballplayers and at the same time castigated Johnson for telling the world about them.

Comiskey told reporters that he was so upset with the performance of the White Sox that he went to see Heydler early in the morning after the first game. Comiskey talked with Heydler again after the second game more convinced than ever that certain players were throwing games.

Reporters also found Heydler at Comiskey Park that Sunday. He was in Chicago preparing for his appearances before the grand jury. Asked to verify Comiskey's story, Heydler referred to notes he had prepared for the grand jury and said: "Comiskey was all broken up and felt something was wrong with his team in the first game. To me such a thing as crookedness in that game didn't seem possible. I told Comiskey I thought the White Sox were rather taken by surprise that perhaps they had underestimated the strength of the Cincinnati team.

"The matter was dropped for a time. That day the Reds won again and we moved to Chicago for the third game. Comiskey called me on the telephone early that morning and with John Bruce, secretary of the National Commission, I went to his office at the ballpark. Once more he stated he felt sure something was wrong.

"Still I couldn't believe it. Among other things he told of a Chicago fan who had gone to Cincinnati and wagered on the White Sox, but after getting some 'inside' information from gambling friends, this man had switched and wagered on Cincinnati.

"Comiskey said his manager, Kid Gleason, felt convinced someone had 'reached' the Sox players, and that they had talked the matter over and felt an investigation should be made. I still believed he was mistaken, but I took the matter up with Ban Johnson later, at the game. Johnson replied with a rather curt remark that made me drop the matter.

"After the series an article appeared in one paper hinting that the series was fixed. I went to Johnson and said the affair should be taken up and cleaned up at once. But Johnson agreed to investigate the affair, and I thought it was really his case and that he would handle it correctly."

Heydler chose not to mention that Comiskey's secretary, Harry Grabiner, also had called him during the Series explaining what he heard about the possibility that the Sox had been reached.

From New York that Sunday Babe Ruth issued a complaint. He wanted something done about the intentional pass. The Babe who had hit 51 home runs, said, "I scored only 23 men ahead of me. The reason was that when there were men on the bags, the pitchers usually passed me."

It didn't take long for Johnson to answer Comiskey's charges that he said the Sox dare not win the pennant. The next day Johnson said a reporter had come to his home the previous Wednesday and asked if he had heard a report that the White Sox dare not win the American League pennant, that certain players were in the grip of the gamblers and should they win, the fraud of last fall would be exposed. "I had heard of such a report, I replied. There were vague rumors of that sort. That they could not be given credence. I am amazed that the papers should give ear to the vaporing of a man whose malice and vindictiveness for the president of the American league have been so long and thoroughly known."

That Monday the White Sox nipped Detroit, 2 to 0, behind Kerr to remain only a half game back of Cleveland. After 2 out in the sixth inning, Tiger pitcher George Dauss "soaked Weaver in the middle of the back with a loose chuck." Eddie Collins pulled a single to right and Jackson lined a smash to left-center scoring Buck and sending Collins to third. When shortstop Bush let Cobb's throw get away from him, Collins legged it home with the second run. It was the White Sox final home game of the season and it was destined to be the last game Buck would ever play for the Chicago White Sox.

The Sox had only three games left in St. Louis and wouldn't start the series until Friday. In the meantime the Indians would play the Brownies twice while the Sox were idle. Then they would finish the race with 4 games in Detroit. While the Indians held only a half game lead, they were up 2 games in the all-important lost column. The Sox would have to sweep St. Louis while Cleveland lost 2 of 6 for the Sox to even edge into a tie.

Suddenly news from Philadelphia drew attention away from the sizzling pennant race. A second rate gambler, former boxer, auto mechanic and perhaps former ballplayer named Bill Maharg sought out sportswriter Jimmy Isaminger of the Philadelphia *North American* and spilled his version of the World Series gambling scandal. He hoped to collect on Comiskey's promise of a $10,000 reward for information leading to corrupt players. The *North American* headline blared on Monday, September 27: "THE MOST GIGANTIC SPORTING SWINDLE IN THE HISTORY OF AMERICA: Gamblers Promised White Sox $100,000 To Lose." By late afternoon Chicago newspapers carried Maharg's confession. The White Sox players read the sordid details in the clubhouse, then went out and got drunk.

Maharg's confession tallied with the information obtained by the grand jury. Maharg said he and Bill Burns "were the pioneers in the conspiracy." Burns, who once pitched for the White Sox for a brief interval in his mediocre major league career, was now a successful oil man in Texas. But he was not averse to a crooked safe bet.

Maharg said Cicotte approached Burns and himself at the Ansonia Hotel in New York and offered to fix the series for $100,000. He assured the gamblers that a group of White Sox players would be in on the deal. The former feather-weight boxing champion, Abe Attel, emerged as the head man for the gamblers. At first Maharg and Burns arranged a meeting with Arnold Rothstein at the Astor Hotel in New York but the bankroller and mastermind of the New York gambling crowd said "he did not think such a frameup could be possible." Later Burns encountered Attel in New York and he agreed to take on the project. Attel, who hung around with Rothstein acting as his bodyguard, told Burns that Rothstein had reconsidered and wanted in. That wasn't true at the time but Burns swallowed the bait and wired Ma-harg: "Arnold R has gone through with everything. Got eight in. Leaving for Cincinnati at 4:30."

Attel, leading his own stable of gamblers into Cincin-nati, welched on his agreement with the ballplayers, only delivering $10,000 of the promised $100,000 and cleaned up on his own bets.

When the White Sox went on to win the third game, Maharg told Isaminger, "Burns and I lost every cent we had in our clothes. I had to hock my diamond pin to get back to Philadelphia. . . .

"Attel is the man the Chicago grand jury wants. . . ."

As for Rothstein, unbeknownst to Burns and Maharg he would make his own arrangements for getting a piece of the action.

All the efforts of the grand jury paled by comparison with the Maharg confession. That really opened up a can of worms. The next day Cicotte cracked. Accompanied by man-ager Gleason, he trudged to Comiskey's office where both Comiskey and Comiskey's attorney, Alfred Austrian, waited.

"I don't know what you think of me," Cicotte blubbered,

"but I got to tell you how I double crossed you. I'm a crook. I got $10,000 for being a crook."

"Don't tell it to me," scowled Comiskey. "Tell it to the grand jury."

Reported the Chicago *Daily News* that same day: "Cicotte told it to the grand jury in tears and in shame slowly, haltingly, hanging his head, now and then pausing to wipe his stream of tears.

" 'Risberg and Gandil and McMullin were at me for a week before the world's series started,' he said. 'They wanted me to go crooked. I didn't know. I needed the money. I had the wife and the kids. The wife and the kids don't know this. I don't know what they'll think.

" 'I bought a farm. There was a $4,000 mortgage on it. There isn't any mortgage on it now. I paid it off with the crooked money.

" 'The eight of us . . . got together in my room three or four days before the games started. Gandil was the master of ceremonies. We talked about throwing the series—decided we could get away with it. . . . Then Gandil and McMullin took us all, one by one away from the others and we talked turkey. They asked me my price. I told them $19,000. And I told them that $10,000 was to be paid in advance.' "

In a mishmash of contradictory statements, Joe Jackson also offered his confession to the grand jury the same day. Cicotte and Jackson were not represented by any attorneys, thinking their interests were being protected by Austrian. Austrian's major task was to keep Comiskey's name clear. He wasn't worried about Cicotte and Jackson. He convinced both players to sign waivers of immunity, which meant they were liable to stand trial and anything they told the grand jury could be used against them.

The year of suspicion, accusation, doubt, innuendo, rumor, unconfirmed fact and hearsay reached a new crescendo with the Chicago *Daily News* banner on the front page, Tuesday, September 28: "EIGHT OF WHITE SOX INDICTED." Pictures of all eight players were emblazoned on front page center. Said the *Daily News*: "Seven White Sox players and one former member of the team were named in true bills following a statement by Eddie Cicotte involving all of them in a conspiracy to throw the world's series last fall."

Within a few minutes after the indictments were announced, Comiskey, through Grabiner, issued a statement indefinitely suspending Joe Jackson, Eddie Cicotte, Happy Felsch, Lefty Williams, Swede Risberg, Chick Gandil, Fred McMullin and Buck Weaver.

Comiskey immediately sent a wire to each of the indicted players. Some received word of their suspension before they learned of their indictments: "You and each of you are hereby notified of your indefinite suspension as a member of the Chicago American League Baseball Club. Your suspension is brought about by information which has just come to me, directly involving you and each of you in the baseball scandal now being investigated by the Grand Jury of Cook County, resulting from the world series of 1919.

"If you are innocent of any wrong doing, you and each of you will be reinstated; if you are guilty, you will be retired from organized baseball for the rest of your lives if I can accomplish it." Comiskey now was posing as a self-sacrificing martyr even though his ball club was being wrecked by other forces. "It is due to the public that I take this action even though it cost Chicago the pennant."

Within minutes of getting notice of his suspension Buck publicly denied ever receiving any money handed out by gamblers and said he knew nothing of any deal to throw the World Series. He was hiding the complete truth. According to Bill Veeck Jr. in his fascinating and wry account in *The Hustler's Handbook*, Weaver was offered $5,000 but Buck didn't want any part of it.

Buck said, "Any man who bats .332 (actually .324) is bound to make trouble for the other team in a ball game. The best team cannot win a world's championship without getting the breaks. The Athletics were the best team in the country in 1914 but they lost four straight to the Boston Nationals because the breaks were all against them. And nobody accused them of laying down."

Comiskey wanted everyone to believe that evidence collected in his investigation from the previous October led to the indictments. Grabiner released the following statement to the press: "Mr. Comiskey has been investigating for the past year, under the direction of Mr. Austrian the reports implicating members of the White Sox team in the world's series of last fall, and the moment anything concrete or substantial in the way of evidence was procured, immediately conveyed it to the grand jury and to the chief justice.

"We presume it was this evidence that caused the indictments to follow."

Comiskey stayed in his office most of the day. A reporter wrote, "He looked broken and worn and old—old for a man who always carried his years lightly."

The Old Roman told the press: "I would rather close my ball park than send nine men on the field with one of them holding a dishonest thought toward clean baseball—the game John McGraw and I went around the world with to show the people on the other side." With what Comiskey knew then he should have closed the ballpark in 1920.

Comiskey said, "We are far from through yet. We have the nucleus of another championship team with the remainder of the old world's championship team." Comiskey was hallucinating. The White Sox wouldn't even reach the first division again until 1936 when they finished in third place. And the Old Roman had long passed from the baseball wars.

That afternoon, Tuesday, September 28, about 2 o'clock, a bunch of lily-white White Sox players—Eddie Collins, Eddie Murphy, Amos Strunk and Nemo Leibold—took an automobile ride down to the Criminal Courts Building. One of the occupants was Sam Pass, an ardent Sox fan, a Chicago manufacturer who had lost heavily on the series. He had testified before the grand jury without contributing anything noteworthy. Pass went up to the courtroom. Learning of the indictments, "he flew down the stairs to the waiting automobile and imparted the news." The players hugged each other and playfully jabbed and swatted one another on the street where they had parked the car not far from the Criminal Courts Building. They telephoned Ray Schalk, Red Faber, Shano Collins and Dick Kerr. Since the Cubs were also in town they called Zeb Terry and Tom Daly, former White Sox teammates, to join their celebration at a dinner at a downtown restaurant.

"No one will ever know what we put up with all this summer," said a member of the White Sox. "I don't know how we ever got along. I know there were many times when things were about to break into a fight, but it never got that far.

"Hardly any of us have talked with any of those fellows, except on the ball field, since the season opened. Even during practice our gang stood in one group, waiting a turn to hit, and the other gang had their own group. We went along and gritted our teeth and played ball. We had to trail along with those fellows all summer, and all the time felt they had thrown us down. It was tough. Now the load has been lifted. No wonder we feel like celebrating."

Eddie Collins admitted, "We've known something was wrong for a long time, but we felt we had to keep silent because we were fighting for a pennant."

After dinner downtown, the players rode to Eddie Collins' apartment on the south side. More teammates joined them. At midnight they sent out for "cheese and cold chicken and pickles and other things."

So the lily-white players had shared in the cover-up. They too knew what was going on. Eddie Collins said as much to the press. Instead of blowing the whistle on their unfaithful teammates, they chose to remain tight-lipped. And what of manager Gleason? Gleason unburdened himself as well: "I am glad this thing has come to a head and wound up the way it did. This, of course, was an awful blow to me. I have felt for a long time that some of my players were not going at the speed they should be going. We will go out and play ball with the honest members we have left, and we still must not be considered out of the pennant race.

"We are going to try to finish the season without another defeat, regardless of what transpired today."

Gleason could not be absolved from all blame. He could have headed off the scandal almost from the beginning of the World Series. When he became aware of the situation he could have benched his suspect players. Or he could have given them a severe tongue-lashing, letting them know he knew the score and ordering them back on the straight and narrow. He chose silence.

Reporters during the day interviewed Judge Landis, whose name had been prominently mentioned as a desirable member of a new baseball commission. Described as being stunned by the indictments, he said, "My opinion of baseball gambling and baseball crookedness is well known.

"I know nothing of the evidence in the case and do not want to talk about it until I have a chance to absorb the facts."

In the meantime Cleveland pulled a full game ahead of the idle White Sox with Jim Bagby winning his thirtieth game against St. Louis.

On the morning of Wednesday, September 29, Buck arrived at Comiskey's office about 8:30. He hoped to convince the White Sox owner of his innocence. He stayed for an hour but "left the ball park with his head down and declined all requests for a statement as to the results of his conference."

That night Buck visited the state's attorney's office and sought advice from assistant state's attorney Replogle. Weaver, trying to clear himself of the scandal, sought to tell his side of the story to the grand jury. But he discovered Replogle and Comiskey wanted him to confess before the grand jury as three of his teammates had done. Buck would have none of that. Earlier in the day Lefty Williams confessed his role in the conspiracy before the grand jury. His testimony led to the first two indictments of gamblers, one being a key figure in the plot, Joseph "Sport" Sullivan from Boston. He was first approached by Chick Gandil and later acted as an agent for Rothstein. Before going before the grand jury Williams told Austrian about a meeting the players and gamblers had at the Warner Hotel on the south side where many of the players resided. Austrian asked, "Was Weaver there?"

"Yes."

"Do you know how much Weaver got?"

"I could not say."

"Did he tell you how much he got?"

"He never did."

Buck quickly retaliated: "I've been wrongfully accused and I intend to fight. I shall be in major league baseball next year, if not with the White Sox, then with some other team. They have nothing on me. I'm going to hire the best lawyer in Chicago to defend me, and I'm going to be cleared.

"Look, I know you have to put in local color in an interview. But print what I say, and don't say I'm prematurely aged over this thing. Don't say my shoulders are drooping, my head hanging and my back humped. I'm no condemned criminal and I don't like being pictured as one!"

The next day Cub president, William Veeck, told Austrian he would have given Comiskey $75,000 for Weaver before the exposure.

As told in Asinof's *Eight Men Out,* Buck met with Risberg, Felsch and McMullin in Joe Kauffman's tailor shop on Thirty-Third Street and Wentworth Avenue to plan their defense. By Saturday, October 2, Buck and his cohorts found someone to take up their cause. He was a young attorney named Thomas D. Nash. It was peculiar for Weaver to associate himself in any way with Felsch and Risberg. While Felsch did not sign any written confession, he blurted to a reporter, "I'm as guilty as the rest." He said he hadn't done anything to help lose the Series but he admitted to taking $5,000. Risberg appeared to be a major perpetrator of thrown games. Perhaps Buck joined the others to help pay lawyer's fees.

Judge McDonald extended the life of the September grand jury into October. It would exist as a special body to continue its investigation of the baseball scandal. While courtroom drama and its reverberations dominated the baseball scene in Chicago and the nation, the White Sox still harbored hopes of catching Cleveland. But on Wednesday, September 29, the Sox chances grew a little dimmer as the

Indians scalped the Browns to conclude a four game sweep and edge out to a game and a half lead.

The White Sox would have to win all three games at St. Louis while Cleveland broke even in a four game series at Detroit for the Sox to maneuver into a first place tie.

Going to the mound for Chicago that Friday, October 1, was Red Faber, the winningest pitcher on the staff. He had notched 23 victories while losing 12 times. The Sox went into the game with a lineup of Eddie Murphy at third base. He was batting about .340 in 55 games but he was mainly an outfielder and pinch hitter. Nemo Leibold, who played right most of the season, shifted to center field. Eddie Collins at second base was swatting the ball close to .370. Shano Collins had replaced Gandil at first base all summer and was hitting about .300. Rookie Bib Falk covered right field and was destined to get 3 hits in the game including a double. Reserve outfielder Amos Strunk went to left field. Harvey McClellan, a rusty benchwarmer, took over at shortstop. Schalk would receive Faber's delivery.

It wasn't exactly a hopeless situation, though it was a patchwork lineup. With a little bit of luck the Sox may well have won the first game of the series. They jumped off to a three run lead in the first inning. Unfortunately, Faber stopped a hard smash in the second inning which numbed his pitching hand. He gallantly came out to pitch the third inning but the Browns clobbered him for 6 hits and 5 runs before he retired the side.

The Chicagoans went down to an 8 to 6 defeat in a game reeled off in the unbelievable time (by today's standards) of only 1 hour and 40 minutes. In Detroit the Indians moved out to a two game lead by splitting a doubleheader with only two games left to play. If the ill-fated players had remained in action until the close of the season, it would have been unlikely that the final outcome would have been different. The White Sox beat the Browns, 10 to 7, on Saturday, but the Indians skinned the Tigers, 10 to 1. On the final day of the regular season, in meaningless games, St. Louis swamped the Sox, 16 to 7, and Detroit beat Cleveland,

6 to 5. The New York Yankees finished in third place, only one game behind the White Sox.

As for Buck, he had had his most sensational season at the plate, batting .333 in 151 games to lead all third basemen in hitting in the American League. Larry Gardner of Cleveland trailed Weaver with a .310 average. None of the others reached the .300 mark. Despite being acknowledged by just about everyone as a brilliant third baseman, if not the greatest at the time, statistically Weaver was dead last. He committed 31 errors. Gardner topped all third basemen with an average of .976 with only 13 miscues. But Gardner was seldom if ever mentioned in the same breath with Buck. So much for statistics. Weaver had still put in 25 games at shortstop.

Babe Ruth pounded out an incredible 54 home runs to almost double his output of 1919, when he established a new record of 29 round trippers. No one in either league came near him.

With the season's end, Comiskey chose to show the public that he could be genuinely magnanimous to his players. He issued checks of $1,500 each to players not involved in the scandal. In his letter to the players he wrote: "As one of the honest ball players of the Chicago White Sox team of 1919, I feel that you were deprived of the winner's share in the world's series receipts through no fault of yours . . . I therefore take pleasure in handing to you $1,500, this being the difference between the winning and the losing players' shares."

The players who received the unexpected largesse from Comiskey responded with an open letter of thanks. "To the Fans of Chicago: We the undersigned players of the Chicago White Sox, want the world to know the generosity of our employer, who, of his own free will, has reimbursed each and every member of our team the difference between the winning and the losing share of last year's world series, amounting to approximately $1,500."

The players were rather diplomatic in the matter since the actual difference between the winners' and losers' shares in the World Series was almost $2,000. But why make waves? Comiskey, who hedged a bit, didn't have to dole out anything extra to his players. Anyway it was a great public relations gesture and probably stirred up sympathy for the Old Roman, who certainly coveted it.

When the grand jury resumed its deliberations after taking a recess during the World Series, a grand entrance was made by Arnold Rothstein, the reputed mastermind of the conspiracy. He volunteered to appear before the grand jury on Tuesday, October 26. On the way into the grand jury room he told reporters: "Attel did the fixing. . . . I've come here to vindicate myself. If I wasn't sure I was going to be vindicated I'd stayed home. As far as my story is concerned, I've already told most of it, but I guess the grand jury wants it on the official record.

"The whole thing started when Attel and some other cheap gamblers decided to frame the series and make a killing. The world knows I was asked in on this deal and my friends know I turned it down flat. I don't doubt Attel used my name to put it over. That's been done by smarter men than Abe. But I wasn't in on it, wouldn't have gone into it under any circumstances and didn't bet a cent on the series after I found out that it was underway. My idea was that whatever way things turned out, it would be a crooked series anyhow, and only a sucker would bet on it.

"I'm not going to hold anything back from the jury. I'm here to clear myself and I expect to go out of here with a clean bill of health."

In the grand jury room, Rothstein demonstrated that the best defense was a great offense. As told in Seymour's *Baseball: The Golden Age*, Rothstein indignantly wailed: "Gentlemen, what kind of courtesy is this? What kind of a city is this? I came here voluntarily, and what happens? A gang of thugs bars my path, with cameras, as though I was a notorious person—a criminal even! I'm entitled to an apology. I demand one! Such a thing couldn't happen in New York. I'm surprised at you!"

Apparently Rothstein convinced about everyone within earshot of his self-proclaimed innocence. State's attorney

Hoyne, who had joined his assistant Replogle in presenting the case, believed Rothstein as did Austrian, who said Rothstein "had proved himself guiltless." The grand jury believed him. He was never indicted.

Also on the witness stand that last day of testimony were St. Louis Browns' second baseman, Joe Gedeon, and Harry Redmon. Both volunteered to testify at the behest of J. G. Taylor Spink, publisher of the *Sporting News*. Gedeon, who incidentally had the best fielding average at his position in the league in 1920, beating out Collins by one point, admitted being tipped off by a White Sox player to bet on Cincinnati before the Series started. He also told of being invited by his gambler friends to attend a meeting at the Hotel Sherman in Chicago after the third game. In attendance were Abe Attel, Bill Burns, Harry Redmon and Carl Zork, a St. Louis shirt manufacturer and Attel's former fight manager. What Gedeon said before the grand jury about the meeting was not revealed. Redmon told the grand jury that the gamblers decided to raise a pot of $25,000, part of which would go to the players. Redmon said he was asked to contribute $5,000. "I refused to donate to the pot and had nothing more to do with them after this." He claimed he lost $6,500 betting on the Sox.

Redmon also revealed the discussions he had with White Sox officials after the World Series in East St. Louis and again in Chicago with Comiskey, Grabiner and Austrian, telling them the Series was fixed.

Grabiner immediately fired off a statement to the newspapers trying to counter Redmon's damaging testimony: "Redmon never gave anyone connected with the club evidence upon which the club could act. The club was informed last winter that Redmon had lost heavily on the series and had learned the games were thrown and would be willing to give evidence upon which the guilty persons could be convicted, if the club made good his losses.

"He could not, however, tell anything definite. He had only rumors and hearsay stories. His seemed to be merely the hard luck yarn of a loser. Still every effort was made by the club to verify his hearsay reports. None was obtained until the deliberations of the grand jury brought out the confessions."

But Redmon's testimony stunned the *Sporting News* which, ignoring Grabiner's statement, tore savagely into Comiskey on November 4. First a picture of Comiskey was featured on page one with the caption: "NOT THE NOBLE ROMAN OF OLD." Then the story ripped Comiskey apart unmercifully: "The climax of the grand jury investigation, however, was not the digging up of more evidence of gambler—player plotting but the disclosure to the American public that one of its magnate idols—Charles A. Comiskey—is not the noble figure that he was supposed to be. The brief brutal story as told is that Comiskey, who was given information of the rottenness within his ball club, suppressed it, because the players involved had 'cost him a lot of money.' He protected his investment at the expense of the public, to the shame of baseball, and to his own final confusion and confounding—all the dust he could stir up by posing with his associates as a 'reformer' has been blown aside and the scene is laid before the world."

The *Sporting News* described Redmon as a businessman and gambler who was as "square as a die and his word as good as his bond."

The grand jury concluded its hearings on October 29 and presented indictments charging a number of conspiracies against the eight suspected White Sox players and a bunch of gamblers—Abe Attel, Joseph "Sport" Sullivan, Hal Chase, Bill Burns and a rather mysterious person, a reputed gambler named Rachael Brown. The name Brown had been an alias for Nat Evans, a Rothstein henchman, who was active in the conspiracy. Rachael Brown, a woman, may have been an employee of Rothstein's in one of his New York gambling houses. Apparently the ruse worked well since Evans was never indicted.

After the indictments Buck Weaver and his attorney, Thomas D. Nash, appeared in Criminal Court to post a $10,000 bail bond. They were accompanied by Weaver's dentist, Dr. Raymond B. Prettyman and his tailor, Joe Kauffman, who signed the bonds.

16

The New Baseball Czar

Against the backdrop of the sensational grand jury proceedings of the Black Sox scandal, another drama was being played out in the world of baseball. The stage was set for a bitter struggle over control of major league baseball. The outcome would affect all the White Sox players charged by the grand jury but especially Buck Weaver. By 1920 the internecine battles had raged for years. Many of the owners had become disenchanted with the National Commission, especially with the self-righteous, dictatorial rule of American League president Ban Johnson. In their eyes, Johnson had usurped his position as one member of the three-man National Commission.

The National Commission was established as the ruling body after the American League was recognized as an equal by the older senior circuit in an agreement signed January 3, 1903, between Johnson and the president of the National League, Harry Pulliam. Pulliam committed suicide in July, 1909, due in part to the pressures of his office. But Johnson and Pulliam agreed on the choice for the chairman of the commission—August Garry Herrmann, owner and president of the Cincinnati Reds. Herrmann remained in office until he resigned under pressure in February 1920.

With the post of chairman vacant and Johnson's authority severely shaken by hostile owners, the major league magnates had begun serious reconsideration of the Lasker plan offered by Albert D. Lasker, a Lord and Taylor advertising executive and minority Chicago Cubs stockholder. (Lasker has been credited with being the father of modern advertising.) The plan called for an impartial board comprised of three distinguished Americans who were not connected in any way with baseball. They would adjudicate all of baseball's problems. Names tossed about in the press as attractive candidates for the proposed board included former president William H. Taft, Generals John "Black Jack" Pershing and Leonard Wood, California U.S. Senator Hiram Johnson, former Secretary of the Treasury William McAdoo (President Wilson's son-in-law), and Judge Landis.

With the grand jury investigation shedding light on the dark cesspool of corruption that engulfed baseball, the owners realized they had to speed up the tempo to get their own house in order or they would totally lose the confidence of their fans. In Chicago to testify before the grand jury, Heydler, in speaking about the moribund commission, said: "It was all right in fair weather but too frail to weather a storm. . . .

"If President Johnson of the American league should ask me now to confer with him on the appointment of a new chairman for the National Commission I would tell him I consider it a waste of time and effort for the present form of government has outlived its usefulness."

Heydler was in Chicago for another reason besides grand jury hearings. A host of baseball luminaries were meeting intermittently for a week in the offices of Alfred Austrian. Among those attending one or more of the conferences were Heydler, Wrigley, Veeck, Comiskey, Grabiner, Dreyfus, Stoneham, McGraw, Ruppert, Huston and Frazee. Together they discussed the Lasker plan with its architect and, when the meetings were over, they all endorsed it.

Two days after the last confab in Chicago on October 5, Heydler was back in New York, holding a meeting of all National League owners in his office where they unanimously voted for the Lasker plan. Then they asked Heydler to invite all American League owners to a joint meeting in Chicago on October 18 to work on the new plan.

With five clubs—Cleveland, Detroit, Philadelphia, St. Louis and Washington—remaining loyal to Johnson and refusing the invitation, the American League president wired Heydler to call the October 18 meeting "premature." Johnson told the press: "I do not care to attend any conference to discuss a new baseball tribunal until the report of the special grand jury . . . is made and [reveals] whom it indicts. . . .

"Judge McDonald is honest in his determination to expose all dishonesty in baseball, and I am willing to give him all the aid in my power. I think all the friends of baseball ought to stand by him and await the decision of this grand jury before taking any further action.

"I believe in a thorough housecleaning before starting to remodel the house."

Heydler wired Johnson back telling him the invitation by the National League was unanimous. "Our people will be there," Heydler told Johnson. "They are firm in the belief that the public sentiment will brook no delay where such vital matters as the good repute of the national game, the protection of all honest players, and the protection of immense property rights are concerned.

"In my judgment it is a fortunate coincidence the Cook county grand jury is to continue its investigation during the time of our meeting. This gives us the ideal opportunity to aid the court."

The eight National League teams joined by the three "insurrectionist" ball clubs of the American League met in Chicago on October 18 and formally voted to end the National Commission and adopt the Lasker plan. Then they gave the Johnson loyalists until November 1 to join them or the eleven teams would form a new league. As the *Tribune* bannered the next morning: "BASEBALL WAR LOOMS; 12 CLUB LEAGUE MAY BE FORMED."

One of the five loyalists, Connie Mack, manager and part-owner of the Philadelphia Athletics, fired a returning salvo the next day: "We are the American League and when the time comes the league will meet on call of its president and no doubt will take action that will help baseball; that will help raise its standard and prevent scandals in the future. . . .

"If all the American League clubs had supported Johnson as they should, the present baseball scandal would never have occurred. Years ago he wanted to take measures to stop gambling, but never received proper support."

President Johnson did call for a meeting of the American League board of directors for October 29 in his Chicago office. The board was made up of four of the five clubs loyal to him. At the meeting were Phil Ball of St. Louis; Frank Navin of Detroit; Clark Griffith of Washington and Thomas Shibe of Philadelphia.

Their statement, without much doubt the voice of Johnson, said they turned down the Lasker plan because they did not want men who had "no experience in the management or conduct of baseball, and the wisdom of permitting men inexperienced in practical baseball affairs, no matter how eminent, to be empowered to take over even temporarily under any circumstances the management of baseball properties in which large sums of money have been invested is gravely doubtful. . . .

"The idea of the sponsors of the so-called Lasker plan seems to be that this evil in baseball (gambling) can be entirely avoided in future by the creation of such a commission. We have no confidence in such a commission being any more able to stamp out gambling than the National Commission has been."

Instead of the acceptance of the Lasker proposals, Johnson and his board of directors issued a counterproposal. They suggested the establishment of a committee of nine men—three from the American League and a like number from the National and minor leagues to study the issues and come up with another plan which would include the interests of the minor leagues.

Of course these ideas were lightly brushed aside by the

Lasker eleven. At the Congress Hotel in Chicago on November 8, the three insurgent teams of the American League—Chicago, New York and Boston—bolted the American League and joined the National League! The new league then offered Kenesaw Mountain Landis a $50,000 a year contract as "chairman of the new board of control for professional baseball." A twelfth team would be named later. Landis was given ten days to decide.

That same day Landis responded: "A thing of that kind is something that I cannot decide in a hurry. It is a big thing. It is a big job. I deeply appreciate the honor which those gentlemen have conferred upon me in offering me the chairmanship, but I told them I would have to give them my answer later. . . .

". . . all I can say now is that I am a fan and love the game and admire clean sport, and that I would do everything in my power to help make baseball worthy of the name it has borne all these years as the cleanest sport we have."

In Kansas City the next day, November 9, at the minor league meetings, which both major league factions attended trying to court support, Johnson gave vent to his opinion of Albert D. Lasker when he disdainfully said from the podium that Lasker "has not shed his swaddling clothes in baseball.

"It is my thought that baseball should remain in the hands of men who have given their lives to its development."

That may have been Johnson's thought at that moment since Landis was about ready to be named a commissioner. But for months Johnson had been laying the groundwork for his friend, Charles A. McDonald, chief justice of the Cook County Criminal Court, to become chairman of the National Commission.

But now time had run out for Johnson to influence the structure and the personality of the new commission. The major league moguls of both circuits held a peace counsel in Kansas City and repudiated Johnson as a major league arbitrator, relegating his authority to the confines of the American League. Johnson would now bide his time in his effort to destroy Comiskey.

The major league operators turned around and traveled back to Chicago to accelerate Landis's decision. Eight club owners entered his courtroom while he was trying an income tax evasion case on November 12. Reported the *Tribune*: "As the magnates filed into the courtroom, hats in their hands, the judge sharply banged his gavel down and ordered them to make less noise.

"When informed of their mission, he had them escorted to his chambers. There they were kept in waiting for forty-five minutes before the judge would listen to the offer which increased his annual salary from $7,500 a year to $50,000.

"While the magnates waited, the judge conducted the bribery trial in his usual vigorous fashion, and gave vent to some scathing remarks about the men who falsify their income tax returns.

" 'The penitentiary is too good for them.' "

The eight powerful baseball dignitaries whom the judge treated as menial supplicants were Charles Comiskey of the White Sox; William Veeck of the Cubs; Jacob Ruppert of the Yankees; Clark Griffith of the Senators; Charles Ebbets of the Dodgers; Garry Herrmann of the Reds; Barney Dreyfus of the Pirates and John Breadon of the Cardinals. They were later joined by Connie Mack of the Athletics, Robert Quinn of the Browns and James Dunn of the Indians.

Judge Landis accepted the offer, provided he could keep his federal judicial robes. The baseball bosses agreed feeling that as a federal judge he would be in an even better position to keep crooks out of baseball. Landis also volunteered to accept ony $42,500 from baseball since his federal post paid $7,500.

After the meeting, Landis escorted Griffith, a personal friend, to a nearby window: "Griff, I'm going to tell you just why I took this job. See those kids down there on the street? See that airplane propeller on the wall? Well, that explains my acceptance.

"You see, that propeller was on the plane in which my son, Major Reed Landis, flew while overseas. Reed and I went to one of the world series games at Brooklyn. Outside the gate were a bunch of little kids playing around. Reed turned to me and said, 'Dad, wouldn't it be awful to take baseball away from them?'

"Well, while you gentlemen were talking to me I looked up at his propeller and I thought of Reed. Then I thought of his remark in Brooklyn. Griff, we've got to keep baseball on a high standard for the sake of the youngsters—That's why I took the job, because I want to help."

Landis issued the following statement to the press: "I have accepted the chairmanship of baseball on the invitation of the sixteen major league clubs. At their request and in accordance with my own earnest wishes, I am to remain on the bench and continue my work here. The opportunities for real service are limitless. It is a matter to which I have been devoted for nearly forty years. On the question of policy, all I have to say is this: The only thing in anybody's mind now is to make and keep baseball what the millions of fans throughout the United States want it to be."

There was talk of adding a second and third member of the commission as suggested in the Lasker plan. Judge McDonald was mentioned as a second possible member but as time passed no further consideration was given to any more commission members. Chicago became the headquarters of the supreme court of baseball with Judge Kenesaw Mountain Landis presiding. Ban Johnson's days as the czar of baseball were over.

When Landis became the first sole commissioner of baseball he was already fifty-four years old. He had presided as a federal judge for the United States District Court for Northern Illinois since 1905 when he received an appointment from President Theodore Roosevelt. His performance on the bench earned him as many detractors as admirers. Far and above any other decision, his judgment in the Standard Oil case in 1907 brought him his greatest publicity.

In a case involving railroad rebates on the shipment of oil, Landis fined Standard Oil an astronomical $29,240,000. He even tweaked oil tycoon John D. Rockefeller by forcing him to come to Chicago to testify. While the decision caused a sensation, Landis's verdict was subsequently reversed by the Supreme Court.

Landis's decisions were often unpredictable, capricious and inconsistent. In Washington there was even talk of impeaching the irascible jurist. In one case he set free an eighteen year old messenger boy who stole $750,000 in Liberty bonds. The bonds were eventually found. Landis reacted to ridicule and criticism heaped upon him from across the country by saying: "I wish I had the power to jail the men who sent him out with $750,000 in bonds." He also found a young man not guilty after he had confessed to stealing money orders and checks from the mails. He threw the letters and envelopes down a sewer. Landis declared that the government had paid the young man too little which led to great temptation. Commented the Pontiac, Michigan, Press: "Landis's decisions frequently are imbued with a homely wisdom and sentiment that warms the hearts of the common folk. Sometimes we are inclined to think he has gone farther toward warming the hearts than he has towards satisfying the brain."

Landis, however, was extremely harsh with war dissenters. When the Industrial Workers of the World were found guilty of obstructing the war effort, he handed out multi-million dollar fines and prison terms as long as twenty years. President Calvin Coolidge commuted the sentences in 1923.

Landis, a bitter and hysterical foe of radicalism, as shown in his behavior in the trial of the native American I.W.W., and a hater of anything German during the World War, presided over a trial that sent a U.S. congressman, Victor Berger, to prison. Berger, an Austrian-born socialist, was editor of the Milwaukee Leader and wrote editorials branding the war a capitalist conspiracy. He and a few fellow socialists were found guilty of giving aid and comfort to the enemy in wartime. Landis handed out the longest sentence he could—twenty years in Leavenworth. The Supreme Court overturned the decision, disqualifying Landis for "prejudicial conduct before the trial." The defendants had charged that Landis had said, "One must have a very judicial mind, indeed, not to be prejudiced against the German-Americans in this country. Their hearts are reeking with disloyalty."

17

The Trial

Whatever the outcome of the indictments, Buck Weaver and Helen still had a life to live. Buck was now thirty years old. He was in his prime as a ballplayer and could look forward perhaps to at least a half dozen more years in a major league uniform if he could clear his name. But he knew one way or another he couldn't play baseball forever. Buck had already shown a sense for business, having owned a pool hall and barber shop. Years earlier on the White Sox and New York Giants' tour of the world, Buck had been elected to bargain for his traveling companions on both teams as they shopped for souvenirs in the exotic markets. Helen's sister, Annetta Marie, was married in 1917 to William Scanlan, a pharmacist and store manager for Walgreen drugstores. By 1920 Scanlan decided to strike out on his own. He offered Buck a chance to invest in a store and help him operate it. Buck accepted and went into business with his brother-in-law at Halsted and Sixty-Ninth streets in November.

Several days after the purchase of the drugstore, Buck mulled over the idea of instituting a civil suit to collect his salary for the coming season, his last of a three year contract, if he were successful in his defense against the indictments.

Buck's fertile, imaginative mind, together with his long established flair for the dramatic and natural bent to play to the crowd, caused him to consider a novel approach to explain his case before the public. He was supposed to have contacted a Dan Arnstein to plan a tour of local theatres. Buck would present a monologue designed to prove his innocence in the scandal. Theatre managers were said to be interested in Buck's project. However, nothing developed beyond the talking stage. Most fans probably would have wanted to believe Buck.

Two weeks before the grand jury concluded its hearing, the *Sporting News* of October 14 headlined over two columns: "CHICAGO FANS GRIEVE MOST FOR WEAVER AND STILL HOPE FOR HIM; Buck Was Idol of South Side Rooters, Who Can't Yet Make Themselves Believe He Really Belongs Among Comiskey's Outcasts."

Oscar C. Reichow, a Chicago *Daily News* sportswriter and contributing baseball writer to the *Sporting News*, described the painful predicament: "What Buck Weaver is alleged to have done in the world's series games of 1919 between the White Sox and Cincinnati Reds has shattered the local fans faith in baseball as much, if not more, than anything that has developed out of the scandal. Weaver's connection—which he denies—with the affair has been a severe jolt to the fans who were not only surprised but shocked when his name was mentioned. They could hardly believe it and there are many here today who still believe he was not a party to throwing any games to the Reds.

"Weaver was an idol on the South Side not because of his personality, but because of the aggressiveness with which he played. Few more aggressive ball players ever have been in the American League. It was thought he could not loaf in a ball game if he tried because he loved to win too much. He always tried, was ever ready to take advantage of an opponents' mistake and enthused beyond compare when it fell to his lot to drive home a run or win a ball game. It was this unlimited interest, this determination and this dexterity that caused the followers of the White Sox team to place much implicit faith in his honesty.

"Throughout the summer there were rumors going about that the series of 1919 had been framed. Naturally guesses were made as to which of the White Sox players were guilty. Weaver's name was one which was never mentioned. Fans thought it was impossible that he would figure in any such rotten affair like that, knowing his disposition to fight for ball games every second he was on the diamond. They refused to link his name with the scandal in any way, and therefore were stunned when his name was involved by the players who confessed their guilt.

"Weaver insists that he is innocent. Nothing could be more pleasing to the followers of baseball in Chicago, but they declare he made the mistake of his life when he did not rush up to President Comiskey after the first game was played in Cincinnati and explain to him what was being pulled off, if he knew what was being done, and it is said he did. He should have protected the fair name of the national game and at the same time kept the finger of suspicion from pointing strongly at him."

Reichow did not spare Comiskey: "Comiskey, I think, erred when he did not bring the matter before the annual meeting of the American League and insist that the league itself take some drastic action. He should not have permitted his unfriendliness with President Ban Johnson to stand in his way. That is a poor alibi. He had too much at stake to even think of that. He should have gone into the gathering with the bit between his teeth and said; 'Gentlemen, here are the facts. Get busy. Let's have some action. Baseball is being wrecked by a lot of piker gamblers and something must be done whether it wrecks my ball team or not."

In the same article Reichow praised Eddie Collins: "It was a rough and rugged road for him to play on that ball club all year and not throw up his hands in disgust. The same could be said of Schalk."

Collins did report to Comiskey his suspicions of crookedness in the last series in Boston but Comiskey did nothing. What made Reichow think Comiskey would have sprung into action if Buck had talked? Should Collins and Schalk have reported their suspicions to higher authority than Comiskey?

On December 9, the *Sporting News* reported that Harvey McClellan would be "taking care of the position so long held by Buck Weaver, who is running a drug store on the South Side and still hopes to get back in baseball by proving that he was in no way guilty of throwing games in 1919."

Most of the time Buck was managing the drugstore, handing out over-the-counter drugs and sundries and mixing delectable concoctions from the soda fountain. One evening New York reporter James L. Kilgallen visited Buck. Kilgallen was the father of Dorothy Kilgallen, who became a popular gossip columnist and television personality in the fifties and sixties. He watched as Weaver took an order: " 'Yes madam two chocolate sodas and a pineapple sundae.' "

Kilgallen observed: "The young man with the broad shoulders and the boyish smile strides vigorously from the table to the soda fountain. In a few minutes he is back with the order.

"Buck talked freely: 'I'm keeping myself busy. My brother-in-law has just bought this place. How'd you find out I was here?'

"A big chap with a red face came in—a cowboy at the stockyards. 'Why, hello if it ain't Buck!' he exclaimed, gripping Weaver's hand.

" 'That's the way my friends come in all day—giving me the glad hand,' said Weaver happily.

"Buck's place of employment is on the south side, not far from the White Sox ball park, and in a neighborhood where everybody is a rabid Sox rooter. Buck is staying here—right with them—because he says they all know he is innocent of ever having 'thrown' a ball game.

" 'I will prove myself innocent at the trial and I will be back in uniform next year,' Weaver declared . . .

" 'If I knew for sure the series was fixed and was in on it I could have bet a lot of money, couldn't I? I didn't bet a nickel on the series. The only bet I made was with Louis Comiskey—a pair of shoes that we'd beat the Reds. That was after we lost the first two games.' "

" 'Cicotte said you went to that meeting in the Warner Hotel where the series was fixed, how about that?' "

" 'Suppose,' Weaver replied, 'you are invited to come and hear a proposition and you go and hear it. Then you say absolutely no—and then you go ahead about your business and play ball. Are you a crook?'

"A woman came in for some aspirin tablets. Weaver got them quickly. 'Pleasant evening,' he remarked as he rang up the register.

" 'Comiskey said if I prove myself innocent I will be reinstated,' Weaver resumed. 'I am dead anxious for this trial.

" 'Don't say Buck Weaver is cringing, that he's hanging his head, that he's trying to run away. Just ask the public to withhold judgement until they hear all. I will tell everything about myself, but there is one thing I won't do and that is say anything against anyone else. I hate a squealer. I know in my heart I never helped throw a game. If my conscience wasn't clear in this respect I would never think of taking a ball in my hands again.'

" 'How about the report that McMullin left some money on your center table?'

"Weaver smiled broadly. For some reason this question amused him."

" 'Wait till the public finds out what was in that package,' he replied.

" 'What was it—a bottle?' "

" 'No,' he laughed—adding criptically [sic], 'You wait till it comes out.' The contents of the package were never revealed.

"Then he called attention to his record in the series. He said he batted .333 and didn't make an error. [Buck never seemed to get his 1919 batting average straight. He hit .324 in the series and .333 during the 1920 season.] He suggested the reporter go back over his record and see how he played, and look up the reports of baseball writers who said he was one of two players on the Sox team who fought to the very end.

"As for the cliques on the club, he said every club has cliques. The Sox cliques were poker cliques—the 'tightwads and those who wouldn't bet without having four aces.' "

Buck knew of what he spoke. He had been an avid poker player at least since his days in San Francisco. Poker helped pass the time in hotels and during boring, uncomfortable train rides. One night he and his teammates suffered the embarrassment of being arrested for engaging in an illegal game of poker in a Los Angeles hotel. They had neglected to lower the window shade in their room and were reported by some busybody. They were hauled to the central police station where they each deposited $15 bail. There was a time when Manager Rowland prohibited poker games because he felt the gambling caused some disharmony among the players.

"There was a voice from the rear. 'Time to close up for the night, Buck.' "

Buck bid Kilgallen a cheery goodnight and locked up.

Publicly, Buck maintained a confident, optimistic demeanor. He always effused confidence about being back in the big leagues. Attending a six day bicycle race at the Chicago Coliseum with a bunch of friends near the end of January 1921, Buck offered to bet $500 with one of his companions that he would be playing with the White Sox next summer.

"I'll prove to everybody that I am innocent of the charges against me. I have a contract with the White Sox and I will be a member of the team next season. They can't start the trial too soon to suit me. When it's over I'll be cleared."

Landis caught Weaver's comments in the *Tribune*. "I saw where he wanted to wager he would be a member of the White Sox next season. I wonder why Weaver is talking that way. I understand he has an attorney and I would naturally suppose a client would not talk unless instructed by his attorney. If the attorney thought he had a strong case, I wouldn't think he would want him to talk. Maybe he isn't paying attention to his attorney."

The wheels of justice rolled slowly with sudden stops and starts for weeks and would continue to do so well into the summer. On February 14, Weaver, attending the arraignment with other accused players Jackson and Williams, entered the courtroom midst rousing cheers. Buck bubbled: "They oughta build bleachers and charge admission."

The players were represented by Michael Ahern, Thomas Nash's partner, who requested a Bill of Particulars, a list of specific details of the charges of conspiracy. In the request, Weaver, Jackson and Williams declared "that they never made any admissions such as has been charged to them; that they never 'threw' ball games, or conspired to 'throw' them."

The banner headline in the Chicago *Daily News* that day pointed to the peculiar development: "JACKSON, WILLIAMS AND WEAVER IN COURT REPUDIATE ADMISSIONS." It was rather bizarre that Buck's lawyers lumped him together with Jackson and Williams. After all, they were retracting their confessions. Buck never confessed or admitted to any wrongdoing.

Two days later Judge William Dever turned down a request to grant Buck a separate trial. Buck was indicted on conspiracy charges facing all the ballplayers and would stand trial with them. The judge ordered a Bill of Particulars be given the defense by March 1. The day's session did not pass without some fireworks. Assistant State's Attorney George Gorman tried to read excerpts of the confessions by Jackson and Williams, but Ahern shouted, "Why don't you indict them for perjury, if that's what you are attempting to get at?"

"I want to tell you, they're running dangerously close to the border line on that very thing!" Gorman fired back.

Defense attorney Ben Short found an opening for his own blast at the magnates for giving the public the impression that they were shelling out "huge salaries" to the players: "They lead the public to believe players get about $10,000 or more a year, here we find out they get $2,600. At the end of the season they have nothing left but a chew of tobacco, a glove and a uniform. And yet some people pity those 'poor' magnates."

By the time the trial date, March 14, approached, Judge Dever was bedridden with a cold. His clerk reported that the judge would not give "much more than a month's delay. Then an attorney named George Barrett entered the court proceedings when he was retained by Ban Johnson to represent the interests of the American League at the trial. He wanted a six month delay so he could become familiar with the case.

Landis, who watched all this with a jaundiced eye, decided to change his original thoughts about not taking any action on the status of the players. He first told a reporter, "Don't you think it would be an injustice to players who are facing trial on criminal charges for the baseball commission to take any action in the matter in the place where the jurors who are to try the cases will be chosen?" With new delays and postponements, the comissioner had enough of continuous procrastination. "INDICTED PLAYERS INELIGIBLE," the *Tribune* headlined on March 13. Said Landis, "I deeply regret the postponement of these cases. However, baseball is not powerless to protect itself. All of the indicted players have today been placed on the ineligible list." That meant regardless of the decision of the court, the players would have to get a clean bill of health from the commissioner before returning to the diamond.

For the next weeks, the serpentine intricacies and complexities of the criminal justice system which made folks wonder if a trial would ever come to pass were played out by lawyers and a judge on a stage called a courtroom. Sanborn wrote on March 14: ". . . there is more behind this movement to postpone action on the cases of the indicted players than appears on the surface. There is a lot of politics in it of the baseball variety. There has been plenty of time since last October to round up all the evidence necessary if it could be obtained." Thomas Nash pressed for an immediate trial for Weaver and his other clients. But the prosecution suddenly requested that the case be stricken from the call, a motion to delay the start of the trial. Gorman revealed the stunning news that the state had lost the testimony of Cicotte, Jackson and Williams. The confessions of the three players had mysteriously disappeared. The prosecution said it needed a delay to build a new case. Judge Dever, recovered from his cold, overruled the motion and ordered the lawyers to appear on March 17 for the purpose of setting a new trial date.

Comiskey, just returned from California to attend the trial scheduled for March 14, complained he would have remained on the West Coast had he known of its postponement. But wasting no time following Landis's ban of the players, the White Sox owner said: "Those indicted players are on my ineligible list. It was not necessary for Judge Landis to put them on his, but I'm glad he did as it justified my position. There is absolutely no chance for any of them to play on my team again unless they can clear themselves to my satisfaction of the charges made against them by three of their teammates." Comiskey seemed to be talking as if Landis didn't exist. Three days later a *Tribune* headline showed that Comiskey was practicing upmanship with Landis: "BLACK SOX RELEASED UNCONDITIONALLY; JOBLESS FREE AGENTS!" Comiskey had sent formal notices to all seven players (Gandil was already no longer with the team): ". . . the undersigned hereby notifies you of your discharge from any and all employment." Comiskey couldn't allow anyone harbor the thought that in the back of his mind, he was still trying to protect his players. Yet one had to wonder who was paying the fees of those expensive defense attorneys.

Back in court on March 17, Judge Dever ordered the prosecution to be ready for trial no later than May 2. State's Attorney Crowe already contended he needed more time for his office to prepare new evidence to supplement the work of the previous administration. Besides, the state's attorney's office learned that copies of the testimony given to the grand jury earlier were being offered for sale by the New York

Herald Tribune. Therefore, Crowe entered a motion to drop the case. The motion granted, the state's attorney immediately started a new inquiry the next day before the grand jury. In one week the ballplayers were indicted for the second time. In addition to the five original gamblers indicted, Crowe found five new targets who had been part of Abe Attel's crowd in Cincinnati at the Sinton Hotel. They included Carl Zork of Des Moines and Benjamin Franklin, David Zelser, and two Levi brothers, Ben and Lou, of St. Louis. Small fry indeed.

The gamblers who were the big fish all squirmed off the hook. In California, Hal Chase had been taken into custody but was released on a writ of habeas corpus and never appeared in Chicago. In New York, Abe Attel wriggled free in habeas corpus proceedings by simply claiming he was not the Abe Attel identified in the indictments. Sam Pass, the close friend of several White Sox players who joined in their celebration of the Black Sox indictments, was brought to New York to identify Attel. Attel's lawyer, William J. Fallon, known as the "Great Mouthpiece," did his work well. He paid Pass the $3,000 he lost in the Series, and Pass suddenly discovered that he could not identify Attel. Pass said his testimony before the Chicago grand jury identifying Attel was all hearsay. Sport Sullivan skipped to Canada. Nat Evans (alias Brown) seemed to have vanished into thin air, though Asinof reveals in *Eight Men Out* that Evans was arrested under his real name in St. Louis as a suspicious character and released on insufficient evidence. Bill Burns, it was reported, had returned to Mexico. Even among the small fry gamblers, two claimed to be "too sick" to attend the trial. But on the threat of contempt of court, they suddenly recovered.

Of the original five key gamblers indicted, one would appear in court and play a major role in the trial. Bill Burns would be drawn back not as a defendant but as the state's star witness. Ban Johnson would see to that. Johnson was a driven man. He was determined to destroy Comiskey and show up Landis whom he felt didn't take an active enough role in the case. In fairness, Johnson did want to get to the bottom of the crooked series. He had warned the owners for years to clean up the gambling situation. Johnson contacted Billy Maharg in Philadelphia and induced him to leave his auto factory job by paying his wages and travel expenses to go search for Burns along the Texas-Mexico border. The extra bonus for Maharg was Johnson's promise to win him immunity from prosecution. Maharg found Burns along the Rio Grande River and notified Johnson, who came down to see Burns and convinced him to return to Chicago to testify as the state's star witness on the promise of immunity.

While the proceedings for the preparation of the trial continued at a snail's pace, most of the indicted ballplayers formed the nucleus of a baseball team in April called the Major Stars. They received financial support from an investment banker named George K. Miller and were to play in Chicago, northern Indiana and Wisconsin. On the team were Jackson, Felsch, Williams, Risberg and McMullin. They tried to convince Weaver to join them, but Buck sought to keep his distance from the other players. He wanted to make it clear to everyone that his predicament was not the same as theirs. The Major Stars had their troubles. Several semi-pro organizations issued orders that any players or teams competing with the Black Sox would be barred from further play. However, by May the five former White Sox players formed another team called the South Side Stars and were playing every Sunday on Chicago's south side. Then the judiciary committee of the city council stepped in and voted to revoke the license of the owner of the ballpark unless the five players were dropped from the team.

Finally, Chief Justice Charles McDonald assigned the baseball trial in June to Judge Hugo Friend, a young man of thirty-nine who had been on the circuit court bench for less than a year. Friend immigrated to the United States with his parents from Prague, Bohemia, at the age of two. While preparing for a law career he became a track star at the University of Chicago and earned a berth on the 1906 U.S. Olympic Team which competed in Athens. As a south sider and a sportsman, he probably was a Sox fan. Friend died in 1966 at the age of eighty-three from a heart attack suffered while listening to a White Sox-Cleveland game.

When Buck entered the courtroom on June 27, he did not join any of the other White Sox on trial. He sat apart. Just as he didn't join them on the Major Stars' team, he sought to maintain his distance from any of the players who allegedly had taken money. He didn't even make an effort to greet his former teammates.

As the trial continued to move slowly, with the attorneys analyzing a vast number of candidates for jury duty, a strange occurrence took place in the courtroom on July 11. The *Tribune* headlined: "WHITE AND BLACK SOX PLAYERS SHAKE HANDS." Into the courtroom had come Gleason, Eddie Collins, Dick Kerr, Red Faber, Ray Schalk, Roy Wilkinson and Harvey McClellan. What followed after the seven were quietly seated made it appear that the unindicted players—the co-called "lily-whites"—had come on a goodwill mission to assuage the Black Sox. Suddenly Swede Risberg yelled jovially, "Hello Kid, how's the boy?"

Gleason answered pleasantly, "Pretty good, Swede—how's yourself?" The two shook hands. "And there's old Bucko!" Gleason perked. "Stacking up pretty good, Buck?"

"Sure," Weaver said. Before Buck could say anymore, he was being tickled by Faber and Kerr. Just about everyone knew Buck was ticklish.

Editorially, the press reacted instantly and negatively. The newspapers questioned the propriety of the clean Sox fraternizing with the soiled ones in the courtroom. Comiskey ordered Gleason to deny any such goings on. Gleason dutifully complied: "Nobody had tickled Weaver. Perhaps he's been tickling himself. . . ."

By July 5, the eight White Sox defendants had been reduced to seven. Fred McMullin, the reserve infielder, was released from prosecution for lack of evidence. Only four of the five second-rate gamblers remained on trial.

Then on July 15, after almost two weeks of examining nearly 600 candidates for jury duty, the defense and prosecution agreed on twelve men. "When [the] last four jurors walked into the jury room, the cheers of the other eight, some of whom have been locked up since a week ago Tuesday, could be heard throughout the building." The twelve men were Stephen Schuben, a merchant; Joseph Vesley, a foreman for the Air Motor Company; Harry Willis, a heater for Inland Steel Company; Andrew Jackson, a store fixtures salesman; Edward Linman, a clerk; William Barry, a hydraulic press operator; Paul J. Zieski, a florist; Emil J. Groskopf, a clerk and a suburbanite from Harvey; William H. Deutcher of suburban Forest Park, an automobile mechanic; Paul E. Luedcke, an employee of the telephone company; Michael F. Lidgen, a clerk for the elevated lines and Herbert J. Jordan, a stationary engineer for the Congress Hotel.

Only one of the jurors claimed to be a White Sox fan who attended one or two games a week. He was Stephen Schuben, who said he bet on Cincinnati to win the World Series because he thought they were a better team. None of the others said they were baseball fans.

The jury would decide whether the prosecution could prove any or all of the five conspiracy charges in its indictment: conspiracy to defraud the public, conspiracy to defraud Ray Schalk, conspiracy to commit a confidence game, conspiracy to injure the business of the American League and a conspiracy to injure the business of Charles A. Comiskey.

It was Monday, July 18. With the temperature oozing up into the mid-nineties, the courtroom was jammed with men, women and boys. The boys were out of school for summer vacation. The crowd overflowed into the corridors. Despite the suffocating heat and humidity people were intent to see and hear legal pyrotechnics promising to be as exciting as any action on the diamond.

The roll call of witnesses began with Comiskey. His testimony proved neither critical nor relevant. The great white hope against the Black Sox for the prosecution was Sleepy Bill Burns. On the day Comiskey testified, Burns was granted immunity. He would not be prosecuted just as Johnson promised. The former big league pitcher became the state's star witness. Burns took the stand at 2:35 in the afternoon, Tuesday, July 19.

Wearing a dark green checked suit and sporting a lavender shirt and bow tie, Burns seemed nervous. He used a handkerchief to constantly wipe his face. He compulsively moved his hands over the bald spot on his head. Burns spoke in a low voice that could barely be heard as he leaned forward, resting his chin on his right hand. He shed his coat soon after taking the witness stand. Assistant State's Attorney Edward Prindeville did the questioning.

With minor exceptions, Burns repeated the story that Maharg told almost a year earlier to a Philadelphia sportswriter. For three days Burns testified in the heat of a sweltering Chicago summer, repeating what he knew of the plan to throw the World Series. During the first day of his testimony he named Weaver as one of the White Sox players at the meeting the night before the first game at the Sinton Hotel in Cincinnati.

Q: When did you meet the ballplayers?
A: At the Sinton Hotel in Cincinnati.
Q: Do you remember the number of the room?
A: I think it was room 708.
Q: Who was there?
A: There were Gandil, Fred McMullin, "Lefty" Williams, "Happy" Felsch, Eddie Cicotte, "Swede" Risberg and "Buck" Weaver.

Buck had hoped to defend himself in this trial, take the witness stand, tell his side of the story, but the defense attorneys, including his own, decided the best strategy was to remain silent. None of the players would say anything. Was it the best strategy for the players or for Comiskey?

On July 25, with the prosecution pushing hard to put the confessions of Cicotte, Jackson and Williams into evidence, Judge Friend excused the jury while he allowed a private session of the three players with the attorneys on both sides. After listening to the questioning of the three players, Friend decided that the players' confessions were made voluntarily and could be admitted in court. But Friend said the confessions could be used only to implicate the players who confessed. Since the original confessions had been mysteriously removed from the state's attorney's office, the court would rely on carbon copies and the transcriptions of the court reporter at the grand jury hearings.

That same day Johnson, who had originally felt Rothstein innocent of any wrong in the World Series scandal, charged that the arch-gambler had paid $10,000 to someone in the district attorney's office during Hoyne's term for the original copies of the confessions. Johnson said Rothstein should be the target of a grand jury investigation. He claimed that the New York gambler turned the confessions over to a New York newspaper after he learned he was not implicated by them. Rothstein threatened to sue. Johnson dared him, but he never did. On the day after Johnson accused Rothstein of masterminding the theft, Rothstein's lawyer, William J. Fallon, chimed, "The minutes were not stolen. I got them from my Chicago representative, attorney Harry A. Berger. I understood attorney Berger got them from the state's attorney's office."

Berger, another former assistant state's attorney now on the defense team in the trial, immediately denied Fallon's statement: "I did not act as his representative here."

There was no further investigation into the missing confessions but they showed up in Alfred Austrian's office in 1924 when Joe Jackson filed suit for $18,000 in back pay. Afterwards, they mysteriously disappeared again.

On July 27, Judge Friend announced he would grant new trials to Buck Weaver, Happy Felsch and gambler Carl Zork even if the jury found them guilty. He said, "There is so little evidence against these men . . ." He also released two of the gamblers, Ben and Lou Levi, for lack of evidence. Only two "minor league" gamblers remained on trial.

There was a parade of witnesses for the state along with Burns. Maharg repeated his story. A host of White Sox players were subpoenaed off the road to testify on July 28 but their testimony did not add to the case. Dick Kerr complained, "I came nine hundred miles to tell this!" Finally, the last man to testify in the trial was White Sox secretary Harry Grabiner. He was brought to the stand by the defense to show that the Sox gate receipts from 1919 to 1920 had nearly doubled from $521,175.75 to $910,206.59. The defense felt it had scored a final point since one of the charges against the players was conspiracy to injure the business of Charles A. Comiskey. All it really showed was that the conspiracy failed. It did reveal that Comiskey was running a successful business operation and that White Sox fans apparently forgave their heroes for blowing the 1919 World Series. Attendance for 1920 was slightly over 200,000 ahead of the previous pennant winning year.

In summation on July 30, one of the assistant state's attorneys, Edward Prindeville, fired away: "I say, gentlemen, that the evidence shows that a swindle and con game has been worked on the American public. The crime in this case warrants the most severe punishment of the law. The crime strikes at the heart of every red blooded citizen and every kid who plays on the sandlot.

"This country is for sending criminals to the penitentiary whether they are idols of the baseball diamond or gangsters guilty of robbery with a gun. The state is asking in this case a verdict of guilty with five years in the penitentiary and a fine of $2,000 for each defendant!"

For the defense the legal implications of the indictments were spelled out by Defense Attorney Ben Short on August 1: ". . . The state failed to establish criminal conspiracy. There may have been an agreement entered by the defendants to take the gamblers' money, but it has not been shown the players had any intention of defrauding the public or of bringing the game into ill repute. They believed any arrangement they may have made was a secret one and would, therefore, reflect no discredit on the national pastime or injure the business of their employer as it would never be detected!"

For many people the niceties of this argument escaped

them. But Judge Friend made the same point in his final charge to the jury the next day: "The State must prove that it was the intent of the ballplayers and gamblers charged with conspiracy through the throwing of the world series, to defraud the public and others, and not merely throw ball games!" Judge Friend spent considerable time with instructions to the jury explaining the state's burden in proving conspiracy. The prosecution had to show that the ballplayers did what they did to intentionally defraud the public and the baseball owners. That aspect of the problem had not been touched by the state.

It was left to the defense attorney for the gamblers, A. Morgan Frumberg, to throw the spotlight on the man many thought should have been on trial but who had escaped prosecution. He asked why Rothstein was not indicted. After all, the star witness for the state, Bill Burns, had named Rothstein as the money man for the fix. He wondered why Chase, Attel, Sullivan and Brown were not brought before the bar of justice.

At 7:52 P.M. on Tuesday, August 2, twelve men proceeded from the jury box to the jury room to ponder their decision.

As Buck walked down the corridor outside the courtroom he felt exuberant. Two weeks short of his thirty-first birthday, he still looked boyish. He grinned widely with a cigar hanging from his mouth. He mingled with the crowd which hung on, waiting expectantly for the jury's verdict. "Good luck, Buck!" friendly voices shouted.

It only took 2 hours and 48 minutes to reach a verdict at 10:40 P.M.; only one ballot was necessary. Three knocks on the jury door signaled the jury was ready to announce its verdict. Judge Friend had to be called from the Cooper Carlton Hotel. The jury returned to the jury box. The babel of tongues in the crowded courtroom hushed with anticipation. The foreman of the jury, William Barry, handed the verdict to Edward Myers, the chief clerk. At 11:22 P.M. Myers announced, "We, the jury, find the defendant, Claude Williams, not guilty."

The spectators cheered. The bailiffs pounded for order.

For a while they were successful, as the clerk read the roll call of "not guilty" for all the ballplayers and two gamblers. All pandemonium broke loose among the 500 male spectators after the last "not guilty" call. At first the bailiffs tried to get the crowd quieted, but they noticed Judge Friend smiling as he headed for his chambers so they joined in the whistling and shouting. It was as if the White Sox had just won a pennant or World Series. Cicotte jumped up and slapped Jackson on the back. Williams shook hands wildly with everyone, his palms hot and moist. Cicotte rushed to the jury box before any of the other players and shook hands with William Barry, the foreman. "Thanks," he shouted, "I knew you'd do it."

It was a New Year's celebration in the heat of summer. Players, jurors, lawyers and spectators "clapped each other on the back and exchanged congratulations." Members of the jury lifted the ballplayers on their backs and paraded around the courtroom while photographers caught the madcap scene. Weaver and Risberg danced. Felsch and Williams kept laughing.

Buck, smiling, said: "I knew I'd be cleared. And I'm glad the public stood by me until the trial was over." Weaver caught up with Judge Friend and shook hands, saying, "Everybody knew I had nothing to do with the conspiracy. I believe that I should be given my old position back. I'm going to fight for it." In the euphoria of the moment Buck ignored the fact that the players in the conspiracy were also declared not guilty.

Buck's attorney, Thomas Nash, confidently declared: "I'll put him back in organized baseball."

As for the prosecution's reaction, it was summed up by George Gorman, who said cryptically, "We did our best."

That night the ballplayers joined together to celebrate their apparent triumph at an Italian restaurant on the west side not far from the Criminal Courts Building at 54 W. Hubburd Street. By strange coincidence the jurors also met at the same eatery but in an adjoining room. Neither group supposedly knew of the other's plans. But now they partied together, eating and drinking well into the morning.

But only one of the players saw himself back in the big leagues even with the favorable jury verdict. The one man who would struggle for reinstatement was George Buck Weaver. Not only had he been cleared in court, he knew in his heart, in his entire being, that he had done nothing wrong, nothing to be ashamed of. He didn't touch a penny of the gamblers' money, nor did he purposely play to lose the World Series. Sure, he had thought about it, considered it; but in the final analysis, with all the chips down, he played his brand of baseball to the limit of his skills and talent and fiery spirit.

Therefore, the announcement made by Judge Landis the day after the trial must have given Buck a severe jolt. Bannered the Chicago *Daily News* on the front page: "NO BASEBALL FOR EX-SOX, LANDIS DECREES." Landis issued this ukase: "Regardless of the verdicts of juries, no player that throws a game, no player that undertakes or promises to throw a ball game, no player that sits in a conference with a bunch of crooked players where the ways and means of throwing games are planned and discussed and does not promptly tell his club about it will ever play professional baseball."

Landis concluded: "I don't know that any of these men will apply for reinstatement but if they do the rules I have just stated are at least a few that will be endorsed. Just keep in mind that regardless of the verdicts of juries, baseball is entirely competent to protect itself against the crooks, both inside and outside the game."

In the history of organized baseball, gambling and crooked games had always been a threat but only players caught offering bribes or accepting bribes to throw games were banished. Commissioner Landis was adding his own ex post facto laws.

18

More Foul Play?

Buck pursued a busy schedule after the end of the trial. He was occupied in the drugstore, made an effort to play semipro ball and laid plans for his fight for reinstatement. Above all, he would fight to get back into a major league uniform despite Landis's forbidding dictum. Weaver was convinced he could persuade the tempestuous judge to understand his dilemma and restore him to active duty. If the White Sox wouldn't use him, McGraw told him during the trial he would love to have him on the Giants. Buck joined a local south side semipro team called the Woodlawn Lions and took pre-game practice before a game in Kenosha, Wisconsin, against Nash Motors on Sunday, September 12. The fans cheered when they saw him but he did not play. Perhaps the blackball policy banning players and teams from associating in any way with the Black Sox players was still making itself felt with some semipro teams. It would be years before Buck would be permitted to play even semipro ball regularly.

While Buck sought to satisfy his hunger for baseball by trying to play semipro ball, Chicago baseball fans demonstrated their love for their favorite third sacker. Members of the Masons in the Chicago district lodge gathered 20,000 signatures on petitions to Judge Landis, requesting that he reinstate their Mason brother. A delegation of petitioners met with Landis but they couldn't move him anymore than they could move a mountain. If Chicago fans felt disillusioned by the Black Sox players, they didn't all show it. In the *Tribune's* "Inquiring Reporter" column, five out of seven people interviewed on the street believed the eight ousted ballplayers should have been reinstated.

In his battle to restore his own respectability, Buck went to court on October 19 and filed papers to collect his back pay due him for the 1921 season, the last year of a three year contract. "At the trial there was no evidence to connect Weaver with the gambling scandal," Buck's new attorney, Charles A. Williams, told the municipal court. The lower court turned a deaf ear to Weaver's plea so his attorney appealed to the federal district court. Again Weaver became a victim of circumstance when Judge George A. Carpenter dismissed the suit on November 21 after Buck's lawyer failed to appear. To add to his woes Weaver was ordered to pay court costs. But Buck wouldn't let go. With the ferocity and tenacity he displayed on the field, he would fight on and eventually get his back pay.

The greatest quest of his life, his intense and determined struggle to wear a major league uniform again, began in December, 1921. Weaver met Landis in the commissioner's office for the first time at the invitation of the new baseball czar. Weaver recalled the encounter for James T. Farrell: "He was a funny man. I'd come in. He'd say, 'Sit down, sit down.' He had that big box on his desk full of tobacco. He knew I chewed tobacco, too. He'd give me a chew of tobacco."

Weaver unburdened himself. He readily admitted again that Cicotte approached him during the season of 1919 about a proposed fix of the World Series. But he quickly turned Cicotte down. As for the meetings he attended, nothing seemed to be settled. Players didn't discuss their decisions with their teammates. No one knew for sure who was in and who was out. In the end Weaver did make up his mind and told Gandil he was out. But Weaver couldn't inform on the other players. He wouldn't peach. It was one of the most compelling virtues taught youngsters in the small towns and farms of America: you don't squeal on friends. What if Weaver had ignored that time-honored counsel? Who would he tell? Comiskey? What would he tell? Would the owner jeopardize his wealth in the ball club by self-destruction? If Comiskey confronted the players with Buck's accusations, and they simply denied them, where would Weaver stand in the eyes of his fellow ballplayers? He had played with those guys for years. He couldn't do it.

By the time Weaver sat in Landis's office, spilling his guts, it had become generally known that the lily-whites were aware that some of their teammates had taken a dive. They admitted as much on the afternoon of the announcement of the original indictments when they went out to celebrate. Before the fifth game of the tainted Series Gleason tore into the team in a clubhouse meeting, issuing a tongue-lashing for their suspiciously poor play. Yet not one player said a word, not the conspirators nor the clean players who knew or were keenly suspicious that foul play was afoot.

Buck told Farrell that Landis "didn't have the guts to tell me to my face" what his decision was. "He said he'd send me a letter. He didn't have the guts to tell me to my face."

The newspapers got Landis's message before Buck did. Pulling an old bromide out of his hat, the commissioner said, "Birds of a feather flock together. Men associating with gamblers and crooks could expect no leniency." It took one full year before Weaver received Landis's detailed conclusion, again by press report: "Indictments were returned against certain members of the team, including Weaver. On the trial of this case, a witness for the prosecution gave what he claimed was a detailed account of his meeting with the indicted men and arranging with them for the throwing of the world's series games.

"The report showed that Weaver was present in court during the testimony of this witness, who most specifically stated that Weaver was present at the conference, and yet the case went to the jury without any denial from Weaver from the witness stand.

"If the incriminating evidence was false, the baseball public had a right to Weaver's denial under oath. Of course, it is true that a verdict of not guilty was rendered in Weaver's favor. It was also likewise true that the same jury returned the same verdict in favor of Cicotte, Claude Williams and Joe Jackson.

"Weaver denies he had anything to do with the conspiracy as alleged in the confessions, which were introduced at the trial. However, his own admissions forbid his reinstatement."

What Landis apparently ignored in his pronouncement were the efforts Weaver made for a separate trial. He had expected to take the witness stand and tell his side of the story. But, denied a separate trial, he was forced to go along with the other defendants, though Judge Friend made special note if the jury found Weaver guilty he would reverse its verdict. The battery of defense lawyers decided the best strategy for all the ballplayers was to remain silent. Their silence would also serve Comiskey well. Weaver would not be allowed to answer his accusers.

There was one bit of personal consolation and satisfaction for Buck when his court battle for his 1921 salary ended successfully. Comiskey paid off in an out-of-court settlement in 1924. Weaver recalled in his Farrell interview, "I sent a letter to the Commissioner. I says Mr. Comiskey settled for my 1921 contract. But that shows that they're wrong and I'm right. But they still paid it and I can't do nothing about it." Landis never answered Buck's letter.

Buck continued to earn a living in the drugstore and on weekends he would sometimes see his old teammates play semipro ball, never giving up hope of playing in the big leagues again. During one summer afternoon Buck was sitting in the stands at White City Park on the south side when Risberg and Felsch approached Buck and asked him to play. He raised his arms. "Nothing doing. I'll be back in the majors soon, and you guys will still be semi-pros."

Buck must have thought his prospects brightened when, a few months later, Landis rescued pitcher Rube Benton.

Benton had admitted "guilty knowledge" of the fixed World
Series at the grand jury hearings and had wagered on Cincinnati. But he was allowed to continue to pitch for the
Giants. In 1921 he was sent down to St. Paul of the American Association. In early 1923 Benton was claimed by Cincinnati but Heydler sought to keep him out of the league
because of his past indiscretion. Landis, however, blocked
Heydler, ruling if Benton could pitch for St. Paul, he could
pitch anywhere. At this late date Landis said Benton should
not "be deprived of his livelihood" because of "alleged irreg-
ularities" committed in 1919. Landis seemingly ignored Benton's own confession and the affidavits of two ballplayers
who said they overheard him boasting of winning World
Series bets on a tip from Hal Chase. Landis already kicked
Joe Gedeon, the St. Louis Browns second baseman, out of
baseball for "guilty knowledge" of the tainted World Series.
One thing Buck could count on was the unpredictability and
inconsistency of Landis's decisions.

But the years began to slip away. Hope to return to the
big time became a faint glimmer. Then suddenly, towards
the end of 1926, a long forgotten episode found the light of
day. It eventually afforded Buck Weaver a stage to make his
most dramatic and emotional appeal for reinstatement. Again
the baseball world was rocked by the suspected mixed brew
of gambling and fixed games. Involved were two of the greatest names in baseball, Ty Cobb and Tris Speaker. It started
innocently enough. On November 2, Cobb resigned as manager of the Detroit Tigers. Coming off a sixth place finish
after being Tiger boss for six years, no one thought it unusual for baseball's greatest hitter to step into retirement.
After all, he had been a rough and tough campaigner since
August 30, 1905, when he came up from the Augusta,
Georgia, club in the Sally League at the age of eighteen.

Exactly one month after Cobb left the Tigers, the baseball community was shocked by the sudden resignation of
Speaker, who had been the Cleveland manager since 1919.
In 1920 the Indians beat the Brooklyn Dodgers 5 games to 2
in the World Series. In the season just ended Cleveland

chased the New York Yankees down to the wire, finishing in second place only 3 games behind the pennant winners. On the surface there didn't seem to be a logical explanation for Speaker leaving his ball club.

But on December 21 Landis released two letters and a hundred page report to the press that shed some light on the Cobb-Speaker mystery. Hubert "Dutch" Leonard, the former Boston Red Sox pitcher who finished his major league career with Detroit, originally possessed the letters, which were written to him by Joe Wood, Detroit center fielder, and Cobb. The letters concerned betting on a Tiger-Cleveland game on September 25, 1919, the same week that the World Series was being fixed. The Wood letter indicated that he had won $420 betting on the Tigers, allowing Leonard, Wood and Cobb to each collect $130, since Wood gave a clubhouse employee $30 to place the bet. The Cobb letter expressed regret that he and Wood could not get a bet down in time: "Wood and myself were considerably disappointed in our business proposition, as we had $2,000 to put into it and the other side quoted us $1,400, and when we finally secured that much money it was about 2 o'clock and they refused to deal with us, as they had men in Chicago to take up the matter with and they had no time, so we completely fell down and of course we felt badly over it.

"Everything was open to Wood and he can tell you about it when we get together. It was quite a responsibility and I don't care for it again, I can assure you."

In addition to the two letters Leonard, in a written statement, indicated that Speaker told him a day before the September 25 game: "Don't worry about tomorrow's game. We have second place cinched, and you will win tomorrow." Detroit needed a victory to beat out New York for third place to collect a share of the World Series' gate receipts. Fourth place was still excluded. With that assurance, according to Leonard, the bets were made. Detroit did beat Cleveland, 9 to 5, and in defeat Speaker collected 3 hits including a triple. Cobb was held to 1 single in 5 trips. Neither Wood nor Leonard played.

Leonard originally gave the two letters and his statement to Ban Johnson. Then the American League pressured Cobb and Speaker to resign quietly without publicly embarrassing the two great stars. Why did Leonard take so long to expose the incident? No one knows for sure. Leonard may have borne a grudge against Cobb and Speaker. In 1925 Cobb released Leonard to the Pacific Coast League. Leonard had hoped that when Cobb placed him on waivers, Speaker, his former teammate from Boston Red Sox days, would pick him up. It didn't happen, and Leonard shuffled off to the West Coast.

Johnson turned the information over to Landis, never expecting all the details to be made public. As far as he was concerned the matter was closed. But not for Landis. The commissioner interrogated Cobb, Speaker and Wood in his Chicago office on November 29. Cobb and Wood admitted writing the letters. Wood felt he had done nothing wrong because he said it was common practice to bet on your own team. Cobb said he was trying to place a bet for Leonard and that he personally never bet on a game. Speaker protested that his name was not even mentioned in the letters and said: "I know nothing of the wagers being made in this contest or any fixing. The only thing they have against me is the word of a man behind this flare-up, Leonard. I have requested repeatedly that Leonard be brought in to face me, but he has positively refused to come into the meeting."

Landis decided for the good of baseball to release the facts to the public to quash all kinds of rumors and innuendos. For Landis, unlike Johnson, the matter was not closed. He prepared to study the issue. Again Landis and Johnson became bitter antagonists. However, before the commissioner could deal with the Cobb-Speaker case, he was diverted by another purported baseball scandal.

One of the readers of the latest diamond expose was Charles "Swede" Risberg of the 1919 Black Sox. He was now living the quiet life of a tenant dairy farmer near Rochester, Minnesota. A wire service reporter quoted Risberg: "Why I could tell Judge Landis of a lot worse things pulled by baseball players than the little $440 (sic) betting deal for which Cobb and Speaker are kicked out." The *Tribune* quoted Risberg as saying on December 29: "I can give baseball's bosses information that will implicate 20 big leaguers who never before have been mentioned in connection with crookedness. Landis will never ask me to tell him what I know. The facts are there, but they don't want to know them."

Risberg was wrong. Landis immediately wired Risberg to come to Chicago and tell his story. On New Year's Day 1927, Risberg and Landis faced each other for two hours in the commissioner's office at 122 N. Michigan Avenue. The *New York Times* called it a semi-open meeting. Besides the press, only one other player was present, and that was Buck Weaver. Buck sat in on the meeting as an observer, refusing to get involved in the questioning. He was looking for an opening to plead his case for reinstatement. Risberg told another story of thrown ball games in 1917. This time the White Sox were allegedly the recipients of four straight sloughed off games by the Detroit Tigers on September 2 and 3, 1917, in Chicago in two consecutive doubleheaders over the Labor Day weekend. Risberg charged that the White Sox later took up a collection of approximately $45 a man to pay off several Tiger players, especially the pitchers. Then in 1919, Risberg said, the White Sox returned the favor to Detroit by dropping two games to them so they could capture third place ahead of the New York Yankees.

Risberg told this story, which was taken down by a court reporter:

"Clarence Rowland met me near the dugout before the first of the four game series with Detroit in 1917. We were fighting for first place. We needed those games. 'Don't worry,' Rowland told me. 'Everything's all fixed.'

"It was common talk among all of us on the club that Detroit was going to slough off four games. We faced them in double-headers and won all four.

"After the series was over Rowland said we ought to do something for the Detroit players. It was my understanding he meant pitchers.

"Chick Gandil and I were appointed to collect $45 from each of the players. We got the money together one afternoon while we were staying at the Ansonia Hotel in New York. That was about two weeks after the fake series which was played on Sept. 2 and 3.

"I remember Collins (Eddie) saying as he gave his money: 'I don't like to do this. I'll never do it again.'

"Red Faber gave us a check drawn to cash. His check covered the contributions of four or five of the fellows who were short of cash.

"When we had all the money Chick and I went over to Philadelphia where Detroit was playing. We went to the Aldine Hotel and found Bill James, George Dauss, Donie Bush and others playing poker. Chick called James outside the room and said, 'Here's a little donation from our boys.'

"James took the money, between $1,000 and $1,100, and said he would take care of the boys. He mentioned Howard. He meant Howard Ehmke, one of the pitchers. Others were Boland, Dauss and Cunningham.

"Well, that's all that happened then, but two years later, when Detroit was fighting hard for third place, I remember some of our boys saying I guess we ought to be good to Detroit. They had helped us out once, and we ought to do it then.

"So the last two games we had with Detroit we sloughed off."

Landis asked Risberg if he knew of any other games the Sox sloughed off.

"I always thought," Risberg said, "there was something funny about our last series in Boston in 1920. We whipped the Yankees to a standstill and went into Boston in first place. And there we lost three straight."

"What did you see that looked funny?

"Well, the balls went past me a mile a minute and away out of reach. It looked to me as if something happened to our pitchers."

Landis asked Risberg if he had ever heard of White Sox

players collecting money and giving it to Detroit pitchers for defeating Boston.

"I never did. The White Sox players gave that money simply because Detroit let us win." That was Swede's parting salvo. Landis remained silent.

Shortly before that New Year's Day hearing ended, Risberg interjected that Buck Weaver did not contribute to the $45 pot. He said Buck gave Oscar Vitt a handbag. Buck nodded agreement but told Landis the handbag was a Christmas present.

As the hearing came to a close the commissioner asked Swede if it was a common practice for ballplayers to help each other to make base hits.

"Sure," Risberg replied. "Stuffy McInnes was always begging us to let him hit."

Risberg's startling accusations galvanized Landis into lightning-like action. Landis sent telegrams to thirty-eight players of both the White Sox and Tigers, ordering them to appear before him in his office on January 5. They were not bound legally to appear but the commissioner's office would pay their expenses. Among those who answered the call were Clarence Rowland, Eddie Collins, Donie Bush, Ty Cobb, Howard Ehmke, Ray Schalk, Oscar Stanage, Kid Gleason, Red Faber, Dick Kerr, John Collins, Harry Leibold, Eddie Murphy, Joe Benz, Harry Heilmann, Bob Veach, George Dauss and Buck Weaver.

Buck appeared to be almost oblivious to the Sox-Tiger controversy swirling about him. He was simply obsessed with clearing his name. He sought to use the hearing as a platform for his quest for reinstatement whenever the opportunity arose. His gift of a handbag to Oscar Vitt would be easily explained.

Buck sent Landis a telegram on January 4 that he would be present. He told the press: "I have been cast out of baseball, but I have no grudge. I only have an ambition to get back into the game. I'm going to apply for reinstatement every time I have a chance. I'm innocent of wrongdoing. I was innocent in 1919 and I got railroaded on the flimsiest of charges. All I ask is a fair hearing.

"During that 1917 series I was on the bench with a broken finger and had nothing to do with any crooked deal. I can't tell the judge about any wrong deal because I wasn't in on any."

From many former White Sox players came hostile denials that they formed a pool to pay off Detroit for sloughing off a four game series to them. Risberg was attacked as an out and out liar. Rowland, now an American League umpire, said, "I knew nothing of that deal. If Risberg says I had anything to do with framing of games he lies."

Rowland advised reporters, "Look at the box scores of the games and they'll tell you in plain language that I had no knowledge of anything having been arranged.

"Nobody seems to have given thought to the fact that if I was in on any kind of a deal, as Risberg declares, I certainly would not have used about every good pitcher I possessed. If the games were fixed and I had knowledge of it I could very easily have bluffed my way through by working some of the second-raters."

Eddie Collins admitted in a press interview on January 2 that a collection was made but to award Detroit pitchers in particular for beating the Boston Red Sox in 3 of 4 games. He said, "Risberg's charges that I contributed to a fund with a view to bribing players on the Detroit team is an atrocious lie. It is a complete surprise to me that he should even make such insinuations, and I agree with Donie Bush and Hughie Jennings in saying that the series he mentions was perfectly regular in all respects.

"I presume the incident which Risberg is charging was bribery is in reference to a fund which was raised at the end of the season as a gift to Detroit pitchers who had trounced Boston in a series by taking three out of four games.

"That Rowland or anyone else had anything to do with the fund I did not know. The only thing I remember is that when we got back to Chicago almost at the end of the season and had the pennant cinched, Gandil asked me for a contribution to be used as a gift to the Detroit pitchers.

"This action was first spoken of more than a month as I recall it, after the series in which Risberg says the fund was used. There was no intimation or suggestion that the series had been thrown, and it was hard fought, as I remember it, with nothing out of the ordinary.

"In those days it was nothing out of the ordinary to give a player on another team some sort of a gift if he went out of the way to turn in a good performance against one of the team's leading rivals in the race. That the contribution which Gandil asked from me was for this purpose alone it never entered my head to doubt.

"Knowledge that this fund was raised and the purpose it was raised for had been common property for some time, and there seems no reason except a personal one on Risberg's part, why it should be brought up again."

On the other side of the coin Chick Gandil said he was coming to Chicago to support Risberg's version of the payoff for the sloughed off series. He would be Risberg's only corroborating witness. Though Gandil was hardly the most desirable character witness he also said, "I want to help Buck Weaver, too. He's a square fellow, and he wasn't mixed up in that 1919 scandal. Some of these fellows who let him be forced out of baseball, knowing that he was no more guilty than they, are still posing as pure boys."

Buck also got a boost from John W. Keys, a reporter for the Chicago *Daily News*, on Wednesday, January 5, the day the dramatic hearings opened: "The only one of the outlawed 'Black Sox' who answered the morning roll call was Buck Weaver. They never did have much on Buck when the 1919 world series scandal broke, but they cleaned him out along with the others. Now he's fighting to get back in the big leagues."

Out in the hall of the conference room Buck ran into Cobb for the first time since he was dropped by the White Sox. They shook hands warmly. Buck spoke first with genuine emotion, "Gosh, Ty, I'm sorry to hear you got mixed up in this thing. But I believe in you."

"Thanks, Buck, old boy," said Ty. "Does look like they got me down for the present, but I'm going to come out all right. My conscience is clear anyway."

Eddie Collins walked over to greet Cobb and slapped him on the back. "Well, well, well," Ty smiled, "so you're one of us now, too. Welcome to our midst."

The commissioner's office took on the atmosphere of a courtroom, except cigarette smoke choked the air. Near the window of the long room which overlooked Lake Michigan, Judge Landis lodged himself at his desk. "Judge" now was an honorary title, since he resigned from the federal bench amidst criticism for holding two prestigious positions in February 1922. He chewed grimly at the end of a half-used cigar. For this special event Landis was attired in a high wing collar "which threatened to rise up and surround his head." At the opposite end of the room facing the commissioner were about forty newspapermen and photographers seated around a long table. Between the commissioner and reporters were chairs for the witnesses. Leslie O'Conner, the commissioner's secretary, sat to the right of Landis, facing the lake. Witnesses sat to the right of the secretary and another chair still farther to the right was reserved for Risberg. The hearings were supposed to start with Risberg as the first witness at about ten A.M. But he telephoned that he would be late and would be there about 1:30 in the afternoon. It was getting close to 2 o'clock and Risberg had not yet made an appearance. "Does anyone know where Mr. Risberg is?" asked the judge.

"Downstairs trying to sneak into the building without causing a riot," a voice perked.

Reported the *New York Times*: "All of Chicago it seemed was jammed on the sidewalk before the People's Gas Building where the Landis offices are housed. The overflow had swarmed into the corridors—everybody craning for a look at the celebrities.

"At 1:50 there was a stir in the outer room and Risberg

appeared, smoking the inevitable cigarette, a ghost of a smile on his face. He was wearing a gray overcoat and light gray cap which he took off after he had walked to the Commissioner's desk. He smiled at the stenographers—a forced smile, it seemed—and adjusted himself in the witness chair."

Then Landis instructed one of his assistants to call Eddie Collins, Donie Bush, Ty Cobb, Ben Dyer, George Dauss, Howard Ehmke, Ray Schalk, Pants Rowland and Oscar Stanage to take chairs facing Risberg. First Risberg repeated the story that he told Landis on New Year's Day. He went on to say: "There was only one remark that I heard during the whole four game series, and that was passed by Eddie Collins when Dyer booted the ball, he said, 'My God that is terrible.' " Dyer, the Detroit shortstop, stared at Risberg from his chair across the smoke-filled room. Only two days earlier Dyer denied he purposely booted the ball in the alleged fixed Series in 1917. "If I booted the ball," he said, "it was just a bad break. I certainly knew nothing of the deal, as I was only a rookie on the team."

Landis relished the prosecutor's role. He would alternately point his finger sternly under the noses of the witnesses and pace back and forth behind his desk. He fixed his piercing eyes on Risberg: "And what was your judgment as to whether or not the Detroit ball club did lay down to you?"

"Well, I thought the pitchers did not put anything on the ball and some of the fielding was not up to what it should have been, and there was quite a lot of base-stealing."

"Quite a lot of base-stealing by Chicago players?"

"Yes, sir."

"Who was catching for Detroit?"

"Oscar Stanage."

When Landis later quizzed Stanage that day, it was learned that the White Sox stole 19 bases in 4 games (actually 21 bases), 8 in 1 game. Stanage maintained he tried his best. "That's quite a crop of stolen bases," said Landis.

"It's happened to me lots of times," said Stanage and laughter filled the room. In defense of Stanage, when Gandil testified he said bases were often stolen on the pitcher not the catcher. That of course favored Risberg's charge that Detroit pitchers were laying down for the White Sox.

Risberg finished his testimony by repeating his story that the White Sox sloughed off two games to Detroit in 1919 to help them gain third place. Said the Swede: "We paid Detroit by sloughing off two games to the Tigers. I know I played out of position, and Jackson, Gandil and Felsch also played out of position."

Rowland then led a long parade of witnesses contesting Risberg's testimony. Landis asked, "What do you think of Risberg's testimony?"

Rowland replied heatedly, "It's a damned lie. I made no such remark to Risberg as 'It's all fixed.' " The commissioner admonished the former White Sox manager "to refrain from the use of superlatives here."

Then Landis interrupted the questioning when he noticed one of the country's leading celebrities sitting in the rear of the room. It was Will Rogers, the popular movie and stage star who also doubled as the mayor of Beverly Hills, California. Landis invited Rogers to "come up here and be more comfortable." Rogers rejected the offer saying he "had been able to keep out of this thing so far." Rogers knew Buck and Helen personally from their winter visits to California.

Rowland continued his testimony denying Risberg's entire story. After Rowland, Eddie Collins took the witness stand. He spoke "in a cool, incisive voice." He denied he ever said, "it was terrible" of the error made by Ben Dyer, Detroit shortstop. Collins went on to say he didn't learn of a pool until the team got back to Chicago to prepare for the World Series.

"It was not until we went back to New York and finished the series there that I paid Gandil the money, and I have a check book here which shows the checks cashed in the Ansonia Hotel, with the notation in it that I gave Gandil $45. That was after the world's series was over. If he said that I gave any money before that time he is a damned liar."

The audience applauded as Collins's voice choked with emotion.

The first Detroit player to take the stand, shortstop Donie Bush, denied that the Tigers sloughed off the series. He was followed by Ray Schalk who also admitted contributing $45 to the Gandil collection but only for rewarding Detroit pitchers for their effective work against Boston.

Then Ty Cobb, already under a cloud because of Dutch Leonard's accusations which cost him his job as Detroit manager, went to the stand. According to the *New York Times,* "Cobb gave Landis a hard, unfriendly stare as he walked towards the inquisator's desk."

Landis opened: "There has been given here some testimony by Mr. Risberg to the effect that the Detroit ball club sloughed off four ball games in Chicago September 2, 3, 1917. What have you got to say about that?"

"There has never been any ball game that I ever played in that I know of that was ever fixed."

Landis also asked Cobb about the two games the White Sox supposedly sloughed off to Detroit in September 1919, in "gratitude and appreciation to Detroit, having sloughed off four games in 1917. What do you know about that?"

Cobb said simply, "Well, to my knowledge, I never heard anything about it."

Detroit pitcher George Dauss, who didn't pitch in the twin doubleheader series in Chicago, testified he got $180. He said he understood that "any pitcher that would beat Boston would receive $200 from the White Sox. He got $180 and the other $20 was to make up a gift of $60 to the catcher, Oscar Stanage. The money was handed to him by Detroit pitcher Bill James, who in turn was paid by Chick Gandil.

Five long dreary hours of testimony elapsed before Buck Weaver was called. Up to that time the monotonous repetition of questions and answers was only twice interrupted by a flareup of tempers. When Bush left the stand, he walked over to Risberg, shaking his fist in Swede's face, called him a liar. Landis ordered him to sit down. Later, when Detroit pitcher Bernie Boland was testifying, Risberg whispered to

Landis that Bush was nodding agreement to the witness. That led to a verbal fusillade among Boland, Bush and Risberg. Boland in a final sally thrust his chin near Risberg and said sharply, "You're still a pig!"

Risberg could only yell back, "I am not a pig."

When Buck took the witness stand it was almost 7 o'clock. Buck denied Risberg's story in every detail and pointed out he refused to give any money to the Detroit pool.

"How about the 1919 series Risberg says was sloughed to Detroit by the Sox?" Landis asked.

"I know nothing about it, Judge," Weaver said. "I was always in there to win and I don't remember ever hearing anything about laying down to Detroit."

Buck appeared "jovial over the box score account of his play in the alleged 1919 "sloughed series" in Chicago. Maybe it was because he didn't see much action in the three games. Buck played only four innings as Detroit won the first match, 10 to 7. He collected 1 hit in 2 trips and committed 2 errors. But miscues were also turned in by Eddie Collins, Nemo Leibold, reserve catcher Joe Jenkins and second-string pitcher Lefty Sullivan. On the face of it those 6 errors might look mighty suspicious but it was tight defense by comparison as the Tigers floundered around for 8 errors.

Since the White Sox already had won the pennant, Gleason inserted his second-line pitchers throughout the series, which wasn't unusual. Should he have been accused of helping to "slough off" the series? Detroit won the second game, 7 to 5, in ten innings. Buck got a hit in his first at bat in the first inning and left the game soon after. The Sox rallied in the tenth with 2 hits, but Sanborn reported they "ran themselves to death on the bases."

In the finale, which the Tigers won, 10 to 9, the *Tribune* headlined: "GLEASONS GIVE LAST GAME TO TIGERS . . ." Buck had lashed out 2 triples and a single and messed up one play. Sanborn revealed: ". . . the Sox would have tied the score . . . in the ninth if they had not tried to steal with little chance of success."

Buck concluded his testimony by saying he "had no

recollection of Risberg, Felsch, Jackson and Gandil playing 'out of position' " in the series.

Landis then excused Weaver. But Buck, who had bided his time patiently for days, anxiously preparing for this moment, turned towards the judge. Facing the commissioner almost eyeball-to-eyeball, before a host of his peers, "sixty great and past great of baseball" and scores of reporters, Buck reached new dramatic heights in his unrelenting efforts to regain his major league status when he suddenly blurted out, "As far as baseball is concerned, your Honor, I do not owe baseball a thing, but I do think baseball owes me something. As I told you before I knew nothing about the 1919 world's series and therefore, I am asking you today to be reinstated. That is all I have to say, Judge."

Weaver's request stunned Landis and everyone else in his crowded office. Silence enveloped the scene. Several seconds elapsed. The commissioner, seldom at a loss for words, struggled successfully to recover his composure. "Well, drop me a line to that effect and I will take the matter up." Buck then left the hearing room.

Weaver returned to the witness chair on Friday, January 7, to respond to testimony from Risberg and Gandil that he had given Oscar Vitt a traveling bag. Buck admitted he gave Vitt a traveling bag at Christmas. Buck said it was his custom to spend the winter months with Vitt in the California mountains where they had exchanged gifts for years.

Shortly thereafter Vitt confirmed Weaver's story. Landis turned to Vitt. "It was testified here the other day that you received a hand bag from Buck Weaver of the Sox on the Christmas following the 1917 season. Will you tell me about that?"

Vitt told Landis he received a hand bag from Weaver about Christmas time and that there was nothing unusual about getting a holiday gift from Buck who was "reciprocating for hospitality shown him at my place in the mountains of California." Vitt supported Buck's statement that they spent several winters there from 1914 to 1920.

When Gandil told Landis his version of the collection of

$45 from each of the Sox players during his appearance on the witness stand during the second day of the hearings, he admitted Buck did not contribute to the fund. Gandil said Weaver objected to the idea in a clubhouse meeting in Chicago. Landis asked: "What did he say?"

"Well, Buck Weaver told me that he didn't like to do it; he didn't want to do it, and he said that I believe he would send to Oscar Vitt a Christmas present."

Gandil's story supported Risberg's testimony that the White Sox rewarded the Detroit Tigers for sloughing off those four games on September 2 and 3 in 1917. Gandil also backed Risberg's contention that the White Sox handed the Tigers two games on September 27 and 28 of 1919 to help them win third place.

Bill James, the Detroit pitcher who would join the White Sox in 1919, took the stand and admitted accepting money from Gandil and Risberg but called it "an absolute lie" that the Tigers were being rewarded for laying down for the White Sox. Just as all the other players claimed, with the exception of Risberg and Gandil, James said the money had been given to reward Detroit pitchers for beating the Boston Red Sox.

The hearings were over. Landis would now hide away for four days preparing his findings. In the meantime Buck must have been elated by a story in the Chicago *Daily News* on January 8: "Another by-product of the Gandil-Risberg attempt to get revenge on the game that has cast them out probably will be the reinstatement of Buck Weaver who came out of the Landis investigation with flying colors. There has always been a sentiment among baseball fans that Buck was sort of human sacrifice back in 1920, when everybody who was even suspected of participation in the 1919 World Series sellout was kicked out of the game."

Two days later Buck filed a formal request with Commissioner Landis for reinstatement.

Landis evaded pursuing reporters the night of January 11-12, finally returning to his apartment at the Chicago Beach Hotel at 3:00 A.M. Wednesday morning. Still he wouldn't announce his verdict, even though the *Tribune* in an exclusive story reported a day earlier that he had exonerated all the ballplayers. Finally, at 10:00 A.M., Landis read his decision before a group of reporters. No players were present. There was no "tense excitement" as Landis read his 3,000 word five page summary: "To some it may seem inexplicable that Risberg and Gandil should implicate themselves in these alleged corrupt practices. Obviously that self-implication may have been conceived upon the theory that 'they have been incriminated themselves so it must be true.' However, being already on the ineligible list, this would not affect them and it might blacken the 'lily-whites.'

"It is the finding of the Commissioner that the fund raised by the Chicago players about September 28, 1917, was not collected or paid to Detroit players for 'sloughing' to Chicago the games of September 2 and 3, 1917, but was paid because of Detroit's beating Boston, that there was no 'sloughing' of the September 2 and 3, 1917, games, nor of the September 26, 27, and 28, 1919 games, except possibly by Risberg and Gandil . . .

"If the Risberg-Gandil version be correct it was an act of criminality. But if the other version be true there was an act of impropriety, reprehensible and censorable, but not corrupt."

Landis decreed that the White Sox fund given to Detroit was a gift and not a bribe. He recognized that it had been common practice for one team to reward another for doing well against its arch rival. But Landis decided because of the revelations at the hearing that such practices had to be eliminated. The commissioner suggested to major and minor league owners that week that there be "ineligibility for one year for offering or giving any gift or reward by the players or management of one club to the players or management of another club for services rendered or supposed to be or have been rendered in defeating a competing club."

Landis, irritated by indiscretions or alleged indiscretions committed before he became commissioner and being exposed many years later, suggested "a statute of limitations with respect to alleged baseball offenses, as in our state and national statutes with regard to criminal offenses." Under that kind of provision the Cobb-Speaker affair and the Risberg-Gandil charges would have been dismissed without consideration. The baseball owners were quick to accept the commissioner's ideas which soon became baseball law.

Now Landis could turn his attention back to the Cobb-Speaker problem, which had taken a back seat because of the Risberg accusations. As Landis was considering his decision, Ban Johnson rushed to print in the New York Times on January 18: "I know Ty Cobb's not a crooked ball player. We let him go because he had written a peculiar letter about a betting deal that he couldn't explain and because I felt that he violated a position of trust.

"Tris Speaker is a different type of fellow. For want of a better word I'd call Tris cute. He knows why he was forced out of the managership of the Cleveland club. If he wants me to tell him I'll meet him in a court of law and tell the facts under oath . . . As long as I'm president of the American League neither of them will manage or play on our teams." Johnson, long simmering over the growing ascendancy of Landis and his own steep decline of power, directly challenged Landis: "Speaker and Cobb never again will play in the American League, notwithstanding what action Landis may eventually take in this matter."

This and other statements in the press, such as Johnson's dissatisfaction over Landis not taking an active role early in the Black Sox scandal, finally forced Landis's hand. The commissioner had heard enough. He threw down the gauntlet to the owners of the American League: "You've got to take Ban Johnson or me."

The owners took Landis. They decided on January 23 at the Blackstone Hotel in Chicago to finally remove Johnson from any position of power. He would continue to draw his salary as nominal president of the American League but he became only a figurehead as Frank Navin, owner of the Detroit Tigers, took over as acting president. Johnson, in ill health, resigned July 8. Almost four years later he died a sick, broken man. It was a tragic, sad ending to a brilliant career of the founder of the American League. Landis now was the unchallenged, unquestioned czar of baseball.

Landis finally cleaned up the Cobb-Speaker affair on January 27 when he announced: ". . . . These players have not been, nor are they now found guilty of fixing a ball game. By no decent system of justice could such finding be made. Therefore, they were not placed on the ineligible list.

"As they desire to rescind their withdrawal from baseball, the releases which the Detroit and Cleveland clubs granted at their requests, in the circumstances are cancelled and the players' names are restored to the reserve lists of these clubs." Neither Cobb nor Speaker returned to their old ball clubs. Cobb signed with the Philadelphia Athletics and Speaker joined the Washington Senators. Each played two more years. Speaker in 1928 became Cobb's teammate on the A's.

Probably Buck Weaver couldn't help but view these developments with new hope. There were growing signals that he might be welcomed back into organized baseball. Buck was warmed by comments written by his former White Sox teammate, Eddie Collins, who was writing a syndicated newspaper column. In the Chicago *Daily News* on January 19, Collins wrote: "Buck Weaver liked to play ball better than any one I have ever seen. It has always been said that Jimmy Collins was the greatest artist at third of all time. I don't dispute it, but I'd rather have 'Buck' on my team. He played great ball at short, but was a trifle erratic there and preferred third." Exactly one week later, Collins focused on Buck again. "Weaver was a splendid base runner, equally effective hitting right or left-handed and batted to all fields. Though he never attained the high average that Bradley and Collins did, I think he would have been a more dangerous sticker than either had he remained in the game."

Collins' comments are quite revealing. If there was friction between him and Weaver, it didn't stand in Eddie's way of publicly recognizing Buck's talent. As for Jimmy Collins, he was an exceptionally fine third baseman for both Boston teams between 1895 and 1907. He posted a career batting mark of .285. Third baseman Bill Bradley played most of his career with Cleveland in the first decade of the twentieth century. He finished with a .283 batting average. By comparison Buck concluded nine years in the majors with a .272 mark.

In addition to Collins the press generally, if not directly, sought to build up a case for Weaver's return to the major leagues. Only two days before Landis cleared Cobb and Speaker, a Chicago *Daily News* reporter wrote: "The only unfinished business of one of baseball's most sensational 'off' seasons will be the bid of 'Buck' Weaver for the right once more to don a player's uniform . . ."

On the same day that Landis cleared Cobb and Speaker, George Moriarity, a former Detroit and White Sox third baseman and Cobb's replacement as manager, wrote a column in the Galveston *Tribune* recognizing Buck as a superstar when he was cut down. Weaver at third base "immediately began to show flashes of true greatness. He became a sure and sensational fielder, and displayed remarkable ease in coming up clear with hops at either side.

"Being the possessor of a truly marvelous arm, he threw out his victims from all possible angles in and out of position. His fielding of bunts was one of the finest pieces of execution I have seen on the ball field.

"Nor did his qualifications end there, as he was just coming into his own as a clever batsman and baserunner when he was ousted.

"Weaver had all the speed of a Cobb on the bases, and it hardly required an expert's prophecy to picture him as a player about to record the greatest deeds of his career."

A cartoon alongside the story showed Buck as a debonair dresser, with homburg, suit and tie. Captions in the cartoon read: "HIS FIELDING OF BUNTS WAS THE FINEST. WEAVER HAD A BETTER ARM AND WAS FASTER THAN J. COLLINS. BASEBALL LOST ITS GREATEST THIRD BASEMAN WITH THE PASSING OF BUCK WEAVER."

The sports editor of the Milwaukee *Sentinel*, George F. Downer, rallied to Weaver's side: "Evidence against Weaver not as strong as evidence against Cobb, or Speaker" and he mentioned several other players. "All these cleared. Why doesn't Weaver get the same square deal?

"It is reported, and generally believed, that C. A. Comiskey himself was 'tipped off' before the Series started that something was wrong, and was warned and urged not to allow Cicotte to pitch the opening game."

But all Buck could do now, despite all the good wishes of the press and the fans, was wait for word from Commissioner Landis. That word reached Buck on March 12. As he unfolded a long letter he appeared "as lithe and dynamic as when he raked in line drives on the 'hot corner' with the Sox in the years up to 1920."

The last paragraph of the detailed letter rankled Weaver with bitterness: "I regret that it was not possible for me to arrive at any other conclusion than that set forth in the decision of Dec. 11, 1922, that your own admissions and actions in the circumstances forbid your reinstatement . . ."

Landis wrote in part: "In connection with your renewal of your reinstatement application I have carefully examined the records relating to the matters involved.

"1. You testify that preceding the 1919 world series Cicotte, your team's leading pitcher that season, asked you if you wanted to 'get in on something—fix the world series,' and you replied: 'You are crazy, that can't be done!'

"2. The world series then was played and so played that even during the series your manager at a meeting of the players, stated something was wrong. Assuming that your opinion when Cicotte solicited you to come in on fixing the series, was, as you testify, 'that can't be done' what happened during the series must have made you question that opinion. After the series there were persistent reports which had widespread publicity, that there had been crooked work by the White Sox players. People suspected that it not only was possible, but an actual fact, that the series had been fixed even though they had not your knowledge about the Cicotte proposition! You knew your club officials were seeking to ascertain the facts but you kept still . . .

"3. You further testify that during the following season another teammate came to you and said Cicotte had sent him to ask if you wanted to make some money throwing ball games. You said nothing to Cicotte about it, you say, but told his agent to tell him that if he ever repeated the solicitation you would tell.

"4. Later that season the 1919 world series was investigated by a grand jury before which Cicotte and two others of your teammates testified under oath that the series had been fixed for and by gamblers.

"All three testified that you were implicated in this. Indictments were returned against all the players named by them, including you, but on trial of these indictments you made common cause with these three players, who, you knew, had implicated you, and one of whom you say had twice solicited you to join in game throwing. At the trial, you were confronted with a witness who testified that he acted as an agent between the gamblers and the crooked players, arranging the fixing of the series and he also named you as one of the participants. Thus there is on record the sworn testimony of four admitted participants in the 'fixing' that you were implicated.

"It is true that the jury verdict was 'not guilty' and that the idea apparently prevails to some extent that this exonerated you and the other defendants of the charge of game throwing. However, this same jury returned the same verdict as to the three other players who admitted accepting bribe money to throw the series."

Buck writhed with disappointment. Landis's words that he had made "common cause with his four accusers" was a distortion of the truth. Weaver said bitterly, "I begged for a separate trial, but my lawyers advised me against it. I didn't testify because they wouldn't let me." Landis had earlier declared Buck should have taken the stand to refute the charges of his accusers. The *Tribune* of March 13 summarized Buck's

bleak predicament in its headline: "LANDIS WRECKS WEAV-
ER'S HOPE OF PLAYING BALL; Denies Buck's Plea for Reinstatement."

There was one great inaccuracy with the *Tribune* headline. Landis may have denied Buck's plea for reinstatement
but he would never wreck the baseball lover's will to fight
to clear his name. Buck would never surrender to Landis.
He may have been dropped for the nine count but he would
scramble to his feet and struggle on even after Landis's death.

19

"One of the Sweetest Guys"

By spring 1927 Buck, nearing the age of 37, couldn't restrain himself any longer. He had to get back on the playing field, any playing field. Sure, the drugstore was still there, and there were other amusements. He could be seen shooting pool often at Lorimer's Pool Hall on Garfield Boulevard, one block west of South Parkway, near the "el" track. Upstairs above the pool hall was the Golden Lily Chinese restaurant which featured dancing as well as food. Helen and Buck, being skilled dancers, probably patronized the establishment. Even in the pool hall, Buck was always laughing and kidding, a big grin on his face. One old-timer remembers Buck as a good player. He carried a bag of fifteen red unnumbered balls which he used in a game called straight pool. Instead of calling his shots by numbers, he would just indicate the ball he was aiming for. "Buck could have been in show business," he said. When Buck had a chance he would go out to the baseball diamonds at Washington Park, only one block west of Lorimer's, and hit fly balls to the kids. They loved Buck and he returned their affection. If the past was any guide, he probably attended the theatre with his beloved Helen. Buck could also find amusement bowling, golfing, hunting, playing pinochle and poker and going to the horse races. Yet his yearning to play ball could not be quieted. In early April representatives of the Midwest

League, a semipro circuit in Chicago and nearby cities and towns, voted unanimously to accept Weaver as a player.

That spring and summer thousands of Chicago fans came out to warmly greet the former third base great of the Chicago White Sox. He had signed on with a Hammond, Indiana, team. Since Hammond is located directly southeast of Chicago, the team performed all over the Chicagoland area. The crowds packed the small wooden stands to watch Buck execute defensive plays with the skill and grace that he displayed when he was years younger. Time had not diminished the magic of his performance; he was still the maestro of the third sack. And he could still sting the ball at the plate.

The *Tribune* gave considerable space to the semipro games complete with box scores. Buck's name appeared in baseball headlines once more. In a two column head on May 9 the *Tribune* reported: "6,000 Semi-Pro Fans in Tribute to Weaver." Admiring fans, who remained convinced that Landis had dealt too harshly with Buck, filled Logan Square Stadium on Chicago's northwest side at Spaulding and Elston avenues. In his first trip to the plate the fans presented Buck with several bouquets of flowers and a shotgun. That same day a record crowd of 52,000 watched the White Sox, who were still in the pennant fight, lose to the Yankees at Comiskey Park, 9 to 0. In 1927 double decked grandstands were built to completely encircle the outfield except for a small center field bleacher section that raised the seating capacity by about 16,000.

Buck may not have been playing in the big show but he obviously was having fun playing the game. One week later the *Tribune* observed that one of the features of the game was "the fielding of Buck Weaver who was a sensation around third base." He also got 2 singles and stole 2 bases in a win over a team called the Bricklayers.

On the following Sunday the *Tribune* wrote that "Buck Weaver was the whole show" as his team beat the Elgin Greyhounds, 8 to 1. "Besides making four hits out of five trips to the plate, Weaver was also the outstanding star in the field, handling eight chances, four of which were most difficult."

On June 13 the *Tribune* headlined: "Weaver Stars as Hammond Wins . . ." Buck had a perfect day at the plate, knocking out 2 doubles and 2 singles. In a 5 to 4 victory over Waukegan, Buck scored three times and "played a spectacular game on defense."

That was the pleasant pattern all summer. Every Sunday capacity crowds flocked to watch Buck play. "An overflow crowd of 4,500 turned out to honor Buck Weaver" with another floral tribute on August 6. The season ended on a high note as the *Tribune* headlined on October 2: "Weaver Bats Hammond to 2 to 1 Victory."

On September 22, not long before the curtain rang down on the baseball season, Helen and Buck attended the heavyweight championship fight between Jack Dempsey and Gene Tunney along with 145,000 others at Soldier Field. That was the famous fight in which Tunney took advantage of the "long count" when Dempsey was tardy in going to a neutral corner after flooring Gene in the seventh round. Referee Dave Barry didn't start the count until four or five seconds had elapsed. Tunney survived and went on to retain the title.

Off season Weaver gave more attention to his duties in the drugstore and in the spring returned to baseball action with the Duffy Florals, a south side Chicago semipro team. Buck became the manager of the ball club and shifted himself back to shortstop. Nearing the age of forty, Weaver may have been playing a far superior game at short than he had years earlier in the majors. He still played with that boyish enthusiasm that impelled him to whoop and holler when he patrolled the outfield for the San Francisco Seals in 1911. He was still the Ginger Kid.

Of course, he was playing mainly on weekends and he didn't have the daily pressures of big league baseball weighing down on him. But Buck had performed in the majors with that same free-wheeling, blithe spirit. Chicago semipro baseball may not have been the majors, but the level of play was quite high. Many players were just as talented and could have played in the big leagues if they had chosen to do so. They preferred staying home and earning more money on a regular job and playing ball on weekends. In any case, Weaver cavorted about the diamond with gleeful abandon. June 3, 1928: Weaver got a "single, walk, stolen base and ten accepted chances at short." June 17 headline: "Weaver Bat Aids Florals to 9-8 Win." Buck's homer in the ninth inning with two men out tied the score. Buck had a perfect day with a double and 3 singles to add to the round tripper. June 25: "Buck Weaver . . . hit a home run," singled, sacrificed, walked, stole a base and made "two sensational plays at short."

Weaver played his last competitive baseball in 1931 when he put together his own team called the Buck Weavers. The team was backed financially by Dennis "The Duke" Cooney, a first ward politician and local vice lord who made millions in bootlegging, prostitution and gambling. "The Duke" was one of Al Capone's early partners. By 1931 Cooney, as owner of the Royale Frolics night club on South Wabash Avenue, was trying to "dissociate his name from the business of the past and to appear as an important figure in the world of glamor [sic]." Though he neither drank or smoked, he was an extravagant and eccentric dresser. He owned fifty suits and 5,000 neckties. He changed clothes three times a day. He could be seen wearing a $200 purple suit and bright yellow shoes. By now he had gained a reputation of being free and easy with his dollars. Perhaps Buck solicited his help. Or Cooney may have offered it.

One of Buck's teammates was an eighteen year old recent high school graduate named Nick Etten. Etten would later climb to the major leagues as a fine fielding first baseman with the Philadelphia Athletics, Phillies and Yankees. In September, 1985, Etten remembered, "Weaver was like a kid around third base. Very agile. He was a good fielder and a very good hitter and was very quick at the time." That summer Buck turned forty-one.

Buck, Etten recalled, was one of those infielders who cut a hole in the pocket of his glove to ensure snaring the ball. The bare skin of the hand was not exposed since the glove has two layers of leather, according to Etten, but only a thin piece of leather remained to protect the hand.

Etten culled one amusing incident from memory. The Weavers were playing the American Giants, a top flight Negro ball club based in Chicago. In the eighth inning Etten was scheduled to bat against a tough left-hander named Willie Foster, the son of the great black player, Rube Foster. Buck advised Etten, "I'm going to bat for you." Etten remembered, "I talked him out of it. I batted and struck out on three pitches. I didn't even see the last pitch. Buck came over to me and told me that I would never talk him out of it again. Buck was a dandy. Something special."

By 1931 Buck faced problems that dwarfed the playing of baseball. The stock market crash of October 1929 and the ensuing Great Depression engulfed almost everyone in some way. Buck was no exception. His brother-in-law, William Scanlan, who had parlayed his first drugstore (of which Buck was part-owner) into a chain of six pharmacies on Chicago's south side, lost almost all of them. Buck's share of the business evaporated as well. Scanlan managed to hold on to one of the stores on a contract sale. But in 1931 Scanlan neglected to be hospitalized for an attack of acute appendicitis. The appendix burst, and an operation followed, but he died a week later of peritonitis. Buck then took into his home his sister-in-law, Annetta, and her two children, Bette, aged 9, and Patricia, aged 4. Helen and Buck had no children, but they helped raise the two girls to adulthood as if they were their own. In addition to this full household, Weaver's brother-in-law and former White Sox teammate, Jim Scott, and his wife, Harriet, Helen's sister, moved in with the Weavers in their south side bungalow for a short time. The bulging extended family was reduced a bit when the Scotts moved to Los Angeles. Jim found a job at RKO Pictures and Republic Studios as best boy, the chief electrician for shooting a motion picture. Shortly afterward, Buck, Helen, Annetta and the children moved into a new apartment building at 7814 South Winchester Avenue. Buck would live there the rest of his life.

At home Buck was a devoted husband and loving surrogate father. Helen and Buck would always go out together. They vacationed in the north woods of Wisconsin, living in the outdoors, pitching a tent and going fishing. Buck had taught Helen how to bowl and they were often seen bowling together. Bette recalled, "He was always the most generous of men. When Pat and I were little kids, he would take us to the corner grocery store and have us pick out candy to fill a good-sized grocery bag. Then he would tell us to take it back home and share it with our friends. He also believed that children should have their own spending money and every weekend would give us each a handful of dimes and quarters. He also gave us a large metal bank in the shape of Charles A. Lindbergh's bust. I remember that Lindbergh got most of the change and every Christmas we had enough money to buy Christmas presents for the family. He set a beautiful example."

Buck liked to take the family out for rides in his Chevy, even driving out to the dog races. Weaver would park the car where the children could see the races from the roof of the car under the watchful eyes of one of the adults. The others would take turns going into the dog track to wager on the greyhounds. Buck loved animals. Bette remembers when she was twelve years old, Uncle Buck brought home a beautiful Irish setter named Sandy. Buck had intended to train Sandy as a hunting dog but he turned out to be the family pet for eight years. At one time or another canaries and parakeets resided in the Weaver household as well.

In the meantime, with the drugstore gone, Buck sought other work. For about two years in the early thirties Buck and Helen tried their hand at running a sandwich shop at 2418 W. 95th Street Called "Buck Weaver's," the eatery featured french fried spareribs. The restaurant failed, according to Bette Scanlan, because Helen and Buck never mastered the knack of restaurant management. Anyhow the restaurant's business card was attractive. The back of the card showed Buck smiling in a White Sox uniform in a left-handed batting stance. He later found a job working for the city of Chicago as a painter for $10 a day. Arthur Edelson, an eighty year old retired automotive supplier, recalled in 1987 meeting Buck at a Pixley and Ellers restaurant at 63rd Street and Cottage Grove Avenue in the early thirties. "When Buck came in I went to his table. Buck looked tired and didn't wear a jacket.

" 'How are you Buck?' I said.

" 'I remember you,' Buck said."

Edelson said he used to come to the ballpark every day, sneaking in one way or another. Edelson was twelve years old when he used to get to the opening in the low fence near the third base dugout. "I'd wait there until infield practice was over and then I'd yell, 'Oh Buck, Oh Buck, can I have the practice ball?'

"Buck would toss me the ball. It became a daily habit with me yelling, 'Oh Buck, Oh Buck!' We used the balls in our neighborhood games."

Reflecting on that meeting in the restaurant many years later, Edelson said, "When he told me he was working for ten dollars a day, I was taken by surprise. I'm sorry I didn't offer him a job. Some things you want to do from your heart. He was one of the nicest, kindest guys you'd want to meet."

But Buck found his new niche at the race track. He followed the horses as often as he could. In his trips to the track he met Charles Bidwell Sr., owner of Sportsman's Park race oval on Chicago's southwest side. Bidwell, one of the city's leading sportsmen, was also a sports promoter on a grand scale. Besides the race track Bidwell owned the Chicago Cardinals of the National Football League. Traditionally, the Cardinals were second class citizens in a town dominated by the Bears, their arch rivals on the north side. Many years later—in 1960—the Cardinals would move their franchise to St. Louis. Bidwell was also involved in professional basketball in its early years when teams played in national guard armories and a crowd of 5,000 was a sellout. Bidwell hired Buck as a pari-mutuel clerk. This job remained his chief means of livelihood for the rest of his life, except for a brief interlude when Weaver worked at a war plant job during the early years of World War II. Once employed as a pari-mutuel clerk, Buck had no trouble finding work as the racing season shifted to other Chicago area tracks.

Before long Buck worked regularly at the $50 pari-mutuel window. "Even though he had little schooling, he could just look up a column of figures and add it up in his head. I guess that's why they put him at the fifty dollar pari-mutuel window because he was so good with figures," niece Bette Scanlan reminisced in 1984. "He would bet on horses if at the last minute a lot of bets were placed on a horse. When he won at the races he'd share his winnings. He was a very generous man."

Charles Bidwell Jr., president of Sportsman's Park in 1984, remembered Buck as "one of the sweetest guys I ever knew." Bidwell recalled Buck working and chewing tobacco, spitting the tobacco juices in a nearby coffee can. He described Weaver as a real gentleman who possessed a superior attitude about loyalty and friendship.

Buck and Helen avoided social events and were not often seen in public. Away from the track Buck put in time as a card dealer at an establishment at 79th and Halsted streets. He spent leisurely hours playing pinochole with friends at a saloon at 63rd and Halsted. As for close friends coming to the apartment, Happy Felsch and Oscar Vitt paid social calls. Felsch lived in Milwaukee where he operated a tavern and Vitt, Buck's old buddy from San Francisco days, had become manager of the Cleveland Indians in 1938 and remained at the helm until the end of the 1940 season. He would visit Helen and Buck whenever the Indians played in Chicago. "While I don't remember the Fabers coming to the house," Bette Scanlan said, "I know Uncle Buck and Aunt Helen saw them socially."

It was a rare occasion now for Buck's relatives or friends

from his home towns to visit. But sometime about 1948 two apparent strangers came to the door. Bette answered since Helen was ironing and Buck wasn't home yet.

"Is Danny Weaver here?" It had been years since anyone had called Buck 'Danny'.

Bette answered, "You mean Buck Weaver?"

The two strangers turned out to be Luther Weaver, Buck's nephew, and Douglas Ludwig, Luther's friend, who were in Chicago to participate in a bowling tournament. The two stayed for dinner. According to a story in the Pottstown, Pennsylvania, *Mercury* in 1988, they recalled that Buck "was as cheerful as ever, but still resolute to clear his name."

Luther said, "He was all smiles. That's the way he always was."

"Just a heckuva nice guy," Ludwig said.

With his baseball playing days long over, Buck could still find an outlet for his athletic prowess on the golf course and at the bowling alley. Bette Scanlan recalled, "He never took more than two clubs. He just put them under his arm and off he would go. He also enjoyed hunting and fishing.

"He had a natural gracefulness and he was excellent in every sport he attempted. He didn't go in much for tennis. However, one day I got a brand new racquet and he got hold of an old junky racquet and we went out to a prairie and he just beat me to pieces. He was a good bowler and taught me to bowl."

As for baseball, Buck never went to the ballpark, although he watched all sports on television in his later years.

Throughout the years, Buck did not fold his hand and give up his dream of clearing his name. That battle continued while he played semipro ball. Sportswriters and newspaper columnists sporadically focused on Weaver's situation expressing both sympathy and sorrow. Baseball fans in Chicago, in poll after poll, vouchsafed their confidence in Buck by naming him their choice as the best third baseman in either White Sox or Chicago history. While Buck was still playing semipro ball, south siders set up booths on busy street corners asking passersby to sign petitions asking for his reinstatement. But it was all to no avail.

Weaver and his attorney, Louis B. Rosenthal, who remained Buck's counselor for at least sixteen years, fought on to win his return to the majors. One short newspaper clipping dated May 6, 1930, carried the head: "Buck Weaver Fights For Reinstatement." The story went on to report: "George (Buck) Weaver, White Sox third baseman who was expelled from organized ball as a result of the 'Black Sox scandal' of 1919, is fighting for reinstatement.

"Weaver and his attorney, Louis B. Rosenthal, claim they have unearthed new evidence to prove their contention that Weaver was innocent of the conspiracy charges that banished him and seven other White Sox players. They were charged with conspiring to 'throw' the world series of 1919.

"Weaver has been denied several reinstatement applications by Kenesaw M. Landis, commissioner of baseball. Since his banishment he has been playing semi-pro ball."

Whatever the new evidence was, it was not made public. Nothing of consequence followed that story.

Sometime in the 1930s, the Chicago *American* theatre critic, Ashton Stevens, quoted entertainer-composer-actor George M. Cohan as saying about Buck, "I will never believe that my good friend had anything to do with it," meaning the fixing of the 1919 World Series.

In later years when Bette Scanlan learned of that column, she asked Buck about it. He replied simply, "I roomed with him in New York."

Chicago *Tribune* sportswriter turned columnist, Westbrook Pegler, in an article published November 13, 1932, castigated his fellow reporters, including himself, for not revealing "the reek of the fake" after the first two games of the 1919 World Series. He concluded, "We were terrible." He did take note that fellow writer Hugh Fullerton did report after the Series was over that something was wrong and seven White Sox would not return for the 1920 season.

In the climax of his column, Pegler, hardly recognized

as a sentimentalist, rushed to the defense of the banished White Sox third baseman. "Buck Weaver . . . was the victim of a singularly hypocritical deal in the reform which followed the exposé. Weaver was asked to join in the scheme, but refused, and he not only took no money but he played loyally and beautifully all through the series.

"However, he undoubtedly did have guilty knowledge which, if he had been working for trustworthy employers, ought to have been communicated to them at once. But if Weaver had squealed the plot would have been abandoned, the other players would have 'played their heads off,' the White Sox would have won the series in four games [Author's note: a neat trick since the Series was the best out of nine games] and Weaver would have been accused of stirring up trouble and fouling the fair name of innocent men.

"Remember that Charlie Comiskey and Ban Johnson did not wish to believe that the Black Sox had been bribed, even when evidence began to accumulate. Fullerton was denounced as a suspicious gossip and a destructive critic when he took a chance at the end of the Series. It took ten months for Comiskey and Johnson to admit to themselves that the World Series had been a fake.

"So I do not think Weaver could have saved himself by reporting his knowledge to Comiskey or Johnson. Many a man had been quietly whispered out of the game and many a man has been whispered out since, without a trial, without any accusation against him, merely on the judgment of the magnates that his going would tend to benefit the game.

"So Weaver was just lynched because he happened to be standing around the corner when the posse came yelling along with the rope. He was a great ballplayer, too."

Sportswriters continued to take up the cudgels for Buck. Just two years later, on October 6, 1934, a well-known New York sportswriter, Bill Corum, wrote in a column appearing in the Chicago *American*, ". . . Abe Attel claims that Buck Weaver never was a member of the shameful group of traitors who came to be known as the Black Sox. Since Mr. AA was the man who finally got the Black Sox such paltry monies as eventually they received for their treachery, there is better than a fair chance that he knows whereof he speaks." Of course Corum didn't have all his facts straight. Most of the money the Black Sox received apparently came from the coffers of Arnold Rothstein.

Chicago baseball fans overwhelmingly voted for Buck Weaver as their third baseman on an all-time White Sox all-star team in a poll by the Chicago *American* in February 1936. With 28,640 readers participating, Buck got 24,192 votes. Willie Kamm finished in second place with 2,224 tallies, an 11 to 1 margin for Buck.

As late as 1938, one full generation after the Black Sox scandal, Chicago baseball fans still showed their warm regard for Buck when they voted him as their all-star third baseman for an all-time Chicago team of Cub and White Sox players. The poll was conducted by Lloyd Lewis, sports editor, drama critic and biographer, in his Chicago *Daily News* column, "Voice of the Grandstand."

Stories kept bobbing up in the press about the ill-fated White Sox and Buck in particular. Chicago sports reporter Wayne Otto, writing fifteen years after the exposé, deemed the 1919–20 White Sox a match for any team. "There, brothers, was a team that could get runs most any old time they wanted them! Jackson, Felsch, Gandil, E. Collins, Risberg.

"Buck Weaver was just the sort of a hitter who fitted in perfectly with such an ensemble. He was one of the finest switch batters in the history of the majors and he had plenty of power from either side of the plate."

Ty Cobb named Buck to his all-time all-star team in the February 26, 1942, issue of the *Sporting News*. Said Cobb: "Third base brings us to the White Sox of 1919, doesn't it? You can't leave Buck Weaver and Joe Jackson off a team like this. Buck could do everything, a terrific thrower and hitter. He gets third base . . . Joe Jackson, the greatest natural hitter that ever was, is my left fielder . . ."

Cobb mused, "Yeah, that White Sox team of 1919 was the best baseball club I ever saw play or played against. They could hit and run. They could all hit to right field. Not a weakness on it. Great pitchers and great fielders. Hap Felsch was a wonder. So was Swede Risberg. Chick Gandil was smart and a great man to throw to. Say, they were so good they almost won that 1919 world series when most of them were trying to lose it . . ."

In 1944 Buck's job as a pari-mutuel clerk at the race track gave him a chance to get back on the diamond, albeit a girls' softball league field. His employer at the track, Charles Bidwell, Sr., helped organize a girls' league and appointed Buck to manage his Bidwell Bluebirds. The league, called by the rather pretentious name of National Girls' Professional League, had five local teams. Besides the Bluebirds there were the Chicks, Bloomer Girls, Tungsten Sparks and the Brach Kandy Kids. The girls played nine inning fast pitch with a 12-inch ball; the pitcher's rubber was 35 feet from the plate and the bases 60 feet apart.

Bidwell and his associates took the girls' softball league seriously. So did the fans and the press. The price of a ticket was comparable to an admission to a movie theatre. The newspapers regularly reported the results and standings of the teams and ran feature stories on many of the players. The girls played five nights a week and earned from $25 to $60 in that time. If their teams couldn't meet a payroll, the league guaranteed the girls' pay and they got two weeks' dismissal pay if they were cut. Most of the girls worked in war plants during the day.

For their games, Bidwell bought "a neat little southside park" at 1925 East 75th Street and called it Bidwell Stadium. Crowds averaged about 1,000 fans a night with attendance climbing higher in July and August.

One evening Bidwell rushed on the field to support Weaver's protest against an umpire's call and Edward Prell, a top sportswriter for the *Tribune*, reported: ". . . such screetching as you seldom hear outside a zoo, by a group of girls in satin shorts . . ." In that same game, one of the girls slid into second base. Prell watched Buck: "The old campaigner winced as he felt the skinscraping, and muttered,

'Those girls really have it. Why, a ball player won't hit the dirt unless he has on sliding pads.' "

Buck admittedly was surprised by the skill and talent of the girls. They in turn considered themselves fortunate pupils to be learning the inside of the game from such an outstanding teacher.

While busily occupied with working at the race tracks and managing the Bluebirds, Buck seems to have made another bid to clear his name. The record of this attempt is clouded by omissions and inconsistencies, however. According to the *Tribune* of May 26, 1946, Buck and his attorney, Louis B. Rosenthal, were to leave for Cincinnati the next day to ask for a hearing before baseball commissioner, Albert Benjamin "Happy" Chandler, a United States senator from Kentucky who succeeded Landis after the feisty judge passed away November 25, 1944. Although Asinof and Seymour both mention Buck's unsuccessful attempt to expunge his name from baseball's black list by enlisting Chandler's aid, a letter from the former commissioner to the author dated May 23, 1984, states: "I have no recollection of Buck Weaver ever having applied to me for reinstatement." In another letter to the author dated October 24, 1984, he wrote ". . . I have no recollection of ever having seen Buck Weaver." Whatever the facts they did not alter the reality that Weaver was still locked out of professional baseball.

According to Asinof, Weaver enlisted the support of Judge Hugo Friend, who believed in Buck's innocence and wrote Chandler to consider leniency in Buck's behalf. Judge Friend also submitted a brief to Chandler's successor, Ford Frick, but to no avail. Buck futilely also appealed in a letter to Frick.

Buck publicly denied that he participated in the "fake World Series against Cincinnati" in a radio broadcast on Chicago's WGN sports program, "Spotlight on Sports," on August 2, 1947. "I was not in on the fix and didn't know anything about it. I was barred from organized baseball because they thought I knew about the fix. I batted .330 (actually

.324) and fielded 1.000. Does that look like I was in on it?" Weaver, who had just led a poll for an all-time White Sox team, told the audience that he had applied to Judge Landis for reinstatement twenty-four times and once to A. B. "Happy" Chandler.

Jack Brickhouse, one of Chicago's three Hall of Fame baseball announcers (the others are Bob Elson and Harry Carey) in his autobiography *Thanks For Listening* mentions his interview with Buck Weaver on August 2, 1947. After the program Jack suggested that Buck take a lie detector test. If Buck passed the test, Brickhouse said he would get him enough publicity to "force baseball to clear his name." If Buck failed the test all would be forgotten. Brickhouse wrote, "But for some reason, he turned me down." There were reasons. Buck had already experienced the futility of publicity earlier in his struggle for reinstatement. And the lie detector was hardly foolproof.

Buck by now was almost fifty-seven years old and must have become weary of his quest for reinstatement, but he never surrendered. He still dreamed of coaching or scouting in organized ball. He was particularly pleased that he discovered Nick Etten on Chicago's south side sandlots.

In his last years Buck went about his business working as a pari-mutuel clerk at the race tracks in and around Chicago. One of the nation's distinguished sportswriters, John P. Carmichael of the Chicago *Daily News*, often saw Weaver at the pari-mutuel windows and tried to get him to talk about the 1919 World Series. "But Weaver was very reticent," Carmichael recalled in an interview in 1984. "Never get anything out of him. He'd freeze up." Carmichael said he felt Buck "was pulled in against his will. He thought he might go along but got out."

At home Buck remained a devoted husband, staying close to Helen, especially after she suffered a stroke in 1952. At first confined to bed with 90 percent of her left side paralyzed, Helen proved to be a fighter like her Buck. With physical therapy she eventually was able to walk with the aid of a cane. Because her foot would give way suddenly without warning, she was compelled to wear a brace up to her knee. She wore slacks to cover the brace. Bette bought Buck and Helen a television set and they sat home together watching television every evening. Bette helped her mother, Annetta Marie, do the shopping and cooking besides holding a clerical job with the *Chicago Sun-Times*. By this time Bette's sister, Patricia, had married and moved out of the apartment.

While Weaver did not attend sports events he followed them on television. Buck hadn't seen a major league ball game in person in thirty years. In November 1953, he told Gene Kessler, sports editor of the *Chicago Sun-Times*, "I knew how the game should be played" and according to Kessler Buck flashed "the same cheerful smile which characterized the days when he was an idol on the South Side." Buck continued, "I don't want to see modern players. They are in the game for the money. And they get it. The bat boy today gets more than we were paid to win pennants."

No longer the young, carefree, boisterous spirit, Buck could still enjoy a humorous and funny situation. Bette recalled, "He didn't laugh out loud but you'd know he was chuckling inside because his shoulder would shake."

Public interest in Buck Weaver's struggle did fade in his final years. But if public interest declined, diehard baseball fans, especially White Sox fans from the old days, kept the flame from flickering out all together. One such fan was author James T. Farrell. He interviewed Buck at the Morrison Hotel in Chicago in the fall of 1954. "He was a thin, pale gray man in his sixties. He dressed on the sporty side, and there were small red blotches on his face. He smiled easily and readily. During his playing days, he was always smiling and kidding on the field. Buck's smile as well as his great playing ability made him one of the most popular White Sox players of his time at Comiskey Park."

In the end Buck's years of determined struggle did not win him his reinstatement that he so desperately wanted and keenly felt he deserved—as did many others. Baseball had been his life, but as he bitterly pointed out to author Farrell, "A murderer even serves his sentence and is let out. I got life."

Buck's life came to a sudden, lonely end on a cold, raw winter day in the early afternoon as he walked along 71st Street on Chicago's south side on his way to see his income tax consultant. A passing motorist saw Buck suddenly "clutching at a white picket fence" in front of the house at 1224 71st Street. He got out of his car and raced over to help, but it was too late. Buck had slumped to the sidewalk, dead of a heart attack. It was January 31, 1956.

Two of Weaver's former teammates, Red Faber and Ray Schalk, lived in Chicago and both took the news hard. Faber said: "I played baseball with Weaver and I played cards with him, and I found him as honest as could be. No one can ever be certain about 1919, I guess. Weaver was a wonderful competitor, a fellow who played baseball because he loved it. Buck Weaver and Lena Blackburne were two I knew who never wanted to leave the field not even in practice."

Schalk, referring to 1919, said: "That incident caused Weaver the tortures of hell. It sure was a shame to see him go from this world without getting his name cleared."

Faber reminisced a moment: "He was always laughing. Remember, Ray, one day he threw the ball away. He comes into the bench and sits down beside Rowland and says, 'Teach—we used to call Rowland Teach—don't worry, don't worry Teach, we'll win this one.' That was Buck."

Schalk and Eddie Collins denied that Weaver wouldn't talk to them.

Chicago newspapers gave prominent coverage to Buck's death. The Chicago *Daily News* on February 1 headlined: "Death Ends Long Fight Of Weaver." The melancholy lead told the somber story: "George 'Buck' Weaver's dream of clearing his name may come true someday, but it will be too late." The *Tribune* ran a four column head under its banner on the sports page, stating in large type: "Weaver, Ex-Sox Star Dies."

The next day a short news story from San Francisco in

the Chicago *Daily News* told of Ty Cobb's reaction to Weaver's passing: "Ty Cobb regards Buck Weaver as 'the greatest third baseman I ever saw' and the old Georgia Peach always will believe Weaver got a raw deal in being banned from baseball after the Black Sox scandal."

Cobb had great respect for Buck as a player and tough competitor. As belligerent as he was, Ty did not hold any special grudge against his baseball adversary. Weaver was one player who did not fear the rough and tumble Cobb. He once warned the rampaging Tiger base runner, "If you ever come in with your spikes high, I'll stomp all over you." In later years, at a retirement party for Eddie Munzel, a *Chicago Sun-Times* sportswriter, Buck's niece Bette was approached by an old-time White Sox employee. He was Ernie Carroll, a waiter and chef in the Bard's Room, the posh dining room for the big wheels at Comiskey Park. He stopped Bette briefly during the evening and said, "Buck and Cobb had a big difference of opinion and beggin' your pardon ma'am, your uncle beat the hell out of Cobb under the bleachers." That would have been no small feat. First of all, most players feared Cobb. He could be mean and vicious on and off the field. Cobb stood 6 feet 1 inch tall and weighed close to 200 pounds. Weaver reached about 5 feet 10 inches in height and tipped the scales at about 170.

But their antagonism towards each other on the diamond did not linger off the field after their playing days were over and did not leave any permanent scars of dislike between the two men. Long after both careers became history Buck noticed Cobb's residence in a newspaper story and sent him a Christmas card. Ty answered in a letter that anytime he was asked about all-time greats, he'd name Buck on the team.

Buck's passing merited national attention. *New York Times* sports columnist Arthur Daley devoted a 16 inch story to Buck in his "Sports of the Times" article on February 19. Astride the top of the second column of the story was a picture of an ever smiling Buck, posed batting left-handed in the ancient dark blue traveling uniform of the White Sox. In those days the White Sox really wore white sox. Daley wrote in part: "Perhaps Weaver was the most tragic figure to emerge from the infamous Black Sox scandal. It generally was admitted that he took no active part in throwing the series to the Cincinnati Reds, but he did have guilty knowledge that such a plot was afoot. He kept that knowledge to himself and therefore was barred forever from organized baseball by Judge Kenesaw Mountain Landis, the Commissioner.

"The pity of it was that Weaver might have gained recognition as one of baseball's greatest third basemen, a tenant of the Hall of Fame and a man with the stature of a Pie Traynor or a Jimmy Collins. A scatter-arm shortstop of indifferent skills and a right-handed hitter of little class, he became a brilliant third baseman and a deadly left-handed batter. Suddenly he was out of baseball, his peak still unattained."

One may argue with some of Daley's conclusions. Despite Weaver's banishment, true students of the game recognize Buck as one of the great third basemen and while he may have been erratic at short, he certainly did not show "indifferent skills" at that position. In fact, he was often sensational.

Daley was critical of Buck's refusal to tell what he knew. "One word from Weaver," Daley wrote, "could have settled everything and that's why his silence almost amounted to a criminal act."

Daley's harsh interpretation was in sharp contrast with that of Farrell, whose *My Baseball Diary* was published a year after Weaver's death. Farrell pointed out that Buck had grown to maturity influenced by a code that "cast scorn and opprobrium on a squealer. He must have heard tales and rumors of the thrown games prior to 1919. These, if there were such—as seems to have been the case—were not reported. What should a player like Weaver have done? And had he told of the 'fix' could he have felt safe in his own career? There could have been the word of 7 against one."

Among the ballplayers themselves there was a code of silence in the years before 1919. What shenanigans transpired on the field, they kept to themselves. The owners were willing accomplices, as they chose to look the other way while high rolling gamblers infested the ballparks and associated freely with ballplayers in hotels and bars. The owners themselves mingled with the "sportsmen." In public, baseball executives ranted against the evils of gambling, but they refused to take action which might threaten their considerable—and profitable—investments in players and plant. Buck Weaver could not have missed the futility of Christy Mathewson's efforts, who as manager of the Cincinnati Reds, unsuccessfully tried to get Hal Chase kicked out of baseball for fixing games. If one of the most respected names in the game was ignored by the top brass, why would Buck believe the baseball nabobs might give him any more of a hearing?

Not only in baseball was the informer considered by most people a pariah; it was a standard in American society generally. Joe Jackson told sportswriter Carmichael many years after the scandal that he was taught from childhood "not to peach against anyone." That kind of attitude is still prevalent and is taught in our schools even today. In the October 1983 issue of the American Federation of Labor's Teachers newspaper, *American Teacher*, a first grade teacher proudly tells how she stopped her pupils from tattling on each other.

When Landis ascended to the position of sole commissioner of organized baseball, however, he totally ignored the customs, values and traditions in and surrounding the game of baseball, many of which found their roots particularly in rural nineteenth century America. As a federal judge, Landis handed down decisions that were often unpredictable, inconsistent, sometimes even capricious and at odds with acceptable jurisprudence. Not only were his most popular decisions overturned by the Supreme Court, he became the target of impeachment demands by some members of the United States Congress. The American Bar Association in September 1921 passed a resolution criticizing Landis's dual role as a federal judge and commissioner of baseball. Those demands and criticisms were quieted when he resigned from the bench in early 1922.

Admittedly, baseball desperately needed an arbitrator and overseer who would clean its untidy house. Following the White Sox scandal which was only the tip of the iceberg in the nether world of gambling and fixing, a strong-willed, incorruptible man was required at the helm to restore baseball to unquestioned respectability. Landis appeared to be that man.

For Buck Weaver though, Landis proved a disaster. Landis did not take into consideration the social milieu of the times, the mores and attitudes that shaped men's behavior. More critically, he did not recognize different degrees of culpability. If Weaver was guilty of any wrongdoing, should he have been classed in the same catagory with those who actually agreed to throw the Series and who received tainted money from the gamblers? Did Weaver deserve the same punishment as the others? Wouldn't it have served justice if Buck had been suspended a year or two or even five rather than being banished for life? As newspaper columnist Haywood Broun wrote, "Landis handed out justice with a meat cleaver." As a matter of law, Weaver had done nothing wrong. He may have been unwise in remaining silent. Perhaps he was less than courageous. But in his scale of personal values, squealing ranked as a vile act; he just wasn't going to talk. Tragically, Buck "realized that silence isn't always golden" as columnist Arthur Daley concluded in his piece about Weaver in the *New York Times* three weeks after Buck's death.

Three years after Buck passed away, the White Sox won their first pennant in forty years and Weaver won a tremendous tribute from one of his former managers. Fans were comparing the 1959 Go-Go Sox with the 1917 World Champions, the last Chicago team to win a World Series. Clarence "Pants" Rowland, the White Sox skipper in 1917, was then eighty years old and a vice-president of the Chicago Cubs.

Said Rowland, "It's a little unfair to compare them with the 1917 White Sox because you're matching them against the greatest of all time. In my estimation not even the mur-

derous 1927 Yankees—the year Babe Ruth hit his 60 homers—
would be a match for them. . . .

"Buck Weaver at third was a fine hitter and in my estimation the No. 1 third sacker in the game's history."

That curse of Buck's silence was revived by sports editor Bob Broeg in his column on February 21, 1965, in the St.
Louis *Post Dispatch.* At the time, college basketball was under fire for games in which players shaved points for the
benefit of gamblers. Players had been dismissed from college either for participating, for which they also faced criminal charges, or, like Buck, refusing to tell. Broeg, in a father-
to-son open letter, tried to explain that there were times
when one had to speak up.

"You're taught at home from the time you're chest high
to a coffee table not to snitch or tell tales. At school, you're
an ostracized informer if you tell who put the paper clips in
Mrs. Murphy's paste pot.

"You've had a hard time reconciling this manly silence,
the unwillingness to squeal, with recent developments, first
the dismissal of Air Force Academy cadets who didn't cheat
on examinations, but just didn't turn in those who did." [The
Air Force cadet dismissals struck the author in a personal
manner. One of my former students at Taft High school in
Chicago was one of the cadets dismissed from the Air Force
for not telling. He had been in my honors United States history class and was an outstanding student, a bright, pleasant, outgoing youngster. His older brother had graduated
from the Naval Academy, eventually becoming a commander
of a nuclear submarine.] "And now this, the expulsion and
disgrace of Seattle's (L. J.) Wheeler merely because he
wouldn't blow the whistle on teammates who played to win,
but apparently to win by smaller margins than possible.

"Tough, sure, son, but not really too hard to understand
if you'll remember that when it comes to dishonor, you're
not your brother's keeper.

"Remember that it doesn't pay to look the other way,
just for the sake of being a good fella in the eyes of those
who would put you in a compromising situation.

"Remember what happened to George (Buck) Weaver."

Broeg then went on to review Buck's baseball history. At the top of Broeg's column was the headline "Don't Pass This Buck, Fellas." Weaver's sad fate was serving as an object lesson.

Buck and the Black Sox scandal was the subject of a letter to the editor in the "Voice of the People" column in the *Tribune* on February 16, 1969. The letter related a strange story never mentioned before. It may have been pure fantasy but is presented here as an interesting footnote at least. "A letter from James T. Farrell in today's "Voice of the People" (Feb. 2) about Shoeless Joe Jackson prompts me to recall a rather close acquaintanceship I had with another of Chicago's 1919 'Black Sox.' This was Buck Weaver—and he insisted to the day he died that he took no actual part in selling out to the Cincinnati Reds in that year's world series.

"Buck told me and many other old friends that the night before the series began he found an envelope containing $3,000 tucked under the pillow in his bedroom. There was no note of explanation, but he suspected it was a bribe, so he took the envelope to the team's manager, Kid Gleason, and gave him both the envelope and the money.

"Gleason is said to have admitted this was so, but Weaver was ostracized anyway as one of the eight 'bribed' players. I knew him well enough to know that he was no liar. It won't do Buck any good now, but his name at least should be cleared of any wrongdoing, without further procrastination." The letter was signed G. R. McLaughlin.

Soon after the letter was published, the *Chicago Sun-Times* conducted a poll of its readers to name Chicago's greatest players ever. They were to pick one team representing the Cubs and one for the White Sox. The voting was part of a national effort to mark organized baseball's centennial year. Each city was asked to select the best players that ever wore their hometown uniforms.

Weaver's former teammates, Red Faber and Ray Schalk, still living in Chicago, named Buck as their third baseman.

During the poll, *Sun-Times* sportswriter Bill Gleason made a plea for Weaver and Jackson. "To honor them now will have no meaning for Shoeless Joe and Buck, both long dead, but the gesture does have meaning for White Sox partisans, and it should have meaning for baseball. The series they were accused of rigging was played 50 years ago and even kidnappers, murderers and income tax evaders have been paroled after four decades or so.

"Jackson played so ineptly in that tarnished series, his batting average was no more than .375. Weaver's average was slightly below Jackson's. Both played through the 1920 season before they were given the thumb for all time and so stricken with guilt were they that Jackson batted .382 and Weaver hit .333.

"After their expulsion Jackson returned to the mists from which he had come but Weaver lived out his life in Chicago and I never met a man who believed that Buck was guilty. When I was a kid thousands of my elders signed petitions asking that Weaver be pardoned.

"I'm not trying to influence anyone's vote, please understand. We don't do that sort of thing in Chicago."

Buck finished second in the poll behind Willie Kamm, who played for the White Sox between 1923 and 1931. Willie was no slouch either. He posted a lifetime batting mark of .281. But he was more renowned as a classy fielder. As a reward for his fielding exploits his glove rests in the Hall of Fame.

Sportswriter Broeg again resurrected Weaver and the White Sox in his St. Louis *Post Dispatch* column on April 22, 1978. The single-lined headline, which spanned almost four columns, read: "Collins, Weaver and Black Sox." Broeg had met James T. Farrell at St. Petersburg, Florida, during spring training, and the talk turned to the fixed World Series. Farrell told Broeg that he thought Eddie Collins' ability to wangle a five year contract of $15,000 a year before he would agree to going to the White Sox from the Philadelphia A's had much to do with the eventual sellout by the disgruntled players who thought they too deserved a greater share of the pot.

"Buck used to say, 'Collins got twice as much as I did,

but he wasn't twice as good,' " Farrell remembered, observing: "Eddie actually was a lot smarter and had more class than those other guys, though obviously some were great players. Eddie Cicotte, for instance, was magnificent in that last season (1919)." Actually the Black Sox weren't banished until near the close of the 1920 pennant race. "Shoeless Joe Jackson had what both Babe Ruth and Ty Cobb said—the sweetest swing ever—and he was a natural whose .358 [actually .356] career batting average speaks for itself.

"Farrell spoke with compassion about Weaver . . ," reviewing his struggle. "Why, though, was there such a to-do about Weaver as a great all-round third baseman when he had only a .272 lifetime batting average?

"Farrell nodded. 'Because,' he said, 'Buck was two different hitters. Even though they called him 'Error-a-Day Weaver' early when he was at shortstop, he was outstanding defensively at third base as you've heard. Even Cobb couldn't and wouldn't try to bunt against him. But he was a mediocre hitter who became a good one when he switched.' "

Farrell explained how Weaver learned to switch hit. "First, he just stood up there from the left side with no bat, watching the flight of the ball. Next he strode and swung an imaginary bat. Then, he began to bunt again and again left-handed. Finally, he began to practice from the left side."

In the last four seasons of his major league career, which ended at the age of thirty, Buck batted .284, .300, .296 and .333.

"By then," said Farrell, "he was what you've heard: all-round, one of the greatest third basemen ever."

As far as the home folk in Pottstown and Stowe, Pennsylvania, are concerned, Buck Weaver is still one of their favorites. Ed McEvoy, an octogenarian who remembered Buck playing before he got into organized baseball, said with quiet pride in August 1984: "You know he was one of us. We have a closed mouth but we stand behind him and defend him."

McEvoy was the sole survivor of the founders of the Stowe Oldtimers Baseball Association which was launched in 1928 by former ballplayers to encourage youngsters to play the game. They laid plans for an annual reunion and, more importantly, devised ways and means to provide financial support for local baseball teams.

In the program book for the 55th annual banquet held January 15, 1983, are two pictures of Buck Weaver. On the first page Buck poses in civilian clothes with members of the Stowe Athletic Club baseball team in 1919. He stands in the back row wearing a fedora and an open neck white shirt. Later on in the program book is a picture taken in 1920 of Buck and McEvoy standing together in baseball uniforms.

On another page is a long list of major leaguers' names who have attended at least one of the banquets. Buck Weaver's name rests at the top of the honor roll. Other players include Jimmy Dykes, Jimmy Foxx, Bob Feller, Danny Murtaugh, Mickey Vernon, Richie Ashburn, Claude Osteen, Whitey Kurowski, Curt Simmons, Dallas Green, Lefty Gomez, Bobby Schantz, Bucky Walters, Tim McCarver, Brooks Robinson, Greg Luzinski and Bill White.

Buck's townspeople showed their affection towards him when they elected him to the Pottstown Area Chapter of the Pennsylvania Sports Hall of Fame on May 20, 1981. His grandnephew, Douglas Weaver, a local resident, accepted the honor in Buck's name and turned over the shield depicting a ballplayer to the Stowe Oldtimers Baseball Association where it rests with other baseball memorabilia in a display case located in the West End Volunteer Fire Company Building at Vine and Rice streets.

On a hot August afternoon in 1984, as the author reminisced with McEvoy, the old-timer said with melancholy, about Landis, "He would allow no deviation. Everyone had to toe the line . . . nobody else would have stopped Weaver." After a moment's pause, he said sadly, "Life of baseball thrown away."

McEvoy's view seems to be unwittingly tragic. It is true that Weaver's marvelous career was snuffed out at the height of his powers. Given his enthusiasm for the game and the knowledge of how well he later played semipro ball, he may have played in the majors for another decade and been a sure candidate for the Hall of Fame. But to say that Buck's baseball life was "thrown away" overstates the case. Weaver played with the White Sox nine full seasons and participated in two World Series. Most major leaguers neither last that long nor ever have a chance to play in the Fall Classic.

Even though Weaver's career was cut short, he ranks among the top ten all-time White Sox players in a number of categories. He places ninth in games played (1,254); seventh in at bats (4,810); seventh in runs scored (692); seventh in hits (1,310); eighth in triples (69); eighth in total bases (1,710) and ninth in stolen bases (172).

The Weaver tragedy lies in the fact that he could not win his reinstatement while alive. Now that major league players have committed felonies in drug use, served prison sentences and have returned to major league action, isn't it about time Buck's name was cleared? He didn't commit any crime. No man loved baseball more or had a greater thirst to win. He may have been guilty of poor judgment to even momentarily consider testing the murky waters of corruption, even driven as he was by Comiskey's parsimony through the years. But in the final analysis, he turned down bribery and played to win. If Buck was punished for "guilty knowledge," what about the "guilty knowledge" of a parade of others such as Comiskey, Johnson, Grabiner, Gleason, the "lily-white" White Sox, Heydler, Benton, Weeghman and a host of sportswriters and gamblers? To put it simply, Weaver became a scapegoat for the entire sordid affair. He was denied his civil rights, the right to earn a living at what he could do best. What happened to Weaver could not happen today. If the baseball commissioner were to use the same yardstick that was applied to Weaver against modern day big leaguers who didn't snitch on their teammates for using drugs, how many players would be left to play?

No one played baseball with more enthusiasm and desire to win than Buck Weaver. Not only was he a firebrand on the field, he was a determined leader urging his teammates to victory no matter what the obstacles. Though a keen competitor, he had a great sense of humor and took pleasure entertaining the fans and his fellow ballplayers with his comic antics. His character shows through in his advice to his two nieces, "Don't ever worry about what anyone thinks of you as long as you know what you are doing."

In the name of fairness and decency, the name of George Daniel "Buck" Weaver—the Ginger Kid—should be restored to good standing in the annals of major league baseball. It is not too late to right a wrong. Justice cries out for a posthumous commutation of Buck's lifetime banishment.

Perhaps Buck's niece, Bette Scanlan, should have the last word. She told *Chicago Sun-Times* reporter Art Petacque in September 1988, "To this day, the people who really know baseball know that Buck was a victim of circumstances. He was a standup guy who took it on the chin rather than become an informant. They don't make 'em like that any more."

Bibliography

Alexander, Charles C. *John McGraw*. Viking Penguin Inc., New York, 1988.

Allen, Lee. *The Cincinnati Reds*. G.P. Putnam's Sons, New York, 1948.

———. *The World Series: The Story of Baseball's Annual Championship*. G.P. Putnam's Sons, New York, 1969.

Andreano, Ralph. *The Dilemma of Major League Baseball*. Schenkman Publishing Co., Cambridge, Mass., 1965.

Asinof, Eliot. *Eight Men Out: The Black Sox and the 1919 World Series*. Holt, Rinehart and Winston, New York, 1963.

Axelson, Gustav W. *"Commy": The Life Story of Charles A. Comiskey*. The Reilly and Lee Co., Chicago, 1919.

Barrow, Edward G. with James M. Kahn. *My Fifty Years in Baseball*. Coward-McCann Inc., New York, 1951.

Bartlett, Arthur. *Baseball and Mr. Spaulding: The History and Romance of Baseball*. Farrar, Straus and Young, Inc., New York, 1951.

Berke, Art and Schmitt, Paul. *This Date in Chicago White Sox History*. Stein and Day Publishers, New York, 1982.

Brickhouse, Jack, with Jack Rosenberg and Ned Colletti. *Thanks For Listening*. Diamond Communications, Inc., South Bend, Ind., 1986.

Brown, Warren. *The Chicago White Sox*. G.P. Putnam's Sons, New York, 1952.

Cleveland, Charles B. *The Great Baseball Managers*. Thomas Y. Crowell Co., New York, 1950.

Cobb, Ty, with Al Stump. *My Life in Baseball: The True Record*. Doubleday and Co., Inc., Garden City, N.Y., 1962.

Condit, Carl W. *Chicago 1910-29*. The University of Chicago Press, Chicago, 1973.

Creamer, Robert W. *Babe: The Legend Comes To Life*. Simon and Schuster, New York, 1974.

Davids, Robert L. ed. *Insider's Baseball*. Society for American Baseball Research, Charles Scribner's Sons, New York, 1983.

Dickey, Glenn. *The History of American League Baseball Since 1901*. Stein-Day Scarborough House, Briarcliff, N.J., 1980.

Deutsch, Jordan et al. *The Scrapbook History of Baseball*, Bobbs-Merrill, Indianapolis, 1975.

Durant, John. *The Story of Baseball*. Hastings House Publishers, New York, 1973.

Durso, Joseph. *The Days of Mr. McGraw*. Prentice-Hall, Inc., Englewood Cliffs, N.J., 1969.

Elder, Donald. *Ring Lardner: A Biography*. Doubleday, Garden City, N.Y., 1956.

Farrell, James T. *My Baseball Diary*. A.S. Barnes and Co., New York, 1957.

Federal Writers' Project (Illinois) Work Project Administration *Baseball In Old Chicago.* A.C. McClurg and Co., Chicago, 1939.

Fitzgerald, Ed. ed. *The American League.* John Carmichael, "The Chicago White Sox," A.S. Barnes and Co., New York, 1952.

Frick, Ford C. *Games, Asterisks, and People.* Crown Publishers, Inc., New York, 1973.

Gettelson, Leonard. ed. *Official World Series Records.* The Sporting News, St. Louis, 1972.

Graham, Frank. *The New York Giants.* G.P. Putnam's Sons, New York, 1952.

Grayson, Harry. *They Played the Game: The Story of Baseball Greats.* A.S. Barnes and Co., New York, 1944.

Gropman, Donald. *Say It Ain't So, Joe!* Little Brown and Co., Boston, 1979.

Heise, Keenan. *Is There Only One Chicago?* Westover Publishing Co., Richmond, Va., 1973.

Kahn, James M. *The Umpire Story.* G.P. Putnam's Sons, New York, 1953.

Katcher, Leo. *The Big Bankroll: The Life and Times of Arnold Rothstein.* Harper and Row, New York, 1959.

Lardner, R.W. and Heeman, Edward. *The Home Coming of Charles Comiskey, John J. McGraw, John C. Calahan.* The Blakely Printing Co., Chicago, 1914.

Lardner, Ring Jr. *The Lardners: My Family Remembered.* Harper and Row, New York, 1976.

Lewis, Lloyd and Smith, Henry Justin. *Chicago—The History of Its Reputation.* Blue Ribbon Books, Inc., New York, 1933.

Lieb, Frederick G. *The Detroit Tigers,* G.P. Putnam's Sons, New York, 1946.

_____. *Baseball As I Have Known It.* Tempo/Grosset and Dunlap, New York, 1977.

Lindberg, Richard. *Who's On 3rd? The Chicago White Sox Story.* Icarus Press, South Bend, Ind., 1983.

Lowenfish, Lee and Lupien, Tony. *The Imperfect Diamond.* Stein and Day, New York, 1980.

Luhrs, Victor. *The Great Baseball Mystery: The 1919 World Series.* A.S. Barnes and Co., Inc., South Brunswick, New York, 1966.

McCallum, John D. *Ty Cobb.* Praeger Publishers, New York, 1975.

McGraw, Blanche and edited by Arthur Mann. *The Real McGraw.* D. McKay, New York, 1953.

McGraw, John J. *My Thirty Years in Baseball.* Boni and Liveright, New York, 1923.

Marquis, Albert Nelson. ed. *Who's Who In Chicago; The Book of Chicagoans,* A.N. Marquis and Co., Chicago, 1926.

Meany, Tom. *Baseball's Greatest Teams.* A.S. Barnes and Co., New York, 1949.

Murdock, Eugene C. *Czar of Baseball.* Greenwood Press, Westport, Conn., 1982.

Obojski, Robert. *The Rise of Japanese Baseball Power.* Chilton Book Co., Radnor, Pa., 1975.

Patrick, Walter R. *Ring Lardner.* Twayne Publishers Inc., New York, 1963.

Paxton, Harry T. ed. *Sport U.S.A. The Best From The Saturday Evening Post.* John Lardner, "Remember The Black Sox," Thomas Nelson and Sons, New York, 1961.

Pope, Edwin. *Baseball's Greatest Managers: Twenty of the All-Time Greats, Past and Present.* Doubleday and Co., Garden City, N.Y., 1960.

Reichler, Joseph L. ed. *The Baseball Encyclopedia.* 5th ed., Macmillan Company, New York, 1982.

_____. *The Baseball Trade Register.* Macmillan Company, New York, 1984.

Rice, Damon. *Season's Past.* Praeger Publishers, New York, 1976.

Rice, Grantland. *The Tumult and the Shouting.* A.S. Barnes and Co., New York, 1954.

Riess, Steven A. *Touching Base: Professional Baseball and American Culture in the Progressive Era.* Greenwood Press, Westport, Conn., 1980.

Rickey, Branch, with Robert Riger. *The American Diamond, The American Dream.* Simon and Schuster, New York, 1965.

Ritter, Lawrence S. *The Glory of Their Times.* The Macmillan Co., New York, 1966.

Rosenberg, John M. *The Story of Baseball.* Random House, New York, 1962.

Sandberg, Carl. *The Chicago Race Riots, July 1919.* Harcourt, Brace and Howe, New York, 1919.

Seymour, Harold. *Baseball: The Golden Age.* Oxford University Press, New York, 1971.

Shannon, Bill and Kaminsky, George. *The Ballparks.* Hawthorne Books, New York, 1975.

Smith Robert. *Baseball in America.* Holt, Rinehart and Winston, New York, 1961.

————. *Baseball.* Simon and Schuster, New York, 1970.

————. *Illustrated History of Baseball.* Madison Square Press, Grosset and Dunlap, New York, 1973.

————. *Babe Ruth's America.* Thomas Y. Crowell Co., New York, 1974.

————. ed. *Sports—The American Scene from Sports Illustrated.* Arnold "Chick" Gandil as told to Melvin Durslag, "This Is My Story of the Black Sox Series," McGraw Hill, New York, 1963.

Spink, J.G. Taylor. *Judge Landis and Twenty-Five Years of Baseball.* Thomas Y. Crowell Co., New York, 1947.

Stein, Harry. *Hoopla.* Knopf, New York, 1983.

Sullivan, Ted. *History of the World's Tour: Chicago White Sox—New York Giants.* M.A. Donahue and Co., Chicago, 1914.

Thomas, Joseph. ed. *Lippincott's Gazetteer of the World.* J.B. Lippincott Co., Philadelphia, 1893.

Thompson, S.C. and Palmer, Pete. eds. *All-Time Roster of Major League Baseball Clubs.* A.S. Barnes and Co., South Brunswick, New York, 1973.

Tunis, John R. *The American Way in Sport.* Duell, Sloan and Pearce, New York, 1958.

Vass, George. *George Halas and the Chicago Bears.* Henry Regnery Company, Chicago, 1971.

Veeck, Bill, with Ed Linn. *The Hustler's Handbook.* G.P. Putnam's Sons, New York, 1965.

Voigt, David Q. *American Baseball From Gentleman's Sport to the Commissioner System.* 3 Vols. University of Oklahoma Press, Norman, Okla. and Penn State University Press, State College, Pa., 1966-84.

————. *America Through Baseball.* Nelson-Hall, Chicago, 1976.

Wallop, Douglas. *Baseball: An Informal History.* W.W. Norton and Co., New York, 1969.

Yardley, Jonathan. *Ring: A Biography of Ring Lardner.* Random House, New York, 1977.

Index